Purchased from
Multnomah County Library
Title Wave Used Bookstore
216 NE Knott St, Portland, OR
503-988-5021

D1042300

EDWARD VII

ALSO BY CATHARINE ARNOLD

The Sexual History of London
Necropolis: London and Its Dead
Bedlam: London and Its Mad
Underworld: Crime and Punishment in the Capital City
Globe: Life in Shakespeare's London

EDWARD VII

THE **PRINCE** OF **WALES**

AND **THE WOMEN HE LOVED**

CATHARINE ARNOLD

ST. MARTIN'S PRESS ❧ NEW YORK

EDWARD VII. Copyright © 2017 by Catharine Arnold. All rights reserved. Printed in the United States of America. For information, address St. Martin's Press, 175 Fifth Avenue, New York, N.Y. 10010.

www.stmartins.com

Designed by Steven Seighman

Excerpts from *The Edwardians* by Vita Sackville-West reproduced with permission of Curtis Brown Group Ltd., London, on behalf of the Estate of Vita Sackville-West. Copyright © 1963 by The Estate of Vita Sackville-West.

Library of Congress Cataloging-in-Publication Data

Names: Arnold, Catharine, author.
Title: Edward VII : the Prince of Wales and the women he loved / Catharine Arnold.
Description: New York : St. Martin's Press, 2017.
Identifiers: LCCN 2017006881| ISBN 9781250069146 (hardback) | ISBN
    9781466877948 (e-book)
Subjects: LCSH: Edward VII, King of Great Britain, 1841–1910—Relations with
    women. | Great Britain—Kings and rulers—Paramours—Biography. | Great
    Britain—Kings and rulers—Biography. | BISAC: HISTORY / Europe / Great
    Britain. | BIOGRAPHY & AUTOBIOGRAPHY / Royalty.
Classification: LCC DA567 .A755 2017 | DDC 941.082/30922 [B]—dc23
LC record available at https://lccn.loc.gov/2017006881

Our books may be purchased in bulk for promotional, educational, or business use. Please contact your local bookseller or the Macmillan Corporate and Premium Sales Department at 1-800-221-7945, extension 5442, or by e-mail at MacmillanSpecialMarkets@macmillan.com.

First Edition: July 2017

10   9   8   7   6   5   4   3   2   1

To my daughters, Rose and Alice, with love

CONTENTS

ACKNOWLEDGMENTS

I would like to thank the following for their help in the preparation of this book: the Hallward Library, University of Nottingham; Cambridge University Library; Charlie Viney at the Viney Agency; Charlie Spicer and April Osborn at St. Martin's Press; Kim Lewis; the Victoria and Albert Museum; Getty Images; the Mary Evans Picture Library; Curtis Brown for permission to quote from *The Edwardians* by Vita Sackville-West; the Gardens of Easton Lodge Preservation Trust; and finally, my husband and daughters for their support, tact, and forbearance while I completed this book. There are no words apart from thank you, with all my heart.

EDWARD
VII

INTRODUCTION

As guests thronged into Westminster Abbey to take their appointed places for the coronation of King Edward VII on August 9, 1902, they were greeted by a bizarre spectacle. This was a pew reserved for "the King's special ladies, whose rank did not automatically entitle them to a place in the Abbey," and christened "the King's loose box"[1] by one of the deputy marshals, James Lindsay, Earl of Crawford.

The term "loose box," derived from horse racing, was appropriate enough, although the pew was more like a winner's enclosure than a loose box. "Bertie," as the king was fondly known, doubtless regarded the coronation as another opportunity to display his thoroughbred fillies and thank them for their years of loyal service. But some guests were left shocked and appalled by the sheer effrontery of inviting the royal concubines to the coronation.

"It was the one discordant note in the abbey," wrote one of Queen Alexandra's ladies-in-waiting. "It did rather put my teeth on edge; there was 'La Favorita' [Alice Keppel] of course in the best place, Mrs Ronnie Greville, Lady Sarah Wilson [née Spencer-Churchill, the first woman war correspondent who had covered the Boer War for the *Daily Mail*], Lady Feodorovna 'Feo' Sturt [daughter of the Earl of Hardwicke], Mrs Arthur Paget [Minnie Stevens, the Anglo-American society hostess], & that ilk."[2] This ilk also included Lillie Langtry, Sarah Bernhardt, Jennie Churchill with her sister, Leonie, Sophia, Countess of Torby, Lady Albemarle (Alice Keppel's mother-in-law), and Princess Daisy of Pless, daughter of Patsy Cornwallis and quite possibly the daughter of Bertie, too. Next to Alice sat Baroness Olga de Meyer, whom Bertie believed was his natural daughter by the Duchess di Caracciolo, although Olga's paternity was the subject of much speculation.

The most prominent men and women in the land witnessed the eighty-year-old Archbishop of Canterbury unsteadily lower the imperial crown onto the head of Edward VII, in the presence of the king's past and present lovers. If you can tell a man by the company he keeps, then these ladies tell us everything we want to know about the character of Edward VII, henceforth referred to as "Bertie."

Charming and dissolute, Bertie admired beautiful, spirited women who were good sports, in and out of bed. Bertie loved smart women who sparkled in his company, but he "had a horror of highbrows, particularly writers!"[3] according to his lover Daisy, Countess of Warwick.

The women Bertie loved had one thing in common: they were nothing like his mother, Queen Victoria. Warm, generous, lively, Bertie's women were the polar opposite of the reclusive "Widow of Windsor." Queen Victoria's pathological mourning for her husband, Prince Albert, who died in 1861, might have been endurable if young Bertie had ever felt that his mother loved him. But Victoria seems to have hated her oldest son from birth, and later, after learning of his first affair, wrote that "I never can or shall look at him again without a shudder."[4] No wonder the welcoming arms of any woman, from countess to courtesan, were attractive, after the Queen's *froideur*.

Bertie also possessed a ruthless streak. He was a dangerous man to cross. "Bertie never forgives," as one companion observed after a particularly difficult episode. For all those women who sat in the king's loose box, and the patient Princess Alexandra, or "Alix," who stood by him for all those years and eventually became his queen, there were also victims. These included a lonely woman who died in exile, another confined to a madhouse, and a young widow who was willfully cast aside after falling pregnant. Bertie had no scruples in destroying those who betrayed or offended him.

One wonders what the atmosphere must have been like in the loose box. Did it bristle with a spirit of competition, or, by this stage in Bertie's life, was there a spirit of female solidarity in the harem? Every one of those women knew that Alexandra, the patient Danish princess who had been married to Bertie since 1863, was the queen in every sense. Not a woman there would have deluded herself that she could have displaced Alix; these were the days when royal mistresses were tolerated, even encouraged; it was practically a court rank in itself. No heir to the throne would have stepped aside to divorce and remarry; it would be more than thirty years before Edward VIII abdicated in order to marry "the woman he loved." Bertie was king by divine right and his marriage was sacrosanct, no matter how many dalliances and flirtations he indulged in. It was Alix, when Bertie died, who declared, "But he loved me the best!"[5] For the ladies of the loose box, becoming Bertie's mistress allowed them to revel in a little reflected glory before, inevitably, he lost interest and another woman took their place.

Alix was a woman for whom the description "long-suffering wife" might have been invented. Alix endured Bertie's endless indiscretions from the earliest days of their marriage, when he went off to Paris while she was experiencing a difficult first pregnancy. As Bertie's indiscretions became common knowledge, Alix gained in popularity and adoration. "The Princess of Wales floated through the ballroom like a vision from fairyland,"[6] noted one biographer. "The county idolised her, so beautiful, so pure, so badly-treated. In the public imagination she combined the appeal of Cinderella and Andromeda. Marvelously dressed, radiant, gracious, pouring forth smiles—who could fault this paragon?"[7] The fact that Alix was called "the Princess of Hearts" makes it easy to draw comparisons with the late Princess Diana, but there was to be no divorce for Alix. She stayed with Bertie and took some consolation in a platonic romance with an adoring courtier, Oliver Montagu.

Meanwhile, Bertie, larger than life with king-sized appetites, conducted his liaisons against the glittering backdrop of London society, the Continent, and the stately homes of England, where a strict code of honor insulated the nighttime corridor creepers from scandal. In Paris, Bertie was a regular at the Moulin Rouge music hall, where his nickname was "Kingy!" and the dancer "La Goulue" yelled to him from the stage, "Oi, Wales! Are you goin' to pay for my champagne?"[8]

Much of Bertie's behavior seems born from boredom; denied the throne, as Queen Victoria resolutely refused to abdicate, Bertie was stuck with the path in life that fate had dictated for him. He was faced with two options: to bow to convention or to live life by his own rules. And those rules were not so very different from those of other upper-class men in the late nineteenth century. As Anita Leslie, author of *Edwardians in Love,* commented, it is hard to dislike Bertie. "After all, he merely wanted to go to bed with a lot of women and took advantage of unparalleled opportunities. Would many men act differently if put in his place?"[9]

As well as his affairs with society ladies, Bertie began frequenting brothels early in his marriage. And in defense of Bertie, brothel-going was common for a man of Bertie's class. During the Victorian period, when "respectable" women were not sexually available until marriage, and not much afterward, prostitutes were the ideal solution. Either that or priapic husbands took out their frustration on the servants. Randolph Churchill once wrote to his wife, Jennie, as friends of theirs were facing divorce proceedings after the husband had been caught dallying with the staff, "Tell Mary from me that she is a fool not to forgive Billy. What does one occasional cook or housemaid matter?"[10] In his later years, Bertie would become an honored guest at Le Chabanais, a palatial bordello known as the best "house" in Paris. It was here that the aging Bertie indulged in champagne baths in a copper tub, and entertained his female companions on a specially designed *siège d'amour,* or "love seat," an extraordinary contraption with footholds, padded seats, and stirrups, which lent a somewhat obstetric air to the proceedings. A surreal object, the love seat is certainly a testament to the cabinetmaker's art, and a lasting memorial to Bertie's devotion to duty in the lists of love.

I first had the idea for *Edward VII: The Prince of Wales and the Women He Loved* while talking with my agent about Bertie's notorious reputation as a womanizer and bon viveur. While Bertie certainly had a "type"—usually a curvaceous, lively society hostess, at home in the saddle and in bed—his lovers also embraced a wide field of occupations: There was Lillie Langtry, who went from artists' model to actress and became the first public mistress of the Prince of Wales. Bertie lavished a fortune on Lillie, and once told her that "I spent enough on you to buy a battleship!" to which the lively Lillie retorted: "And you've spent enough in me to launch one!"[11] And Frances "Daisy" Brooke, later Countess of Warwick, the extravagant socialite who embraced socialism and stood for Parliament as a Labour party candidate in 1923. And then, as if to prove that Bertie did not have a "type" after all, came the romance with French actress Sarah Bernhardt, celebrated for her decadent appeal and opium habit, and by total contrast the starchy Agnes Keyser, who founded a hospital for army officers. As Bertie was a serial polygamist, many of these affairs overlapped. Bertie seemed to be able to juggle his women without the women in question taking offense, an enviable state. In fact, I doubt if even Bertie could always keep track of his affairs, and in many cases it was his sentimental side, his habit of writing romantic *billets doux* to his women, that led to more than one scandal. So *Edward VII* does not claim to be an exhaustive list of Bertie's lovers. Instead, I have selected the most outstanding and interesting lives to show "aspects" of Bertie.

Some of the women in Bertie's life had more to say for themselves than others. I have concentrated on the regiment of women who formed Bertie's mistresses in chief: Lillie Langtry, Daisy Warwick, and Alice Keppel, his last serious mistress and ancestress of Camilla Parker Bowles, former mistress, now wife, of the Prince of Wales.

And then there is Jennie Churchill, over whom a question mark always hovers. Jennie was too shrewd to be explicit about their relationship, despite having had over two hundred lovers. Jennie Churchill, née Jerome, was the unhappy wife of Sir Randolph Churchill, a spectacular example of the Victorian cad. Raven-haired, panther-eyed, and smart as a whip, Jennie was an immediate hit with Bertie when they were first introduced at the royal yacht club in Cowes, and following her marriage to Randolph, Bertie's carriage was regularly spotted outside their London home.

Many of Bertie's established romances with society women were played out against the backdrop of the country house weekend. It was this remarkable institution that allowed Bertie and his friends to conduct passionate affairs with impunity, away from the prying eyes of the gutter press and servants who might betray their aristocratic employers for a few guineas. While Bertie might enjoy brief afternoon trysts in the grand houses of Belgravia, the only sign of his presence being the one-horse brougham drawn up outside, it was the smiling and beautiful countryside that offered a safe environment where he could take his pleasures at a leisurely pace. In a country house, Bertie's lady of the moment was also insulated against the vulgar gaze. A secluded setting offered ample opportunities for discreet companionship without the need to risk her reputation; in those days, society women would never dare be caught out at a restaurant or even—the very idea—a hotel!

The country house weekend was properly known as a "Saturday to Monday." The term "weekend," coined only in the late 1880s, was regarded as unspeakably vulgar, as it suggested one was involved in "trade," and had to work for a living and hurry back to London on Sunday night. "Saturday to Monday," on the other hand, emphasized the fact that Bertie's carefree companions had comfortable private incomes. While field sports constituted the alleged attraction, with the great landed estates offering superb opportunities for hunting, shooting, and fishing, sporting activity of a somewhat different nature was the order of the day. In a country house, nestling deep among the rolling acres, scandalous flings could be flung with impunity. Discretion was assured for all parties, as long as one remembered the Eleventh Commandment: *Thou shalt not get found out*. The consequences of discovery, ranging from the vilification of the divorce court to exile and death, were too ghastly to contemplate. In every generation, one or two unfortunate individuals were offered up who suffered such public annihilation. Lady Harriet Mordaunt, who ended her days in a lunatic asylum, was one; Edith Beresford, who lost custody of her children, another. Women, who had the most to lose when their "honor" was gone, were generally the victims. One unfortunate wife, Lady Somerset, who surprised her husband in bed with another man, found that *she* became a pariah for bringing him into disrepute.

A typical Saturday to Monday took place in the early autumn, when the shooting season opened. Eager "guns," having already blasted away at Scottish grouse from the glorious August 12 onward, were ready to shoot partridge from September 1 and pheasant from the start of October, while the fox-hunting season started in earnest from November 1. In Bertie's later years, the Prince of Wales would appear in family photographs like a kind of human trophy, seated at the heart of a group of tweedy men and elaborately dressed women. Landed families loved nothing better than to bag a visit from Bertie. Despite the fact that having him to stay proved ruinously expensive, his presence guaranteed the making of an ambitious socialite or crowned the existing achievements of a great landowner. No price was too great for such an honor, and the fact that Bertie was sleeping with the hostess was discreetly overlooked. It was a brave, even fool-hardy man who intervened between his own wife or mistress and Bertie.

The Saturday to Monday had its own distinctive routine. On Sat-urday afternoon, between twenty and forty guests would disembark from the London train at the local railway station, to be met by carriages for the ladies, and the station bus, with its fusty smell and rattling windows, for the gentlemen. Daisy Warwick, Bertie's mistress for nine years, built a little station for the royal train near her Easton Lodge estate in Essex, so that Bertie could reach her all the sooner.

Upon arrival, the guests would be conducted upstairs to their lux-urious quarters, their cases carried up and unpacked by the servants of the house, or by their own maids and valets if these had traveled up from London with the party. These servants would be received below stairs in the servants' hall with a corresponding amount of ritual.

Once changed, the ladies into tea gowns and the gentlemen into their country tweeds, the guests descended to the drawing room for tea. Tea in Daisy Warwick's elegant gold and white drawing room was always particularly impressive, an elaborate spread of muffins, crumpets, cakes, and scones with jam and cream. No formal intro-ductions were made over tea, as none were necessary. It was assumed that all the guests, drawn from the narrow top drawer of London society, were already acquainted. Everyone who mattered knew everyone else through the byzantine network of family links, the royal court, public school, Oxford and Cambridge, and the army.

But it was at tea that another form of connection was established, as men scanned the drawing room for ladies whom they might "amuse" over the course of the weekend, if the lady seemed interested. Like every other activity in Edwardian England, the licensed promiscuity of the country house weekend was governed by a strict social code. If married couples occasionally got a little mixed up on these excursions, discretion was the order of the day. These men and women were so assured, so certain of their position in society that they would never violate appearances or offend decorum. The penalty for such a blunder was ostracism for life.

As one French writer observed, scandal was deeply unusual in England. Unlike Paris, where adulterous affairs were avenged with pistols at dawn in the Bois du Boulogne, there was no need for such desperate measures in England. "The dominating idea is not the cultivation of virtue, but the prevention of scandal" wrote "An Outsider." "London society can visit any grave offence against it with penalties as severe as the bullet of a pistol or the thrust of a rapier."[12]

While men could do as they liked, as always, women were not supposed to embark on an affair until they were married and had provided their husbands with an heir and a spare. It was the task of the hostess to know who the married lovers were and place them in adjacent bedrooms, and to ensure that the current mistress of the Prince of Wales was never too far from the royal suite. To avoid confusion, and aid navigation, every bedroom door bore a little brass frame with the guest's name written on a card within it.

It was at teatime that those men who had arrived at the country house alone, in search of amorous distraction, took the opportunity to appraise the available married women. If a lady seemed interested, a swift but elaborate courtship would follow, with glances across the dinner table, a hand pat on a gloved elbow, a note on a breakfast tray, or an offer of a walk to the summer house. All these would lead, inevitably, to a late-night assignation.

Prime Minister Benjamin Disraeli, never a fan of the Saturday to Monday, once remarked to Queen Victoria that, as far as he was concerned, country house weekends involved "a great too much both of eating and dressing."[13] Meals were certainly on an epic scale, to fortify the guests for the feats of athletic endurance ahead.

For breakfast, the guests either had a tray in the bedroom or came downstairs to find a dazzling array of silver chafing dishes lined up on the dining room sideboard, containing fried, poached, or scrambled eggs, bacon, sausages, mushrooms, tomatoes, kedgeree, and cold ham. Luncheon often took the form of an elaborate picnic, with massive hampers of game pie, cold meat, and cheese, wine, and beer dragged out to the waiting guns, and spirit stoves lit to warm up tea and coffee.

Shooting was a predominantly masculine activity, although there were one or two enthusiastic "lady guns" among the parties as the years progressed. Alice Keppel, Bertie's last mistress, was a keen sportswoman, happy to tramp across the grouse moors with her royal lover and exchange pleasantries with the beaters. Hunting was popular with both sexes; Daisy Brooke once left Windsor Castle early in the morning to attend a meet of the Essex Hunt, much to the disapproval of Queen Victoria. Daisy, who was still hunting in her forties, and survived several serious accidents, including one occasion when her horse rolled on top of her and broke her arm. By contrast, Lillie Langtry, often invited to country house weekends during her time as Bertie's mistress, did not enjoy the sporting aspect of these occasions. Lillie once watched a stag being stalked, and recalled, "I felt so sick and sorry for the fine beast that I have never forgotten it."[14] The alternative, staying inside with the female guests, did not appeal to Lillie, either. Instead, the lively Lillie found other distractions during the *longueurs* of the country house; on one occasion, her host had to lock away his largest silver tray, as Lillie had insisted on tobogganing on it down the stairs of his stately home.

Late in the afternoon, the guns returned from the moor or the hill to a roaring fire, a well-stocked drinks tray, and an enormous tea. While edible temptation was laid out upon the table, the ladies were tempting, too. Having changed into their third outfit of the day, the women would be draped decoratively around the drawing room like gorgeous butterflies in their long-sleeved "tea gowns," elaborate confections of sable-trimmed velvet, satin, brocade, silk gauze, and lace that contrasted vividly with the hairy tweeds and muddy gaiters of the men. The chief advantage of the tea gown was its ability to display the charms of the lady within, and its ease of access. If a spark of desire was ignited, and a couple stole away to a bedroom before dinner, a tea gown enabled swift and easy intimacy, unlike the long, narrow, whale-boned corsets of more formal dress, which made intimacy all but impossible.

Dinner was the most elaborate meal of the day, with thirty or forty people sitting down to eat at an elaborate dining table. The ladies glimmered in satin and jewels, roses in their hair, while the gentlemen wore full evening dress and military decorations. Their clothes were so perfectly in keeping with their setting that it seemed they had not a care in the world.

A typical country house dinner consisted of ten courses, including hot and cold soup, followed by whitebait and trout, quail and capon, asparagus, cold ham, roast mutton, elaborate puddings, a savory, and ice cream, all washed down with the appropriate sherry, wine, madeira, port, and brandy. The Prince of Wales loved rich, elaborate dishes: quail stuffed with pâté de foie gras, pheasants stuffed with truffles, snipe crammed with forcemeat, all garnished with truffles, mushrooms, oysters, and prawns and served in a thick, creamy sauce. If this was not enough to satisfy the pleasure-hungry guests, a late supper would also be available, with cold chicken and lobster salad, and sandwiches were provided in every bedroom.

After dinner, when the ladies had "retired" to the drawing room, the men were free to engage in the traditional masculine pursuits of card games and billiards, accompanied by brandy and cigars. And late at night, the real amusements would begin.

There is a story, perhaps apocryphal, about an innocent young girl who once told a company of guests lazing in the garden that she believed Easton Lodge to be haunted. The night before, this debutante had seen a figure in white walking down a corridor, who had then suddenly vanished. There was no reaction to this statement, and a long silence followed. The experienced guests knew that the mystery figure was very much of this world and had vanished into a lady's bedroom.

By night, the passageways of the great country houses were alive with the sound of gently padding feet, the swish of dressing-gown cords and gently closing doors as the corridor creepers made their way to their secret assignations, and a certain amount of danger made the game more piquant. At Easton Lodge, Daisy Warwick always warned her visitors that the stable-yard bell rang at six A.M., a signal that ensured that all concerned were safely returned to their own beds before the maids arrived with early morning tea.

These late-night encounters were not always successful. There is one anecdote about the husband who, feeling hungry, carried off the plate of sandwiches that his wife had left outside her bedroom door as a signal to her lover. Or the tale of dashing Charlie Beresford, lover of Daisy Warwick, who tiptoed into a dark room and leaped into bed, only to discover that he was not in the arms of his mistress but those of the Bishop of Chester.[15] There was even a rumor that one night a lady who did not respond to Bertie's charms told him she would leave a rosebud on her bedroom door as a signal. Bertie duly arrived, opened the door, and crept into bed, only to encounter the kitchen maid whom the lady had substituted there instead. In the words of Hilaire Belloc:

There will be Bridge and booze 'till after three
And, after that, a lot of them will grope

Along the corridors in robes de nuit,
Pyjamas, or some other kind of dope.
A sturdy matron will be sent to cope
With Lord _____, who isn't quite the thing,
And give his wife the leisure to elope
And Mrs James will entertain the King![16]

Chapter One

A YOUTHFUL INDISCRETION

I never can or shall look at him without a shudder.
—QUEEN VICTORIA

F ollowing a privileged but loveless childhood, the young Prince of Wales paid dearly for his sexual initiation. Indeed, if Bertie did not pay for it with his life, then he paid for it with another man's life. This would be the verdict according to Queen Victoria, who believed that her son's behavior contributed to the sudden death of Prince Albert at just forty-two years old.

Bertie had led a sheltered life, surrounded by nursemaids and tutors, trained for his role in the British royal family from his earliest years. To assist Bertie in this task, he had a "governor," or mentor, in the form of Colonel Robert Bruce, who had accompanied Bertie on trips to Europe and America and for a year at Christ Church, Oxford, followed by further study at Trinity College, Cambridge.[1] This latter experience of higher education confirmed that Bertie, though bright and alert, would never really be "university material." As a result, Prince Albert decided that the nineteen-year-old Bertie would benefit from a spell in the army, which might be "a good field for social instruction."[2] During the Cambridge Long Vacation, which ran from June until the end of September, Bertie was attached to the

Grenadier Guards for ten weeks at the Curragh, a military camp out-side Dublin.[3]

At first excited by this taste of army life, Bertie was soon crest-fallen to discover that the army was not just about horses, guns, and combat but was set about with rules and the Queen's Regulations. Every moment of his time had to be accounted for, from dawn until dusk. Bertie was whisked from place to place so quickly, his "feet scarcely touched the ground" in the words of another famous cadet.[4] Although Bertie dressed in the uniform of a staff colonel, as a con-cession to his birth, he was required to undergo a rigorous training "in the duties of every rank from ensign upwards."[5] It was confi-dently predicted that within ten weeks Bertie would acquire the skills to command a battalion and be competent "to manoeuvre a Brigade in the Field."[6] Alongside this, he had to acquire the appropriate so-cial graces of an army officer, dining twice a week in the Grenadier Guards officers' mess, once a week in other messes, and hold a din-ner party for other officers. This was a tall order. If the Prince Con-sort had thought that this schedule would serve to keep his son out of trouble, he was wrong. After seven weeks, Bertie's commanding officer considered him to be totally inadequate to perform the du-ties of a staff colonel. To make matters worse, when Bertie's "Uncle George," the Duke of Cambridge, visited the camp, Bertie's CO or-dered him to perform the duties of a subaltern while still dressed as a colonel. When Bertie protested, he was told that his drill was im-perfect and his voice indistinct. "I will *not* try to make the Duke of Cambridge think that you are more advanced than you are."[7] The fact was that Bertie did not want to be a soldier. He possessed nei-ther the inclination, the athleticism, nor the pure enjoyment of army life. It was also abundantly clear that an all-male environment was not for him. But army life did at least offer one compensation. A group of convivial young officers, shocked at Bertie's sexual inno-cence, procured the services of a young Irish actress and good-time girl named Nellie Clifden. Nellie was smuggled into Bertie's quarters and told to wait for him in bed. What happened next was clearly the most successful event of Bertie's brief and otherwise unexceptional spell in the army. Bertie commemorated their subsequent meetings in his diary:

6 SEPT	CURRAGH	N. C. 1ˢᵗ TIME
9 SEPT	CURRAGH	N. C. 2ᴺᴰ TIME
10 SEPT	CURRAGH	N. C. 3ᴿᴰ TIME [8]

Bertie was smitten, and continued to see Nellie when he returned to England, "installing her at lodgings at Windsor."[9] Not only was Bertie grateful to Nellie for his sexual initiation, he seems genuinely to have fallen in love with her. Unfortunately, Nellie, who had also become the mistress of the young Lord Carrington, went around London boasting about her relationship with the young Prince of Wales and even hinting at their forthcoming nuptials. The potential embarrassment of Nellie's presence cannot be overestimated, particularly as a suitable bride had already been selected for Bertie.

The search had been on for a bride for Bertie since the prince turned sixteen. Bertie's older sister, Vicky, now Crown Princess of Prussia, had been delegated to the task by the queen.[10] King Leopold of Belgium and Queen Victoria's trusted courtier Baron Stockmar had also been recruited to search for a wife who would keep Bertie "out of mischief."[11] When Baron Stockmar told Prince Albert that he could not, really, organize an arranged marriage, Prince Albert replied that everyone had told him, "You must marry the Prince of Wales soon, unless you do so he is lost."[12]

During the summer of 1860, Vicky could be found underneath a chestnut tree, studying the *Almanach de Gotha* to find the right bride for her brother. The *Almanach de Gotha,* which might be described as the bloodstock manual for European royalty, was an indispensable authority on monarchies and their courts, reigning and former dynasties, princely and ducal families, and the genealogical, biographical, and titular details of Europe's highest level of aristocracy. Vicky had her work cut out for her as she turned the pages of this royal mail-order catalog. Princesses did not grow on trees, and there seemed to be something wrong with every one of them, particularly as Queen Victoria would settle for nothing less than perfection.[13] The fortunate princess would have to be beautiful, dutiful, clever, quiet, virtuous, Protestant, and royal.

Marie of Altenburg was dismissed on the grounds of dressing badly and being in possession of an offensive mother. Augusta of Meiningen was "a very nice, clever good girl" but too young. There was a choice of Weimar girls, but they had delicate constitutions and were not pretty. The Princess of Sweden was too young, and Princess Hilda of Dessau was too old. Princess Marie of the Netherlands was "clever and ladylike" but suffered from being plain and physically infirm. As for Princess Alexandrine of Prussia, she bore the crippling twin disadvantages of being "*not* clever or pretty." Anna of Hesse looked like a good prospect, and had the "fewest disadvantages" according to Vicky, but even she suffered from twitchy eyes, bad teeth, and an abrupt manner. Marie of Hohenzollern-Sigmaringen was "quite lovely" but ruled out on the grounds of being a Roman Catholic. Finally, Elisabeth of Wied, although somewhat dowdy, was a strong, healthy girl with a fresh complexion but was boisterous and uninhibited. Elisabeth subsequently became Queen of Romania and a prolific writer under the pseudonym Carmen Sylva.[14]

So many princesses having been ruled out, just one possibility remained: Princess Alexandra of Denmark, daughter of Prince Christian. However, despite Alexandra's "beauty, her charms, her amiability, her frank natural manner and many excellent qualities,"[15] there was just one thing wrong. Princess Alexandra was not "Prussian" and Queen Victoria wanted her son to marry a woman of German ancestry.[16] The queen also disapproved of King Frederick VII of Denmark, Princess Alexandra's colorful uncle, who "lived openly in sin and was seldom sober."[17] King Frederick's first two marriages had ended in divorce, and his third wife, Louisa, was a ballet dancer. The king was rumored to be in a same-sex relationship with his close friend, Carl Berling, who had fathered a child on Louisa. But despite his eccentricities, alcoholism, and unconventional private life, King Frederick was much loved. He had the common touch, and could speak to anyone. As King Frederick had no official heirs, Princess Alexandra's father, Prince Christian, a cousin, was appointed heir apparent and succeeded to the throne when Frederick died in 1863.

It wasn't just Princess Alexandra's wicked uncle whom Queen Victoria objected to. The queen had also taken a dislike to Princess Alexandra's mother, who came from the House of Hesse-Cassel, a dynasty noted for being high-spirited, pleasure-loving, and frivolous,[18] characteristics embodied by Princess Mary, so fat she needed two chairs to sit on and was a notorious flirt.[19]

In fact, Princess Alexandra's mother was a devoted homemaker who raised her children to be practical and self-reliant. Princess Louise even had her own rejoinder to the worried comments about Princess Mary, telling Princess Alexandra that if she ever saw her flirt like Mary, she would box her ears.[20]

Despite Queen Victoria's misgivings, it was clear that young Princess Alexandra was a keeper. Mrs. Paget, wife of Augustus Paget, the British diplomat to Copenhagen, confided in the queen that "it would be impossible to find anywhere a Princess better suited than Alix to be the wife of the Prince of Wales."[21] A photograph was procured, and shown to Prince Albert, who took one look at it and said, "From that photograph, I would marry her at once."[22]

Vicky interviewed Princess Alexandra's former nanny, who confirmed that Alix was "the sweetest girl who ever lived, full of life and high spirits, with a good constitution, and had never suffered from anything worse in her life than measles."[23] When Vicky finally got to meet Alix for herself, she was entranced and wrote home that "I never set eyes on a sweeter creature. She is lovely! She does not seem the least aware of her beauty and is very unassuming. You may go far before you find another princess like Princess Alix. Oh, if only she was not a Dane and not related to the Hesses I should say yes—she is the one a thousand times over."[24]

By this point, Queen Victoria was beginning to overcome her initial hostility toward Alix. Apart from anything else, she did not want to lose Alix to the Russian tsar, who had also expressed an interest. "It would be dreadful," Vicky reminded the queen, "if this pearl went to the horrid Russians."[25]

Bertie was finally allowed to have some say in the matter after leaving the Curragh in September 1861[26] when he was invited to meet Alix for himself. Bertie traveled to Germany, where the Christians were staying at their shabby, run-down castle near Frankfurt, and the couple were finally introduced at the Cathedral of Speyer. As the bishop was showing the royal party around the frescoes, the two young people became detached from the party and wandered off by themselves. The next day, Bertie wrote home and told his parents that he had enjoyed meeting "the young lady of whom I had heard so much; and I can now candidly say that I thought her charming and pretty."[27]

There was just one problem. Although Bertie had admired Alix, he now showed a peculiar reluctance to marry her and settle down.[28] Perhaps Bertie entertained some preposterous fantasy of marrying Nellie Clifden; perhaps he was genuinely in love with Nellie, finding her far more appealing than Alix, who was, after all, a sixteen-year-old schoolgirl. Prince Albert, who knew nothing of Nellie's existence, simply reproached his son with a stern letter, telling Bertie that he must marry early because "it would be impossible for you to lead, with any chance of success or comfort to yourself, a protracted bachelor life."[29] Bertie replied that he wanted to meet Alix again before he made up his mind, and was told that if he did so, he must propose to her immediately or release her from any further obligations.[30] Bertie procrastinated and returned to Cambridge to continue his studies, which chiefly consisted of hunting with Natty Rothschild and expeditions to London to see Nellie. It was at this point that Lord Torrington, a courtier and gossip,[31] took it upon himself to inform Prince Albert about Bertie's fling with Nellie.

The scene may be imagined: the queen, who had been supplied with a censored version of events but could understand their significance, called down fire and brimstone upon her firstborn son, while Prince Albert was horrified but characteristically measured and conscientious in his reaction. The prince resolved to find the truth about these allegations, despite being exhausted by a debilitating combination of neuralgia, toothache, insomnia, and anxiety. The prince was also deeply concerned about the effect this news would have on his wife's state of mind. Queen Victoria had recently lost her mother, a "DREADFUL, DREADFUL terrible calamity," causing her "fearful and unbearable outbursts of grief."[32] The queen had retreated from public life, dining alone, spending considerable periods of time sitting in her late mother's rooms, and accusing Bertie of being insufficiently grief-stricken. In addition, Prince Albert's beloved young cousin, King Pedro V, had died of typhoid in Portugal. Now came the news that Bertie had been seduced by Nellie Clifden, already known in London society as "the Princess of Wales," and worries that this would endanger the marriage plans. Prince Albert was appalled, not just because Bertie had gone off the rails, but because Nellie might conceive Bertie's child, or pass off another man's baby as his.

"If you were to try and deny it," Prince Albert wrote to his son, "she can drag you into a Court of Law to force you to own it and there with you in the witness box, she will be able to give before a greedy Multitude disgusting details of your profligacy for the sake of convincing the Jury; yourself cross-examined by a railing indecent attorney and hooted and yelled at by a Lawless Mob!! Oh, horrible prospect, which this person has in her power, any day to realize! And to break your poor parents' hearts!"[33]

Nothing was to be done, Prince Albert concluded, but to confess everything to Bertie's governor, Colonel Bruce. Bertie duly did so, although he refused to give the names of the fellow officers who had smuggled Nellie into the camp, and this was accepted as a matter of principle. Bertie admitted that he had yielded to temptation and that the affair was over. Bertie also apologized fulsomely to his father for the "terrible pain" he had caused. There was only one thing that would satisfy Prince Albert now: Bertie must agree to marriage, as soon as possible. If not, the consequences for England, indeed for the world, would be "too dreadful!"[34]

Two days after writing this letter, Prince Albert went to the Royal Military Academy at Sandhurst to inspect new buildings for the staff college.[35] The day had been cold and wet, and he returned to Windsor tired and aching with rheumatism. The following day, Prince Albert caught a cold, which did not improve matters, and neither did his habitual insomnia. Despite feeling so ill, on the following day, November 25, Prince Albert traveled to Madingley Hall in Cambridge, where Bertie was staying during his desultory studies at the university. It was another cold, wet day, but the prince took Bertie for a long walk and discussed the situation, arriving back at Madingley Hall exhausted. Prince Albert later told Vicky that he was at his lowest ebb, "much worry and great sorrow . . . have robbed me of sleep during the past fortnight. In this shattered state I had a very heavy catarrh and for the past four days am suffering from headache and pains in my limbs which may develop into rheumatism."[36] It was far worse than that. A week later, the prince contracted typhoid.

As Prince Albert lay dying, the queen refused to invite Bertie to Windsor Castle, blaming him for his father's illness. It was Princess Alice who sent a telegram to Cambridge and summoned him to Prince Albert's bedside. Vicky, who was pregnant at the time, was unable to make the journey from Germany. Even then, Bertie had no idea of the gravity of his father's condition. Bertie arrived at Windsor at three o'clock in the morning, in good spirits following a dinner engagement in London, and did not see his father until the following morning. To Bertie's horror, Prince Albert smiled up at him, but was unable to speak. It was left to Princess Alice to say calmly, "this is the death rattle" and then go and fetch her mother.[37] Queen Victoria hurried into the room, and she and her children all knelt beside Prince Albert's bedside.

Queen Victoria said, *"Es ist Kleines Frauchen"* (It is your little wife),[38] and Prince Albert bowed his head. Queen Victoria asked him for a kiss, and he did so. Then she went out of the room, inconsolable, before Princess Alice summoned her back in, to hold Prince Albert's already cold and dying hand. In his last two or three breaths, his fingers clasped hers. And then it was over. Queen Victoria stood up, kissed Prince Albert's forehead, and cried out bitterly, "Oh, my dear Darling!" and fell to her knees in mute despair, unable to utter a word or shed a tear."[39]

Queen Victoria was led away to a sofa in the Red Room, where Princess Alice sat with her arms around her. Meanwhile, Princess Helena stood at the foot of the bed, sobbing violently, while Bertie stood near the sofa, obviously deeply affected, "but quiet."[40]

For the rest of her life, Queen Victoria blamed Bertie for Prince Albert's death. "I never can or shall look at him without a shudder, as you may imagine," she wrote a fortnight later. "He does not know that I know all—Beloved Papa told him that I could not be told all the disgusting details . . ."[41] but the queen clearly sought the information out.

One of Prince Albert's closest friends, Colonel Francis Seymour, tried to persuade Queen Victoria that Bertie's affair with Nellie was little more than a youthful indiscretion, and that Prince Albert's extraordinary personal integrity had made him exaggerate what was nothing more than a normal young man's rite of passage. But the queen was not to be convinced. Bertie, she maintained, had killed his father. Queen Victoria's grief was "something which is too dreadful to describe. Pity him, I do. But more you cannot ask. This dreadful, dreadful cross kills me!"[42]

Bertie tried to comfort his mother but Queen Victoria's hurt ran too deep. Bertie stayed away from Windsor, prompting anxieties that he had fallen out with her. Lord Palmerston intervened, visiting the queen to say that her subjects were "fearful" that she and her son were not on good terms. Queen Victoria responded that this was better than having Bertie loafing around the house, and so it was decided that Bertie would go abroad for a spell, to complete his education with a tour of the Holy Land. In February 1862, Bertie set off for Venice, via Vienna, in the company of Colonel Bruce. There were tears when mother and son parted, and, on Bertie's side, the hope that by the time he returned, the wound might be healed.

Chapter Two

A ROYAL WEDDING

But he loved me the best!
—HRH Queen Alexandra

ertie bowed to the inevitable a year later and proposed
to Alix at her home in Lakean, in conditions carefully
stage-managed by Queen Victoria. Once Alix and Bertie had been
safely betrothed, the queen took Alix under her wing, welcoming
her into the royal family by inviting her to stay at Osborne, the
queen's home on the Isle of Wight. Alix, meekly and uncomplain-
ingly, submitted to her role, to the queen's endless anecdotes of the
late Prince Albert, and carriage rides in the rain.[1] Although this royal
wedding could hardly be described as romantic, Queen Victoria's
spin doctors ensured that it appeared to be a genuine love match.
And Bertie, eager to please his mother after the debacle of Nellie,
played his part like a born actor. "Love and cherish her you may be
sure I will to the end of my life," he told the queen.[2]

The date was set for March 10, 1863, in St. George's Chapel,
Windsor, by which time Alix would be eighteen and Bertie twenty-
one. The royal wedding, the first for many years, was greeted with
enthusiasm by a public ready to celebrate after two years of mourning Prince Albert. The poet laureate, Alfred Lord Tennyson, penned

"A Welcome," with which to greet the future princess when she arrived:

> Sea-Kings' daughter from over the sea,
>> Alexandra!
> Saxon and Norman and Dane are we,
> But all of us Danes in our welcome of thee,
>> Alexandra![3]

Princess Alexandra's arrival in London was greeted with immense pageantry, the sort of event at which the British royal family excels. From the moment she set foot on British soil, Alix proved a hit with the public. She disembarked at Gravesend on March 7 on the royal yacht *Victoria and Albert* to be greeted with deafening cheers from the crowd on the riverbanks and little boats bobbing about in the water as Bertie, ten minutes late, ran up the gangway to kiss her. "It was her smile of greeting that I shall always remember—the wonderful smile which ravished all in the days when she came a girlbride, and with its undying beauty to the end," raved the *Daily Express*.[4] The couple then traveled by train to the Bricklayers Arms station in Southwark, a heavy-goods station that had been converted into a "perfect triumph of the decorative art."[5] After being greeted by representatives of the railway company and civic dignitaries, they boarded a carriage to London Bridge, with an escort of Life Guards, where the procession was joined by the carriages of the livery companies, the lord mayor of London, and the prime minister, Lord Palmerston.

London Bridge had been lavishly decorated by J. B. Bunning, the city architect, with standards bearing the Danish emblem of the raven and the elephant. One hundred incense burners gave off "the most graceful fragrance."[6] A massive triumphal arch had been mounted on the bridge, decorated with royal portraits, coats of arms, allegorical figures, and a representation of Britannia in a chariot drawn by four horses, welcoming Princess Alexandra to Britain.

From London Bridge, the route passed through dense crowds wearing wedding favors and waving Danish flags to the Mansion House, where the Lady Mayoress, attended by eight young women in white dresses, presented the princess with a bouquet.

The diarist Arthur Munby, watching the procession from King William Street in the city, heard the bands approaching and the sound of deep hurrahs coming nearer and nearer:[7]

> *The great crowd surged to and fro with intense expectation. The glowing banners of the City procession reappeared and passed, and the countless carriages full of blue robes and scarlet robes and Lord Lieutenants' uniforms and the Volunteer bands and the escort of the Blues [a Guards regiment]; and the first three royal carriages whose occupants . . . were heartily cheered. But when the last carriage came in sight, the populace, who had been rapidly warming to tinder point, caught fire all at once. "Hats off!" shouted the men; "Here she is", cried the women; and all those thousands of souls rose at her, as it were, in one blaze of triumphant irrepressible enthusiasm, surging round the carriage, waving hats and kerchiefs, leaping up here and there and again to catch sight of her, and crying Hurrah. . . . She meanwhile, a fair haired graceful girl, in a white bonnet and blush roses, sat by her mother, with "Bertie" and her father opposite, smiling sweetly and bowing on all sides, astounded—as she well might be—but self-possessed; until the crowd parted at length.[8]*

There was enormous excitement and genuine enthusiasm for the royal couple, and the immense crowd was generally good-natured, but the shortage of city policemen led to poor crowd control. The men of the London Volunteer Brigade, who were supposed to take up a position outside Mansion House, arrived too late to get through the crowd, and the procession frequently ground to a halt, with carriages unable to get through to take their place in the procession. At several points, the Life Guards had to clear the way with drawn sabres.[9] It later emerged that several people had been crushed to death.[10]

The procession continued up past St. Paul's Cathedral, where seating for ten thousand people stretched from Cheapside to Ludgate Hill, and then along Fleet Street as far as Temple Bar, which had been made into another heavily decorated triumphal arch. At this city boundary the procession ended and the lord high steward of Westminster took over, with the royal party traveling via Hyde Park Corner to Paddington Station, where they took a train to Slough, which would be followed by another carriage procession to Windsor. The young princess took it in her stride, smiling and waving to the cheering Eton schoolboys despite her long and tiring journey and the fact that her carriage arrived in darkness and torrential rain.[11]

Queen Victoria's response was rather different. When Princess Alexandra finally arrived at Windsor Castle, the queen told her that although the wedding would be "the only ray of happiness" in her life since her husband's death, she was too "desolate" to join the young couple for dinner.[12] This approach set the tone for what was supposed to be a gloriously happy occasion. On the day before the wedding, Queen Victoria conducted Bertie and Alix to Prince Albert's mausoleum at Frogmore. "I opened the shrine and took them in. . . . I said, 'He gives you his blessing!' and joined Alix's and Bertie's hands, taking them both in my arms. It was a very touching moment and we all felt it."[13]

There is a photograph, described by one author as "possibly the most repulsive picture in the Royal Archives,"[14] that reflects this curious event. The photograph depicts the young couple standing politely before the bust of the late prince consort, with Queen Victoria, in full mourning, eyes fastened on the image of her late husband while Alix looks self-conscious and Bertie appears to be frankly resentful. The "bust" photographs were not unusual: a series appears in the royal family albums. But this particular photograph casts a long shadow over the wedding preparations, like a wicked fairy's curse in an old folk tale. It was scarcely an auspicious start to Alix and Bertie's married life.

On the morning of the wedding, Queen Victoria dressed in her customary mourning, with long black streamers and white veil, with the badge of the Order of the Garter that had belonged to Prince Albert and a miniature decorated with his portrait. The queen made her way separately to St. George's Chapel, under a covered way constructed for the occasion, which took her into the north side of the altar that had been built by Henry VIII to enable Catherine of Aragon to watch the ceremony of the Order of the Garter and had henceforth been known as the "Catherine of Aragon closet." From this prominent position, Queen Victoria, who was conscious that she was being photographed, stared fixedly not at the ceremony itself, but instead at the marble bust of her late husband.[15]

As nine hundred guests crammed into St. George's Chapel, Bertie, with risers in his shoes, stood five foot seven in his size eight boots and general's uniform. Bertie had been promoted to the rank of general on his twenty-first birthday. From Bertie's shoulders hung the cloak of the Order of the Garter. As he stood between the Crown Prince of Prussia, his brother-in-law, and the Duke of Coburg, waiting for his bride, Bertie kept casting nervous glances up at his mother in the Catherine of Aragon closet, where she appeared "agitated and restless" and in a state of profound melancholy.[16] As Jenny Lind, "the Swedish nightingale," sang in the chorale that had been composed by Prince Albert, the queen threw back her head and looked "away with a most painful expression on her face."[17] "See," commented one observer, "she is worshipping him in spirit!"[18] By this stage, Crown Princess Vicky, Princess Alice, and her sisters were in tears.

In contrast, Princess Alexandra was completely composed, walking demurely down the aisle on her father's arm. Pale from crying and saying good-bye to her mother, Alix wore a white dress trimmed with Honiton lace and garlanded with orange blossom with a long silver train, which had to be held by eight bridesmaids.[19] By the time she reached the altar, Alix was twenty minutes late, setting the tone for the lifetime of unpunctuality that would drive Bertie to distraction. In other unedifying scenes, wedding guests were shocked to see the Knights of the Garter hurrying down the aisle in a giggling huddle, rather than stepping decorously two by two.[20] But the worst behavior came from Vicky's son, the future Kaiser William II. Young children can often be difficult at weddings, but the four-year-old William, clad in Highland dress, kept throwing the cairngorm from the top of his dirk across the choir.[21] William also hurled his aunt's muff out of the carriage window, addressed Queen Victoria as "duck," and bit Prince Alfred on the leg.[22] Benjamin Disraeli, who had dared to look at the queen, had received a cold stare, but still recalled the wedding as "a fine affair, a thing to remember, a perfect pageant . . . the beautiful chapel, the glittering dresses, the various processions . . . the heralds, the announcing trumpets, the suspense before the procession appeared, the magnificent music. . . ."[23]

The royal party lunched separately from the other guests. Queen Victoria did not attend, and ate alone. Later, Queen Victoria watched as the newly married couple's carriage left Windsor Castle for the railway station, en route for their honeymoon at Osborne on the Isle of Wight. The carriage halted briefly under Queen Victoria's window, and Bertie and his new bride looked up at her. Once Bertie and Alix and their guests had departed, Queen Victoria walked down to the mausoleum to pray beside Prince Albert's tomb.[24]

Excited crowds, including many boys from Eton College, flocked to greet the royal carriage as it arrived at Windsor Station. Among these young Etonians was Randolph Churchill, who vividly recalled the scene:

"Nothing stood before us. The policemen charged in a body, but they were knocked down. There was a chain put across the road, but we broke that; several old *genteel* ladies tried to stop me, but I snapped my fingers in their face and cried, 'Hurrah!' and 'What larks!'

I frightened some of them horribly. There was a wooden palisade put up at the station but we broke it down. . . . I got right down to the door of the carriage where the Prince of Wales was, wildly shouting, 'Hurrah!' He bowed to me, I am perfectly certain; but I shrieked louder."[25] Randolph also observed that Alix had strong nerves, because she did not look frightened, just kept smiling blandly as the frenzy continued around her.

There are no intimate details, but it appears that Bertie and Alix did have a genuine "honeymoon period" during which they were said to look "comfortable and at home together."[26] The wedding night might have come as something of a shock to Alix, as it did to so many well-brought-up young girls. But these early days seem to have been satisfactory: according to Crown Princess Vicky, meeting the couple soon after their wedding, "love has certainly shed its sunshine on these two dear young hearts and lends its unmistakable brightness to both their countenances. . . . Bertie looks blissful. I never saw such a change, his whole face looks beaming and radiant."[27] To Queen Victoria's genuine delight, the Alix she encountered on their return to Windsor Castle was "sweet and lovely." It was not to last.

Chapter Three

"GAY PAREE AND LONDON LOWLIFE"

Oi, Wales, are you goin' to pay for my champagne?
—"LA GOULUE" OF THE MOULIN ROUGE

Bertie and Alix embarked on their married life among the splendid surroundings of Marlborough House in Pall Mall. A beautiful Queen Anne mansion, Marlborough House had originally been designed for Sarah Churchill, Duchess of Marlborough, by Sir Christopher Wren. The house had passed to the Crown and had been allocated to Bertie in 1860 and was the ideal royal residence, its high walls lending a secluded air while "its ballroom was large enough to entertain the whole of London Society and its lawns, running down to the Mall, proved a splendid setting for garden parties. . . ."[1] Marlborough House swiftly became an alternative court, where Bertie and Alix lived with "the gay abandon of two children suddenly set free on a floodlit stage, with all the scenery and gorgeous costumes to play with. They went to balls every night of the season, they dined in the houses where Queen Victoria advised them not to go, they attended the opera and theatre dressed in glittering outfits, and gave the crowds their money's worth."[2] These days were the happiest days of their marriage. But within a year, childbirth had begun to take its toll upon poor Alix. Prince Albert Victor was born two months prematurely in 1864, followed by his brother George a year later, four weeks prematurely.[3] In November 1867, another confinement rendered Alix unable to accompany Bertie to St. Petersburg for the wedding of Alix's sister to the Tsarevitch Alexander. During his six-week absence, Bertie's head was turned by the "sirens of St Petersburg."[4] When Bertie returned to England, Alix was undergoing a ghastly pregnancy and suffering from rheumatic fever. As a result, doctors refused to allow her anesthetic and her baby daughter, Louise, had to be delivered without chloroform. Alix suffered serious long-term consequences from rheumatic fever, which left her with a damaged knee and triggered deafness that would become a real problem during middle age.[5] Following the birth of Louise, Alix had two more daughters, Victoria, born 1868, and Maud, born 1869. Prince Alexander John, Alix's last child, was born in 1871[6] but lived for less than twenty-four hours. After the age of twenty-six, Alix never had another baby.

As if this was not enough to put a strain on their marriage, the fundamental incompatibility of the couple's personalities began to emerge. Pleasure-loving Bertie, charming and dissolute, was a very different character from Alix, a natural homebody. Indeed, Alix's character was the embodiment of the Danish word *hygge,* meaning a loving, informal gathering of friends and family. To make matters worse, Alix's health problems made her a poor sexual partner for the demanding Bertie, who began to seek consolation elsewhere, adding to Alix's distress. Lady Macclesfield, one of Alix's ladies-in-waiting, recalled: "the Princess had another bad night *chiefly* owing to the Prince promising to come in at 1 AM and keeping her in a perpetual fret, refusing to take her opiate for fear she should be asleep when he came. And he never came till 3 AM!"[7]

While Alix was recovering from a series of difficult confinements, Bertie was living in style, traveling across Europe with his entourage from hotel to hotel. Luxury suites were kept in preparation for the prince in Paris, Marienbad, Monte Carlo, and Cannes, and he became a familiar figure at opera houses and casinos. Despite his increasing girth, Bertie was always so immaculately dressed and impeccably groomed that even the French admired his sartorial elegance. Bertie changed six times a day, and his style was quickly imitated: when he left the last button of his waistcoat undone to accommodate his expanding waistline, all other men followed suit. The prince had little interest in the formal side of society: enough of his life was already constrained by protocol and consumed by an interminable sequence of receiving lines and diplomatic functions. What Bertie liked was fun, the company of attractive and lively women, cards after dinner, and the carpet rolled back for dancing.[8] Bertie preferred his women bright but not clever. As Daisy Warwick later noted, "The Prince had a horror of highbrows."[9]

Bertie loved parlor games, high jinks and "ragging," and mock duels with soda siphons.[10] Sometimes, Bertie's japes could verge on the sadistic. He took pleasure in humiliating his friend Christopher Sykes, a Yorkshire landowner and MP, by pouring brandy over his head while Sykes repeated over and over again, "As Your Royal Highness pleases."[11]

In London, his anonymity preserved by trusted friends and the fact that photography had not yet made his distinctive features instantly recognizable, Bertie enjoyed the lowlife. Disguised as any other "champagne Charlie," Bertie was free to prowl the demimonde of the Alhambra Rooms and Mott's dancing rooms in Foley Street, acknowledged dens of vice patrolled by the middle ranks of London's fifty-thousand-strong army of prostitutes. Bertie could visit the notorious Cremorne Gardens, a pleasure garden in Chelsea where toffs and swells rubbed shoulders with clerks and pickpockets, and couples disappeared into the bushes for al fresco sex. Bertie relished the freedom to walk about London unrecognized, to be driven in a hansom cab, or, one of his favorite activities, to see a big fire. Captain Eyre Shaw, head of the London Fire Brigade, was under strict orders to report a good blaze immediately to Marlborough House.[12] Other high jinks included "galloping through London in a pink coat with the Royal Buckhounds like an unruly schoolboy, chasing a deer from the Queen's herd known as 'the Doctor' from Harrow through Wormwood Scrubs to Paddington Station where it was cornered in the goods yard in front of the staff of the Great Western Railway."[13]

Bertie had a hand-picked band of accomplices for these exploits, including Lord "Harty-Tarty" Hartington, heir to the Duke of Devonshire, and Sir Frederick Johnstone, a member of the Bullingdon Club at Oxford, notorious even in those days for smashing up restaurants. Lord Dupplin, a Scottish earl, and Lord Hardwicke, MP for Cambridgeshire and the original "Champagne Charlie," were also members of Bertie's entourage, and the Marquis of Hastings, or "the wild Markis,"[14] as he was known in the London underworld, was another favorite. Bertie had met Hastings, "the kind of self-annihilating rake who had flourished around the Earl of Rochester during the Restoration," during his brief period at Oxford. Hastings was a textbook hell-raiser, who at Oxford had breakfasted on claret and mackerel cooked in gin.[15] Handsome and rich, Hastings loved nothing better than to slum it alongside the sailors in the brothels of Rotherhithe. One night at Mott's dancing rooms, Hastings turned up with a handful of sacks, and, just as the dancing was at its height, asked one of his cronies to turn off the lights. At that point, he opened the sacks and released two hundred full-grown sewer rats loose onto the dance floor.[16] It was Hastings who introduced Bertie to cockfighting at Faultless's Pit in Endell Street, Holborn, where he could pit his birds against those owned by the Duke of Hamilton, and ratting, where aristocrats would bet on how many rats a terrier could dispatch within one hour.[17]

In 1864, Hastings had eloped with Florence Paget, fiancée of his best friend, Henry Chaplin, snatching her away from the doors of Marshall and Snelgrove's department store and whisking her off to be married at St. George's Church, Hanover Square. Three years later, Chaplin got his revenge. On an unseasonably cold Derby Day, in May 1867, Henry Chaplin's horse, Hermit, went off at 66 to 1.

Hastings bet heavily on the favorite, taking spiteful side action on Chaplin's longshot horse. In a storybook ending, Hermit charged out of the sleet to win, stunning the oddsmakers and costing Hastings no less than £120,000. Chaplin's winnings were £140,000. A year later, *The Times* announced that Hastings was dead, "ruined in health, in honour and in estate."[18]

In May 1867, while Alix was still recovering from the birth of Princess Louise, Bertie was invited to open the International Exhibition in Paris. Sir William Knollys, Bertie's private secretary, wrote that "the accounts I subsequently heard of this visit were very unsatisfactory; suppers after the opera with some of the female Paris notorieties, etc. etc."[19]

Paris was Bertie's spiritual home. Here, for the remainder of his life, Bertie would be accepted by the worldly French as the consummate *bon viveur,* a connoisseur of wine, women, and horseflesh. Bertie had first visited Paris at the age of fourteen, with Queen Victoria. In 1855, the young Prince of Wales had wowed the French by appearing in Highland dress as he was driven through Paris with Napoleon III.[20] Life back in England must have seemed very tame after that. Paris in 1867 was every bit as exciting as Bertie had remembered, and he soon discovered that Napoleon III's tastes were very similar to his own. This was the man who remarked that he needed a woman, like a good cigar, after every meal.[21] Here, Bertie could find "love treated as an art, a high society which pursued a civilised routine of sexual pleasure, a ready welcome from the most skilful mistresses of Europe."[22] The French attitude to beauty was that it was "a commodity which demanded a certain conventional devotion. There was an admitted objective brutality mingled with the aesthetic admiration. Young men were brought up to appreciate a fine woman by matching her to a catalogue of classic points, as if she were a high-bred horse or a Ming vase. . . ."[23] Men paid court to the *grandes horizontals,* the fabulous courtesans who held sway over art and fashion, wooing them with diamonds and banknotes. It was inevitable that Bertie, with his appetite for pleasure, would fall prey to these shrewd and manipulative women. Parisian courtesans, unlike their more unfortunate sisters operating on the street corners, could pick and choose their followers. It was something of a coup to be accepted by one of these legendary goddesses, such as Cora Pearl or La Barucca. And Bertie was a willing victim.

The first of Bertie's French mistresses was Hortense Schneider (1833–1920), a professional singer who had excelled in Jacques Offenbach's operettas, particularly *Orpheus in the Underworld,* as well as *La Vie Parisienne* and *La Belle Hélène.* Described by the Marquis de Villemer as "exciting, modern, ironic—the froth of the champagne,"[24] Hortense was exactly the sort of woman who appealed to Bertie, and Bertie appealed to her. Hortense had such a great weakness for royalty that she came to be known as *"Le Passage des Princes."*[25] Bertie had to accept that she was not his exclusive property and that her long-term lover was Lord Carrington, with whom he had once shared Nellie Clifden. Hortense Schneider was the first of Bertie's mistresses to have her name linked to him publicly, being mentioned in *The Times,* with a mixture of disapproval and envy, in 1867. At this period *The Times* did not possess the automatic deference of the establishment newspaper. Instead, it shared with other newspapers displeasure with the royal family, ranging from prurient interest about Bertie's personal life to the suggestion that the queen, the self-indulgent "Widow of Windsor," should abdicate, as she did not play a sufficient part in public life. Bertie, for all his faults, it was felt, did at least show himself "more zealous and courteous in the performance of all his duties."[26] Bertie was regularly compared with his ancestors, the Regency rake George IV and the debauched Prince Hal from Shakespeare's *Henry IV Part One.* Bertie's response to the criticism of his relationship with Hortense Schneider was to take his wife, Princess Alexandra, to watch Hortense perform in Paris. The impact of this upon the already long-suffering Alix may be imagined.

Cora Pearl (1835–1886), who had begun life as ordinary Eliza Crouch from Plymouth, once appeared on stage alongside Hortense while Bertie was in the theater. Cora, clad in nothing more than two oyster shells and a five-franc piece, strategically fell over during the performance so that the audience could admire the diamonds on the soles of her shoes.[27] While Cora was no actress, her activities that night had been sufficient to kindle Bertie's interest. Cora, whose antics included being served up for dinner naked on a large silver dish (with a parsley garnish), was an accomplished and spirited young woman.[28]

Bertie was also friendly with another lively expatriate, Catherine Walters, or "Skittles," the former mistress of Harty-Tarty. Skittles had arrived in Paris in 1862,[29] after Harty-Tarty had dumped her in favor of Louisa, Duchess of Manchester. Born in Toxteth, Liverpool, Skittles possessed a compelling combination of blond hair, blue eyes, and a mouth that could make a docker blush. On one occasion, when Skittles was thrown from her horse while out riding in Hyde Park, a gentleman hurried across Rotten Row to see whether she was hurt.

"Hurt be damned!" Skittles replied, rising to her feet and dusting herself down. "Wait til I get my arse on that damned saddle. I'll teach the bastard to go!"[30]

An outstanding horsewoman, Skittles had been spotted by Lord Fitzwilliam while exercising horses for a livery stable and swiftly elevated to the position of mistress. Even the snooty country set accepted Skittles and permitted her to ride to hounds on account of her superb equestrian skills. On one occasion, Skittles cleared the eighteen-foot water jump at the National Hunt Steeplechase course at Market Harborough for a £100 bet, after three other riders had tried and failed.[31]

In Paris, one of Louisa's "protectors" was the young and somewhat naïve Wilfrid Scawen Blunt, diplomat and aspiring poet, who witnessed Skittles's transformation from a healthy English horsewoman to a sophisticated *poule deluxe*, "dressed up and glorified for the world, beset by a crowd of wondering fools."[32] Scawen Blunt suspected that a more powerful lover lurked in the background, but could never be sure of his identity. Widely believed to have been Bertie's mistress, but also known for her discretion, Skittles left a teasing reference to an affair with Bertie in her papers. According to Skittles, Bertie had once commented: " 'You always promised we should be friends some day' and so it began." As Bertie's biographer Jane Ridley states, we don't exactly know *what* began, but Skittles claimed to have possessed a drawer full of letters from Bertie, perhaps set aside as a pension. But these disappeared after she died and were never to be available for posterity.[33]

One of the most beautiful courtesans in Paris, "La Barucci," made an indelible impression on Bertie. Born Giulia Benini (1837–1871) in Rome, La Barucci had black eyes, luxuriant black hair, golden skin, and an air of southern languor. Within months of her arrival in Paris, La Barucci's looks had earned her an apartment on the Champs-Élysées, and a jewel chest the size of a wardrobe, full of precious stones.[34] La Barucci granted her favors to the entire Jockey Club, and somehow managed to remain on good terms with all of them. When Bertie visited Paris in 1867, the Duc de Grammont-Caderousse invited La Barucci to dine with them at the Maison d'Or. Before the meeting, the duke briefed La Barucci at length on the protocol required for the occasion, and warned her, strictly, not to be late, as the Prince of Wales was highly punctilious when it came to timekeeping. As the hour approached for the arrival of La Barucci, the duke and the Prince of Wales stood waiting for her to appear. Ten minutes passed, and then twenty, and then half an hour, and Bertie began that activity that every host feared, drumming his fingers in irritation. At last, after three-quarters of an hour, La Barucci swept in, an unrepentant vision in a blaze of diamonds. "Your Royal Highness," said the duke. "May I present to you the most unpunctual woman in France?" Whereupon, La Barucci spun around, and with one swift movement lifted her skirts and bent over to show Bertie, as one source described it, "the white rotundities of her callipygian charms." When the duke reproached La Barucci for mooning the Prince of Wales, she retorted: "I showed him the best I have—and it was for free!"[35]

As a man of appetites, Bertie did not restrict himself to courtesans. In Paris, as in London, he also had affairs with society ladies such as Jeanne Seillière, the Princesse de Sagan, "an industrial heiress who had made a grand match" by marrying into the grand Talleyrand-Périgord family, who also owned the Sagan estates.[36] In Paris, the Prince de Sagan was known as the *fleur des pois,* "the pick of the crop." He was an elegant dandy, with a caustic wit, and a notorious and completely unregenerate womanizer who "excelled in the art of paying homage to women who showed themselves attentive to him, like a cat, without good-faith or law."[37] Hurt and angry, Jeanne de Sagan passed most of her time at her homes in Cannes and Deauville, and at the Chateau de Mello, about sixty miles south of Paris, which she had spent considerable money on restoring and developing. An enterprising woman, Jeanne de Sagan had built laboratories at Chateau de Mello to distill perfumes, and it was a common joke in her circle that she was using them to find a method to poison her husband.[38] Far from being annoyed by the fact that Bertie was having an affair with his wife, the Prince de Sagan reveled in it, finding it rather chic to be cuckolded by the Prince of Wales. When Bertie visited the Chateau de Mello, the atmosphere was like that when Louis XV called upon Madame de Pompadour, the staff, from the lowliest scullery maid to the butler, whipped into a frenzy of activity preparing for his arrival. When Jeanne de Sagan bore a child, nine years after the birth of her first son, Hélie, he was assumed by all to be the son of Bertie.[39]

Bertie was not popular with one member of the Princesse de Sagan's household. By the age of fifteen, Hélie had conceived such a violent hatred of Bertie that upon one occasion, after finding Bertie's clothes on a chair in his mother's boudoir, he picked the garments up and hurled them out of the window into the fountains. When Bertie emerged from Jeanne's bedroom, it was to find his sopping wet clothes being retrieved from the ponds by hysterical servants. Bertie, as a stickler for correct dress, was annoyed, and had to drive away wearing a pair of trousers "borrowed" from the Prince de Sagan, which were too tight.[40]

Bertie could not have been described as a serial monogamist. The prince of pleasure never restricted himself to one individual woman, but was forever chasing another conquest. By 1867, a pattern had emerged of a sexually insatiable man who loved to surround himself with willing women, short- and long-term mistresses, courtesans, and bona-fide prostitutes. As "a rake of truly catholic tastes,"[41] Bertie was as ready to dally with a harlot as a duchess.[42] And Bertie never seemed to differentiate in the pursuit of his ideal: young, high-spirited, feminine in appearance but somewhat masculine in character. Bertie also managed to remain on good terms with his mistresses once the affairs were over; throughout his life, we see evidence of his kindness and generosity toward his former lovers. This was of course contingent upon the behavior of these women. In certain cases, to remain on good terms was impossible; in one case, it was tragic.

In 1871, Bertie received a letter from a Mrs. Harriet Whatman, who was writing to him through "a sense of duty and loyalty to your Person" and out of concern for her close friend, "a most unfortunate and unhappy lady."[43] This unhappy lady was Lady Susan Vane Tempest, one of Bertie's earliest mistresses following his marriage. Lady Susan had been widowed after her husband, a violent alcoholic, had died in a madhouse, and now she was facing another tragedy. According to Harriet, Lady Susan was facing a "crisis." "The Position is a most pitiable one and most dangerous for all parties. Without *any funds* to meet the necessary expenses and to buy the discretion of the servants, it is impossible to keep this sad secret."[44] In other words, Lady Susan was pregnant and claiming Bertie as the father.

If Lady Susan had still been married, this might not have been a problem. In society, the convention in such circumstances was that the husband would raise the child as his own. This was part of his code as a gentleman. But a single woman who fell pregnant faced social annihilation. Harriet's letter made it plain that Lady Susan's pregnancy was advanced. It was a plea for funds, as Lady Susan's "private means were very small,"[45] and an attempt at blackmail, with the rather threatening statement that "I dread some catastrophe that may awaken public attention to the facts."[46]

The same post brought a letter from Lady Susan herself. "I cannot tell your Royal Highness how *utterly miserable* I am that you should have left London without coming to see me . . . what have I done to offend you?"[47] she wrote, before adding that she had done her best to "obey the orders your Royal Highness gave me the last time I had the happiness of seeing you, but the answer was '*too late* and *too* dangerous.'"[48]

At a time when termination was illegal, the word "abortion" never appears, but Lady Susan's next letter to Bertie makes the situation clear. "Your Royal Highness blames me for not at once going to Dr C. as you desired me, but you can understand it was *most* painful to go to an *utter stranger* under such sad circumstances, when my own doctor had done everything he could for me as long as it was possible to do so with safety."[49] "Dr C." was Oscar Clayton, Bertie's own physician.

Lady Susan went on to apologize for keeping Bertie in ignorance of the facts, hoping that she could deal with the situation herself, but now, obviously facing the prospect of giving birth, she was looking for a small house to rent, away from prying eyes, in "Southend, Surbiton or Ramsgate. Perhaps as the latter is a seaside place it might be the safest, as people would not then wonder why I left town."[50] Lady Susan was subsequently installed in a town house in Wellington Crescent, Ramsgate, to await the birth of a child in late 1871. But on February 3, 1872, she wrote to Bertie's private secretary, Francis

Knollys, asking for more money to pay Clayton's fees, as she was feeling very unwell and could not even set foot out of bed. There is no mention of a birth, suggesting that Clayton had performed a late abortion and Lady Susan was suffering from complications. Lady Susan's last letter to Bertie, sent five days later to congratulate Bertie on his recovery from typhoid, ends on a disturbing note: "Forgive me such a *scrawl* my dear sir as I am a cripple on two sticks and cannot move about!!!!"[51] Lady Susan died just three years later, and the fate of her child is unknown.

Chapter Four

MORDAUNT VS. MORDAUNT

*To sin in secret was one story, to shake the home by getting into the
newspapers or law courts another. . . . Society turned pitilessly
on those who tumbled openly into trouble.*
—ANITA LESLIE, *EDWARDIANS IN LOVE*

In 1869, Harriet Mordaunt, wife of Sir Charles Mordaunt, MP, gave birth to her first child at their country seat, Walton Hall in Warwickshire. Harriet's baby, a daughter named Violet Caroline, was born prematurely and swiftly developed an eye infection. While this is a common-enough condition, Harriet became obsessed with the idea that there was something seriously wrong and that Violet had been born blind as a result of inherited venereal disease. Harriet seems to have developed postpartem psychosis, and servants later alleged that she had even tried to kill her baby. Harriet sent for her husband, Sir Charles Mordaunt, and confessed that she had committed adultery "in open day" with three men: Lord Cole, the Earl of Enniskillen; Freddie Johnson; and the Prince of Wales.[1]

The eye infection was soon cured, and there was no evidence that Violet had inherited venereal disease, but the damage was done. Sir Charles broke into Harriet's desk, found three letters from Bertie, and commenced divorce proceedings. This was an almost unprecedented action in Victorian upper-class society. The convention was that a gentleman would avoid the scandal of divorce at all costs, and accept the "bastard child" into his family. But Sir Charles was not a gentleman, and was unwilling to play by Marlborough House rules.[2]

Bertie's culpability in all this is debatable. Bertie had certainly written to Harriet, sending her those noncommittal little notes that he sent to all his lady friends, lovers or otherwise. There was also a valentine, but perhaps that was a lighthearted gesture. In some respects, Harriet occupied the role of old friend rather than mistress. Bertie had known Harriet from childhood, when she had been little Harriet Moncreiffe, growing up near Balmoral in a family of Scots beauties. Sensitive and highly strung, Harriet was not really mistress material; she lacked "that asbestos lining to the sensibilities that was so necessary for any woman playing sexual hide-and-seek around the Prince."[3]

Harriet had entertained Bertie at the Moncreiffes' London home before her engagement to Sir Charles Mordaunt, MP for South Warwickshire, and Bertie's visits had continued after their marriage. Given Bertie's reputation, Sir Charles's suspicions were understandable. But the Mordaunts had seemed at ease with the Marlborough House set, visiting the theater with Bertie and Alix and even staying as guests at Sandringham. Whether there was something more between Harriet and Bertie was a matter for conjecture. During the divorce trial, servants giving evidence on behalf of Sir Charles claimed that Harriet had entertained male visitors alone at Walton Hall, acting like "a beast of the field."[4] Bertie was just one of those male visitors. In July 1869, Sir Charles returned home unexpectedly from a fishing expedition and found Harriet driving two white ponies, a gift from Bertie, while Bertie stood on the steps and looked on. Bertie left immediately and Sir Charles ordered the grooms to bring the ponies round. Sir Charles dragged Harriet down the steps and shot the ponies dead in front her.[5]

Harriet's family, fearing the loss of their good name, declared that she was insane from the outset and the tales of affairs were nothing more than fantasy. While Harriet's family maintained that Harriet was unfit to appear in court, Sir Charles responded that she was faking her symptoms to avoid a trial. Harriet was examined by medical experts, including the leading and enlightened "mad doctor" Thomas Harrington Tuke and Bertie's personal physician, William Gull, who could not agree on a diagnosis. As a result, the judge, Lord Penzance, ruled that the question of Harriet's sanity would have to be decided upon by a jury, in open court. By the time the case came up, Harriet had deteriorated physically and mentally; her symptoms included hysterical laughter, eating the fluff off the carpet, and daubing feces on the walls.[6] But the legal point was whether Harriet was actually mad when the writ for divorce was served on her.[7]

Bertie found himself in the highly embarrassing position of being subpoenaed as a witness in the Mordaunt divorce trial. No Prince of Wales had ever been subpoenaed to appear in court before, let alone in a divorce case, and the prospect of being cross-examined was dreadful.

"I shall be subject to a most rigid cross examination by [Mordaunt's counsel] who will naturally try to turn and twist everything that I say in order to compromise me," Bertie wrote to the queen. "On the other hand, if I do not appear, the public may suppose that I shrink from answering these imputations which have been cast upon me. Under either circumstance I am in a very awkward position."[8]

The press had already smelled blood. The republican *Reynold's Newspaper* accused Bertie of being "an accomplice in bringing dishonour to the homestead of an English gentleman."[9] As one biographer put it: "the irresponsible gossip spread a misconception of the Prince as a superman of pleasure, who lacked serious interests."[10]

Bertie's family and friends went to great lengths to save him from the embarrassment of having to appear in court. Queen Victoria wrote to the lord chancellor, Lord Hatherley, saying that the court appearance would damage Bertie in the eyes of the middle and lower classes, showing him as imprudent in forming a close relationship with a young married woman.[11] The lord chancellor replied that the law was clear in this respect: even the heir to the throne could be subpoenaed and forced to appear. In desperation, Bertie turned to George Lewis, the most famous solicitor of the day. Lewis was described in *The Dictionary of National Biography* as a solicitor who "obtained what was for more than a quarter of a century the practical monopoly of those cases where the seamy side of society is unveiled, and where the sins and follies of the wealthy classes threaten exposure and disaster."[12] While Lewis appeared in almost every cause célèbre in the London law courts for thirty-five years, his reputation lay not in just his skill in winning cases but in keeping them out of court altogether.[13] On this occasion, however, even Lewis could not keep Bertie out of court. Lewis's advice was: "Accept the summons. Go boldly into the witness box—it is the only way to clear your name."[14]

Bertie was called to give evidence before Lord Penzance and a special jury on February 23, 1870. It had been decided not to cite Bertie as a corespondent but as a witness on behalf of Harriet, who by this time had been declared insane and confined to an asylum. Bertie underwent a seven-minute examination in the witness box by Harriet's counsel, who asked outright, "Has there ever been any improper familiarity between yourself and Lady Mordaunt?" As Bertie replied resoundingly, "No! Never!" applause rang out from the public gallery. Bertie was not cross-examined by Sir Charles's counsel, and Sir Charles's petition for divorce was dismissed on the grounds of Harriet's insanity.

"I trust by what I have said today, that the public at large will be satisfied that the gross imputations which have been so wantonly cast upon me are now cleared up," Bertie wrote to his mother later that day.[15] But the public at large was not so easily silenced. *Reynold's Newspaper* speculated that "even the staunchest supporters of monarchy [must] shake their heads and express anxiety as to whether the Queen's successor will have the tact and talent to keep royalty upon its legs and out of the gutter"[16] upon reading that Bertie was appearing in a divorce court.

Bertie's indiscretions were treated as crimes: he was hissed at in the streets of London, and greeted with boos and catcalls when he arrived at the theater. Princess Alix stood by throughout these events, accompanying Bertie to official functions, and winning hearts and minds of her own on account of her loyalty. On one occasion, at a City of London dinner, when the toastmaster summoned guests to raise their glasses to the Prince of Wales, the guests shouted: "To the Princess!"[17] Three months later, at Ascot, Bertie was met with further abuse, but when one of his horses won the last race, the crowd relented and cheered him. "You seem to be in better temper now than you were this morning, damn you!"[18] Bertie retorted, and the crowd whooped and laughed. All was forgiven. Bertie was the people's Prince once more.

Throughout the Mordaunt divorce case, Bertie demonstrated his extraordinary instinct for self-preservation. Had Bertie undergone a cutthroat cross-examination from Sir Charles's counsel, and somehow implied that he had been involved with Harriet, the consequences were unimaginable. To sin so outrageously against the Victorian moral code could only lead to exile and death, as Oscar Wilde was to discover a generation later. But Bertie neatly sidestepped the allegations and it was accepted that Harriet, far from telling the truth by a confession of adultery to her husband, had been out of her mind. This would not be the last time that Bertie would escape a public whipping and leave a victim bobbing in his wake; he may not have intended to sacrifice Harriet, but that was the consequence.

The real scandal in all this was the fate of poor Harriet. Whether or not Harriet had originally been mad, and her symptoms suggest postpartum psychosis, she had certainly become mad by the time of the trial. Harriet's daughter, Violet, was taken from her, and raised in a cold and loveless fashion at Walton Hall. Harriet never recovered, and spent the remainder of her life in asylums. Mercifully, she was spared the worst excesses of Victorian mental treatment as a patient of the enlightened Dr. Tuke, who ran a progressive and liberal regime at the Manor House Asylum in Chiswick. Harriet later moved on to Hayes Park Private Asylum in Hillingdon, which specialized in distressed aristocrats, and died in 1906. She was buried in Brompton Cemetery.[19] Harriet, mad or not, never had any doubt that Bertie had been responsible for her downfall; the last we see of Harriet is the poor woman hurling a teacup at a portrait of Bertie and screaming: "That has been the ruin of me. You have been the curse of my life, damn you."[20]

Chapter Five

JENNIE CHURCHILL, THE DOLLAR PRINCESS

*Lady Randolph was like a marvellous diamond—a host
of facets seemed to sparkle at once.*
—DAISY, COUNTESS OF WARWICK

O ne of Jennie Jerome's earliest memories was being hoisted onto the back of her father's racehorse, Kentucky, after it won the Saratoga Cup in 1864.[1] This image provides a lasting impression of young Jennie, with her huge gray eyes and glossy black hair: a young girl raised in luxury, seated upon a prizewinning racehorse, the apple of her father's eye. Nothing was too good for Jennie Jerome.

Jeanette "Jennie" Jerome had been born ten years earlier to Leonard Jerome, millionaire property speculator, and his wife, Clara, who claimed Iroquois descent in the days before it was socially acceptable to mention Native American ancestry. Named after the opera singer Jenny Lind, she was raised in New York City with her sisters, Clara (1851–1935) and Leonie (1859–1945). Leonard Jerome was the prototypical American millionaire: flamboyant, generous, larger than life. His passion for the theater and opera was surpassed only by his love of horses, and it was said that when he acquired land on which to build a mansion on Madison Square in 1860 he built his stable before he built his house. The mansion itself was spectacular, redbrick trimmed with white marble, looking like nothing so much as an enormous strawberry pie set amid the chocolate rows of brownstone houses.[2] Above the stable Jerome built a private theater, handsomely adorned, and for years it was the center of fashion. New York's top four hundred families eagerly sought admission to Jerome's fantastic parties, and he "dazzled society with the glitter and novelty of his carriages, the costliness of his blooded horses, and excited its dubious admiration by his extravagance, his fantastic speculation, his scandalous love affairs, his incredible parties."[3] He made, lost, and made again fortunes; he was reputed to be worth more than ten million dollars. Jerome was also a ladies' man, often seen driving around Manhattan in a coach loaded with beautiful women. On Sundays, he would wave to friends strolling to church. "[G]ay and laughing ladies in gorgeous costume filled the carriage . . . with a huge bouquet of flowers attached to his buttonhole, with white gloves, cracking his whip, and with the shouts of the parties, the four horses would rush up Fifth Avenue, on toward the Park," as people said to one another, "That's Jerome!"[4]

Clara Jerome, who had been brought up to spend Sundays at home with the blinds drawn, disapproved of such extravagance and tried to keep her daughters in the country.[5] But in 1867 Mrs. Jerome took the girls to Paris, along with their black nurse, Dobby.[6] Mrs. Jerome was aware that she had three soon-to-be-marriagable daughters and was concerned about their future. Although the Jeromes were wealthy, Leonard's boom–and–bust career was precarious, and the family was considered nouveau riche by the American top drawer. In Europe, their fortunes might be different; indeed, their wealth would be welcomed by impoverished titled families eager to marry "dollar princesses." Mrs. Jerome emphasized their French surname, originally Huguenot, as evidence of their old-world breeding.[7]

In 1867, with the Second Empire at its height, Paris reveled in a daily succession of "royal processions and cavalcades," fetes and parties.[8] Mrs. Jerome organized an exhausting course of cultural activities for her daughters, and introduced them to French high society. Still a great beauty, Mrs. Jerome was known as *la belle Amer-icaine*,[9] while her daughters experienced the French equivalent of the debutante scene at the French imperial court. Clara attended her first ball at the Tuileries at the age of eighteen, dressed in a white crinoline, curtseying to Emperor Louis Napoleon and Empress Eugénie. At a cotillion, resplendent in her white dress with mar-guerites, Clara played *chat et souris* (cat and mouse) and was chased by the Prince Imperial in and out of the crowd of guests, until she caught her foot in the Duchesse de Mouchy's dress and fell over.[10]

But storm clouds were gathering. France went to war with Prussia in 1870 and despite the court apparently carrying on as before, this way of life was about to change. France attacked Germany and suffered serious losses, but kept her spirits high. When the Jerome girls attended the opera, the entire audience stood up to sing "La Marseillaise."[11] Lessons ceased as the maids and governesses disappeared. Mrs. Jerome sprained her ankle and could scarcely walk, and the girls realized that this golden world they had inhabited all too briefly was about to dis-appear.[12] The family fled to the Gare du Nord, Mrs. Jerome hobbling on the arm of Dobby, and caught the last train out of Paris.[13]

The Jeromes arrived in England tired and despondent and made their way to London, where they stayed at Brown's Hotel. Jennie re-called that "a winter spent in the gloom and fogs of London did not tend to dispel the melancholy which we felt."[14] She missed the French court and spent the time playing piano and walking around Hyde Park practicing her German conversation with an Austrian *fräulein*. A former pupil of Stephen Heller, Jennie was a gifted pianist, and Chopin's Funeral March fitted her mood. France was over: some of their friends had been killed, others were ruined. Clara mourned the departure of the French aristocrat with whom she had been in love, and young Leonie was packed off to school in Germany.[15] Jen-nie, a spectacular beauty of eighteen, began to realize that her future lay in England.

This became even more important two years later, when Leonard Jerome's financial empire took a direct hit during a Wall Street crash. Leonard was not ruined exactly, but certainly compromised.[16]

It was a case of in England we trust, and rescue came when Clara and Jennie were invited to the Royal Regatta at Cowes on the Isle of Wight and presented to the Prince and Princess of Wales. Even at this early juncture, Jennie made an impression on Bertie. Later that evening, the girls attended a dance on board HMS *Ariadne*, given in honor of their Imperial Highnesses the Grand Duke Cesarevitch and Grand Duchess Cesarevitch of Russia. It was here that Jennie met her fate, in the form of Randolph Churchill.

At first glance, the twenty-three-year-old Randolph did not seem an obvious match for Jennie. Outwardly cold and reserved, Randolph possessed a slim boyish figure, a weird laugh, and a moustache that seemed to have a life of its own. His round protruding eyes had earned him the nickname "Gooseberry-faced Churchill" at school, and he was accompanied at all times by his pug.[17] But Randolph had the distinction of being the younger son of the Duke of Marlborough; and he was also smitten with Jennie.

The dark hair, the gray eyes "put in with a sooty finger,"[18] and the air of tragedy that hung about her after her European adventures gave Jennie an edge over the English debutantes. Randolph was invited to dinner the following evening, and made a great impression on the Jerome family, apart from Clara, who said straight out that she disliked him. But Jennie cut her short, telling Clara that this was the man she was going to marry. At the same time, Randolph was telling his friend Colonel Edgcombe that he intended to make "the dark one" his wife.[19]

The following evening, Randolph returned to the Jeromes' villa, and, despite being completely unmusical, agreed to play a duet with Jennie. Colonel Edgcombe later commented on the lovely sight of the golden head and the dark side by side over the keyboard.[20] After coffee, Randolph invited Jennie outside into the garden, where he proposed to her, and was accepted.

Winston Churchill, in his memoirs, pictured the scene: "That night, the third of their acquaintance, was a beautiful night, warm and still, with the lights of the yachts shining on the water and the sky bright with stars."[21] When the couple returned indoors, Mrs. Jerome demanded why they had spent so long outside. When Jennie retorted that she had just received a proposal of marriage, Mrs. Jerome replied that she felt the decision "precipitate" and "over-hasty."[22] Jennie must think this through. To which Jennie replied that there was nothing for her to think through. A similar response greeted Randolph when he told his father that he had proposed to an unknown American girl on the strength of three days' acquaintance. Randolph, the future Conservative MP, used all his eloquence, responding that "all I can say is that I love her better than life itself . . . my one hope and dream now is that . . . I may soon be united to her by ties that nothing but death itself could have the power to sever . . ."[23] and he asked for his allowance to be increased so that they could be married. "She is as good as she is beautiful . . . in every way qualified to fill any position."[24] This included being the wife of a Tory MP. Randolph had hitherto been reluctant to seek election to Parliament, a dream that his father had long cherished for him. Now Randolph as good as promised that he would stand for Parliament if he were allowed to marry Jennie. The duke, patriarch of a family that married for status, not for love, remained unconvinced. With the spectacular rudeness that is the hallmark of the British aristocracy, the Duke of Marlborough commented that Mr. Jerome was a "sporting and I should think vulgar sort of man,"[25] a speculator who had been bankrupt once and might be so again. Worst of all, according to the duke, Mr. Jerome was "not respectable," making Jennie nothing more than "an American adventuress."[26]

Over in New York, Mr. Jerome showed a similar reaction when

Jennie wrote him about her betrothal. "You quite startled me," he replied. "I fear if anything goes wrong you will make a frightful shipwreck of your affections. I always thought that if you did fall in love it would be a very dangerous affair."[27] Leonard Jerome's attitude softened, however, in the course of the letter, and by the close he was saying he was prepared to accept this sudden engagement. "I could not object . . . provided he is not a Frenchman or any of those Continental cusses."[28] Unfortunately, when Leonard Jerome learned about the Duke of Marlborough's objections, he withdrew his consent. Jennie was forbidden to reply to Randolph's letters, and Randolph himself was told that, as a test of his affection, the couple were to wait a year before getting married.

Leonard Jerome, investigating Randolph's background, would have heard of the following, discreditable incident. In March 1870, while he was an undergraduate, Randolph was involved in a fracas with two policemen following a dinner at the Randolph Hotel, Oxford. Randolph was fined ten shillings for assault, but acquitted of being drunk and disorderly. And there the matter might have been at an end had Randolph not decided to take out an action against Constable Partridge, one of the arresting officers, accusing him of perjury. A waiter, Alfred Wren, was summoned as a witness and provided an itemized list of the alcohol Randolph had consumed that fateful evening: champagne, hock, sherry, claret, port, and punch. At some point in the proceedings Randolph spilled some wine and threatened the waiter with a wine cooler. The charge against Constable Partridge was dropped, but the affair ended badly. After Randolph threatened that the Churchills would boycott the hotel as long as the waiter remained an employee there, Wren was sacked.[29]

Randolph, who was already becoming a consummate political operator, told Jennie that he would stand for Parliament, but, unless they were allowed to marry, he would withdraw at the last minute, allowing the radical candidate to triumph in a traditional Tory seat.

"All tricks are fair in love and war."[30] The trick worked. Randolph was elected as MP for Woodstock, Oxfordshire, on February 4, 1874, with 569 votes. Randolph's Liberal opponent was George Broderick, a fellow of Randolph's own college, Merton.

The Duke of Marlborough had no option but to agree to the marriage, and the following week Randolph arrived in Paris to see Jennie and the couple were blissfully reunited. Just how blissfully and closely reunited they were is a matter for some conjecture. Mrs. Jerome was a strict mother, anxious to guard her daughter's reputation. The couple were officially not permitted to see each other alone, and Mrs. Jerome attempted to keep Jennie under twenty-four-hour escort. Such were Victorian values. While it was considered entirely permissible for a young lady to go out riding with every Tom, Dick, and Harry, it was considered improper for a single woman to share a carriage with a man, let alone a drawing room. And yet there is the possibility that Jennie managed to give her mother the slip.[31] This was a dangerous business: had Jennie been caught in Randolph's hotel room at the Rue de Rivoli, her reputation would have been in tatters. And yet Randolph wrote: "I like to think of you being in my room. You can't think, darling, how I long to be back—"[32] It would have been an audacious move on Jennie's part, considering that she had so much to lose, and yet it is typical of impulsive, unconventional Jennie that she would take such a risk.

By October 1874, the Duke of Marlborough agreed that the couple could marry as soon as Randolph was elected to Parliament. Leonie, Jennie's little sister, heard the news from a stranger while at school in Wiesbaden. "Last night at the circus someone told me that Jennie would marry the second son of the Duke of Marlborough—a Good Thing tho' he *is* a younger son!"[33]

Jennie would become one of many American heiresses whose money contributed to the upkeep of a stately home and a ruined family. Despite his stock market losses, Leonard Jerome was still a wealthy man and contributed a settlement of £50,000, which he wanted to give to his daughter but which, in the end, went jointly to the couple. Jerome was shocked to discover that Jennie's fortune would be absorbed by Randolph's family, as was traditional. It would be another eight years before the Married Women's Property Act ensured that women were permitted to keep their own money and property. Meanwhile, the Duke of Marlborough settled £20,000 on Randolph and paid off his son's £2,000 debts.[34]

Jennie and Randolph were married at the British Embassy in Paris on April 15, 1874. Although Jennie had wanted a church wedding, this would have involved a lengthy period of residence in Paris to qualify. Leonie, permitted leave from boarding school to attend her sister's wedding, recorded Jennie resplendent in a white satin dress trimmed with Alençon lace and a tulle veil that covered her entirely from head to foot.[35] Clara and Leonie, her bridesmaids, were dressed in pale blue silk and wore their bridesmaids' presents, crystal lockets. The service was performed a second time at the American Legation, and then the happy couple dined alone, as was the embassy tradition, while their guests sat down to a splendid lunch in a room bursting with white floral displays. At two o'clock, Jennie appeared in her "going away" outfit, a dark blue-and-white-striped traveling dress, and a virginal white coat with a white feather.[36] A beautiful carriage with four gray horses and two postilions waited to carry them off to a chateau near Paris called Petit Val, lent by Mrs. Charles Moulton, an American expatriate. Just before the couple left, Leonard Jerome presented his daughter with a beautiful parasol, made of Alençon lace, with a gold and tortoiseshell handle.[37] Bertie and Alix had already sent Jennie a locket of pearl and turquoises.[38]

When the happy couple arrived home from their honeymoon to Woodstock station in Oxfordshire, they were met by cheering tenants from Blenheim estate, who were so pleased to see them that they unfastened the horses from their carriage and dragged the carriage back to Blenheim Palace.

"As we passed through the entrance archway and the lovely

scenery burst upon me," Randolph said, with pardonable pride, "this is the best view in England. . . . Looking at the lake, the miles of magnificent park studded with old oaks . . . the huge and stately palace . . . I confess I felt awed." [39]

But life for Jennie at Blenheim was not an unalloyed pleasure. Jennie was a city girl, urban to her fingertips, and she felt lonely and uncomfortable among the country set. As an American, and a nouveau riche American at that, she was accustomed to a more informal atmosphere. And as the daughter in a close-knit, happy family, Jennie struggled to cope with the cold and distant formality of the Churchills. Jennie's mother-in-law, the Duchess of Marlborough, treated her with disdain. She "ruled Blenheim and nearly all those in it with a firm hand. At the rustle of her silk dress the household trembled." [40]

The Churchill sisters were jealous of Jennie's accomplishments as a gifted musician and horsewoman, and sneered at her "Red Indian" ancestry. Jennie, with her jet black hair and huge eyes, looked as out of place as a panther at a garden party. But even the Churchills had to acknowledge that this magnificent new brood mare brought a healthy streak to an otherwise inbred and delicate bloodline. As one admirer later put it, Jennie possessed "more of the panther than of the woman in her look, her courage not less than that of her husband— fit mother for the descendants of the great Duke." [41]

Like many an American heiress, Jennie was horrified by the austere, unfashionable nature of country house life. In letters home to Mrs. Jerome, Jennie deplored the clunky water jugs and tumblers on the dinner table, the frumpy clothes of the Churchill women, and even their tablemats. She was shocked by the feudal tradition by which the duke and duchess carved the roasts and distributed them to the entire family, including governesses and tutors, with the remains being carried off to the children in their separate quarters. "How strange life in a big country house seemed to one whom until then, had been accustomed to towns!" [42] It was almost like being back in the schoolroom, with every day the same, a cycle of reading, piano practice, and whiling away the time with walks in the garden or visits to neighbors before the long and tedious dinner, which was followed reading or a game of whist. For a high-spirited girl of twenty, the boredom was unendurable.

Jennie soon escaped to London, when she and Randolph moved to their house in Belgravia for a round of dinners, balls, and parties. Jennie was formally presented to Queen Victoria, and the Prince and Princess of Wales. This allowed Jennie to renew her acquaintance with Bertie, who had been so impressed by her beauty when they met at Cowes. And then there were the races, an obvious source of pleasure to Jennie after growing up in a racing household. "We used to drive down in coaches in Ascot frocks and feathered hats, and stay to dinner, driving back by moonlight,"[43] she recalled. At Ascot in 1874, Jennie was the center of attention, wearing her wedding dress, as was the custom. A bonnet trimmed with pink roses completed the outfit, and the exquisite lace parasol, that wedding gift from Leonard Jerome, framed her beautiful features.[44]

As an excellent horsewoman, Jennie drew the grudging admiration of the Churchills for her skill in the saddle. But Jennie's enjoyment was soon cut short when she discovered that she was pregnant. Banned from riding, she was forced to spend every afternoon with the duchess during visits to Blenheim. These visits, to a girl of Jennie's spirit, sound unendurable: "Our return found the drawing room full of lots of people having tea. . . . You cannot imagine how stiff & uncomfortable the first hour of their arrivals are. No one knows each other & so content themselves with staring. . . ."[45] Matters did not improve after dinner, when the time was spent talking "gossip & slander . . . everyone is pulled to pieces & and it is not only the women . . . the men I assure you are quite as bad."[46]

In November, when the shooting season was under way, Jennie joined the guns for their picnic, then followed the men in a pony and trap. On November 28, rattling home from a shoot, Jennie went into labor. On November 30, 1874, Jennie gave birth to a son, Winston Leonard Spencer-Churchill, born some two months prematurely. While this might be taken as evidence that Jennie and Randolph had anticipated their marriage vows, Jennie's second child was also born early, suggesting that Jennie may have had a weakness in the neck of the womb, causing premature labor.

Having produced an heir for Randolph and recovered swiftly from the ordeal, Jennie could look forward with excitement to her third season in London, away from the stultifying gloom of Blenheim Palace. Sadly, the stalwarts of London society had different ideas. Despite the fact that Jennie brought money to the Marlborough clan, she was regarded as a gold digger, while the British upper class revealed its deep-rooted racism by referring to her as a "Red Indian."[47] There was also more than a little jealousy: Jennie appeared to be a potential royal mistress. Bertie, who had sent Jennie a bracelet during the first year of her marriage, had become a regular guest at the Churchills' house in Charles Street, often calling when Jennie was alone. Bertie was also a genuine friend of Randolph's, finding him more entertaining than any other man he knew.[48] But within a year, the Aylesford scandal would see Bertie fall out bitterly with Randolph and ban the Churchills from court. Jennie could do nothing but watch in horror as the scandal unfolded.

Chapter Six

THE AYLESFORD SCANDAL

Poor little Edith and that Churchill cad!
—"Sporting Joe" Aylesford

n October 1875, Bertie set off on an official tour of India, against the wishes of Queen Victoria, who was genuinely concerned about her son's health. Bertie had narrowly avoided death from typhoid in 1871, after contracting the disease at Londesborough Lodge near Scarborough. The drains had leaked into the drinking water, and Lord Chesterfield and a groom had died.[1] The queen also had a low opinion of the companions Bertie had chosen to accompany him on the visit. While among the eighteen men Bertie had enlisted to travel with him were his nephew, Prince Louis of Battenberg, and Colonel Owen Williams, commander of the Royal Horse Guards, the party also included some notable reprobates. The queen particularly objected to Lieutenant Lord Charles "Charlie" Beresford, RN, and Lord Charles Carrington, with whom Bertie had shared Nellie Clifden. Queen Victoria instructed the prime minister, Benjamin Disraeli, to warn both young men against "larks." As Lord Carrington wrote to his mother, wistfully, "no jokes, or any approach to them . . . no whist and no sprees, or bear fights, or anything!"[2] Another colorful character along for the ride was Heneage Finch, Earl of Aylesford, familiar to all as "Sporting

Joe" because of his reputation for "racing, gaming and whoring."[3] Sporting Joe was a close friend of Bertie, and he and his wife, Edith, had entertained Bertie and Alix, at ruinous expense, at their country house, Packington Hall in Warwickshire. Edith was the sister of Colonel Owen Williams, and she and her sisters had all married into the peerage. Bringing up the rear of the Indian contingent was the Duke of Sutherland, who took along his own piper, Alistair, to serenade the party every night after dinner.[4]

Bertie made a good impression in India. The maharajahs admired his sporting prowess and royal bearing, while the Indian professional classes were impressed by his liberal views and refusal to tolerate racism. Bertie wrote angrily to Lord Salisbury, the secretary of state for India, protesting about the "disgraceful habit" of some British officers who referred to the Indians as "niggers."[5] Bertie toured India for five months, shooting elephants, tigers, and cheetahs, attending state receptions, meeting Indian royalty, and even visiting murderers in prison. In February 1876, he reached Nepal, where one thousand riding elephants and a squad of ten thousand soldiers were put at his disposal. On February 21, after shooting six tigers from the back of an elephant, Bertie returned to his lavishly appointed camp to find that a mood of despondency had descended on his companions. Bertie's only reference to the event was recorded in his diary as "Letters!!!" but the word was highly significant.[6]

Ever since the party had arrived in India, Sporting Joe had been writing home to Edith, describing humorous incidents on the tour, and always addressing his wife as "My darling" and concluding "Your most affectionate Joe."[7] Despite his hell-raising lifestyle, Sporting Joe apparently adored Edith and was very much in love with her. They had two daughters, but Sporting Joe was still waiting for the all-important male heir to carry on the title. Edith's replies were few and far between, and it became a standing joke of the India trip that, when the mailbag arrived, there was a letter for everyone apart from Sporting Joe.

The reason for this soon became obvious. Within hours of Sporting Joe writing an affectionate letter home, mentioning sadly that he had received only five letters from Edith in as many months, a letter arrived. Sporting Joe opened it with excitement, as his friends gently mocked him. But within seconds of opening the letter, all the color drained from his face. Edith had written to Sporting Joe that she intended to leave him and elope with Lord Blandford, son and heir of the Duke of Marlborough, and brother of Bertie's great friend Randolph Churchill.[8]

While Sporting Joe had been traveling with Bertie in India, Edith had been carrying on an affair with Lord Blandford. Within days of her husband's departure, Edith had invited Lord Blandford to come and stay with her at Packington Hall, for the fox-hunting season. Lord Blandford moved his hunters to a nearby livery stable and rented a house in the village. Every night, Lord Blandford visited Edith at Packington Hall, leaving footprints in the snow as he headed for a back door to which Lady Edith had given him a key.[9] Lord Blandford made no attempt to cover his tracks and soon everyone knew about the affair: the servants, the grooms, and the entire village. Edith's sisters, fearing for their own position in society, were on the point of informing their brother, Colonel Williams, about Edith's bad behavior, but before they could do so, the colonel was summoned home as his wife was critically ill.[10]

When Sporting Joe told Bertie and his friends that Edith was planning to elope with "that Churchill cad!"[11] Bertie advised him to go home at once and resolve matters. Sporting Joe climbed into a howdah and vanished in the direction of the nearest railhead. As Anita Leslie says, "this was the last the royal party saw of him and there is nothing more melancholy, majestic and uncompromising than the hind view of an elephant."[12] "He has gone home broken-hearted at the disgrace," wrote Lord Carrington, "and the misery it all entails is terrific."[13]

Sporting Joe began his miserable five-week journey back to England, during which his anger grew. He was totally out of his depth. Sporting Joe was a man's man, who "drank hard and gambled away his money and was more popular with men than women."[14] He was one of the greatest huntsmen of his generation, who could fly his horse over the highest fences by sheer technique, a heavyweight who "could ride with hands of gossamer."[15] Alas, Sporting Joe did not possess the same lightness of touch when it came to women. "Certainly the way he had with a horse was not his way with a woman."[16] In short, Sporting Joe loved Edith, in his way, but could not understand what would drive a nervous, insecure woman, four years his senior, into an affair with another man, let alone Lord Blandford. For all his "intelligence, wit and charming voice," Blandford was Sporting Joe's equal in the hell-raising stakes, an attention-seeking self-dramatist said by some to be touched with the reputed Marlborough madness.[17] Humiliated and angry, Sporting Joe wrote to his mother, the Dowager Lady Aylesford, telling her to send for his daughters immediately and to keep them until he returned to England. Edith agreed to renounce her daughters—she had little choice in the matter—and wrote to her mother-in-law a few days later.

Dear Lady Aylesford,

By the time this letter reaches you, I shall have left my home for ever. . . . I do not attempt to say a word in self-defence, but you can imagine I must have suffered much before I could have taken such a step: how much it would be impossible to tell you . . . you do not know, you cannot know, how hard I have tried to win his love, and without success, and I cannot live uncared for. I do not ask you to think unkindly of your son; I know you could not do it, but for God's sake be kind to the children, and do not hate them to hate their wretched mother, let them think I am dead, it will be the best, . . .[18]

When Sporting Joe eventually arrived back in England, he found the Churchills trying to dissuade Lord Blandford from eloping with

Edith, while accepting that it was impossible to get him to give her up, despite the fact that both were married. This created bitter tensions between Lord Blandford and the Duke of Marlborough: "You have displayed to me an untold cruelty of intention," Lord Blandford wrote to his father. "What can it affect you who I marry and who my children may be? In what manner do they come into the circle of your life? What matters it in the future of our things? For what considerations of a worldly character have you thought fit to step in to sacrifice my whole life?"[19] Louisa, Duchess of Manchester, visited Edith and was concerned about her friend's total change in personality since embarking on the affair with Lord Blandford. Edith seemed "bewitched" by him, adopting all his mannerisms and even brandishing a box of poisonous pills to take in case anything happened to him.[20] Louisa described Blandford contemptuously as behaving like a character in a fourth-rate French novel.[21]

Meanwhile, all attempts to keep the scandal from going public were failing. Lord Blandford's brother-in-law, Dudley Coutts Marjoribanks, 1st Baron Tweedmouth, wrote to the Duke of Marlborough, saying: "I don't think anything is very generally known as yet, only the following people are aware of everything. The Duchess of Manchester, the Princess of Wales, the Charles Kerrs and Huntington and Lords Alington and Lansdowne."[22] One might just as well have announced the liaison on the front page of *Reynold's Weekly*. By early March 1876, *everyone* knew, thanks to Sporting Joe, who prowled the gentlemen's clubs vowing to divorce Edith and telling anyone who would listen that Bertie himself had described Lord Blandford as "the greatest blackguard alive."[23]

This scandal was not restricted to the Aylesfords and the Churchills. It had particularly harmful implications for Bertie's reputation. It was common knowledge among the Marlborough House set that Bertie was fond of Edith and had written her three mildly flirtatious letters in 1873.[24] Edith showed Bertie's letters to Lord Blandford, who immediately handed them over to his younger brother, Randolph

Churchill. Randolph quickly seized on the possibilities of these letters. If he could persuade Bertie to forbid Sporting Joe from divorcing Edith, the Churchill family honor might be saved. Otherwise, Randolph would publish the letters. Randolph was proposing nothing less than blackmail.

Randolph's next step was to visit Princess Alexandra at Marlborough House, accompanied by Lord "Bunny" Alington, a racehorse trainer and close friend of Edith, and Edith herself, somewhat against her will, one imagines, as she was keen to marry Lord Blandford.[25] This visit created an additional level of embarrassment for Alix, as she should not have received someone as tainted by scandal.[26] In front of Alix, Randolph insinuated that if Sporting Joe sued Edith for divorce, Bertie's letters to Edith would be made public and Bertie "would never sit upon the throne of England!"[27] Poor Alix was understandably horrified, both by Edith's presence and by the revelation of yet another indiscretion on the part of Bertie. Going straight to the queen, Alix poured out her story, and received a sympathetic hearing. As for the queen, she wrote to Bertie:

> *What a dreadful disgraceful business about Lady Aylesford and Lord Blandford! And how unpardonable of Lord Alington to draw dear Alix into it! Her dear name should never have been mixed up with such people. Poor Lord Aylesford should not have left [Edith]. I knew last summer this was going on. Those Williamses are a bad family. . . .*[28]

The queen's private secretary, Sir Henry Ponsonby, wrote to Bertie's private secretary, Francis Knollys: "Lord R Churchill who had been a very intimate friend of the P. of Wales and Pss also spoke to Her R H'ss about it—and afterwards threatened to publish letters from the P of Wales to Lady A if HRH did not prevent Aylesford bringing an action for divorce. The letters are said to be innocent but containing chaff which might be mis-interpreted."[29] Colonel

Williams, Edith's brother, suspected that the case was unlikely to go to court, as Sporting Joe's own character would not stand up to public scrutiny. "Aylesford is already so unsavoury that it will not do for him to appear in the Divorce Court."[30] Among Sporting Joe's peccadilloes was his habit of visiting Cremorne Gardens after dinner, picking up prostitutes, and going home drunk at three o'clock in the morning.[31]

By this point, Bertie had arrived in Cairo, Egypt, on his journey home to England. In Cairo Bertie was appalled to hear about Randolph and Edith's visit to Princess Alexandra. Bertie's mood degenerated further when Randolph telegraphed asking Bertie to tell Sporting Joe to drop his divorce suit against Edith. Although Bertie had so much to lose if those letters to Edith were ever published, he steadfastly refused to intervene in this private quarrel. However, Bertie had become so incensed by Randolph's behavior that he sent a message back, via Lord Hardwicke, challenging Randolph to a duel.[32] Randolph's infuriating response was to point out that Bertie's father, Prince Albert, had made dueling illegal in England, and to insinuate that Bertie had only offered the challenge because he knew that he could not go through with it.[33] Not content with this response, Randolph added that he blamed Bertie for the whole affair, because he had taken Sporting Joe out of the country, leaving Edith vulnerable and alone.[34] The friendship between the two men, hitherto a good one that had even withstood allegations about Bertie's affair with Jennie, had been utterly destroyed.

Almost forgotten in all this was the forlorn figure of Lord Blandford's wife, "Goosie," daughter of the Duke of Hamilton. Goosie, real name Bertha, seems to have been somewhat naïve. Far from regarding Edith as a rival, she adored her and even copied her style of dress. A great fan of practical jokes, including ink bottles over the door frames and short-sheeted beds, Goosie commented on the scandal in her own, unique manner. One morning, Lord Blandford lifted the cover on his customary poached eggs to discover a little pink celluloid baby. Lord Blandford slammed down the lid in horror and fled choking from the room.[35]

While Lord Hardwicke wrangled Sporting Joe, persuading him not to divorce Lady Edith, the prime minister, Benjamin Disraeli, intervened with Randolph Churchill. In his capacity as leader of the Conservative party, Disraeli attempted to argue some sense into the young MP;[36] he also reminded Randolph that he had known him since boyhood and that he was ruining his prospects with this campaign against Bertie. Meanwhile, the Duke and Duchess of Marlborough continued to be horrified by the scandal, which threatened to leave a blot on the Churchill family name. By the time Bertie returned to England on May 11, 1876, the Aylesford scandal was common knowledge, as was the implication that Edith had been involved with Bertie. Indeed, society people could talk of nothing else. Bertie was so keen to explain himself to Princess Alexandra that he insisted Alix join him on board before he disembarked, so that he could speak to her alone and give her his side of the story.[37] After this, the couple traveled up to London together with their family, and drove past cheering crowds to Marlborough House, in what should have been a triumphant homecoming after Bertie's successful tour of India. That evening, the Prince and Princess of Wales attended a gala performance of Verdi's *Un Ballo in Maschera* at Covent Garden Opera House in a bravura display of family solidarity. It was a brave move, and it worked: as the couple appeared in the royal box, the audience rose to their feet in a standing ovation.[38]

Eventually, Lord Blandford's friends managed to persuade him not to see Edith for a year. Lord Blandford reluctantly agreed, and left for Belgium, where he wrote to Randolph Churchill:

> *Poor little Edith, I telegraphed her from Brussels. I enclose you a letter for her. Please post it at once. . . . I must say though with Edith it is not worth all the trouble to avoid the Divorce Court . . . one thing*

strikes me. If [Sporting Joe] leaves matters as they are between him and Edith I shall only wait till HRH comes back to appear on the scene and then if [Sporting Joe] tries to lick me I shall do my damndest to defend myself and afterwards If I am all right, I shall lick HRH within an inch of his life for his conduct generally, and we will have the whole thing up in the Police Court![39]

This would have been a horrific prospect for Bertie, but he did at least have the support of his mother. Queen Victoria maintained that Bertie's letters to Lady Edith were essentially innocent, "but the publication of any letters of this nature would be very undesirable as a colouring might easily be given and injurious inferences deduced from hasty expressions. The Queen, therefore, regrets that such a correspondence, harmless as it is, should be in existence; but Her Majesty thinks it quite right that His Royal Highness should not interfere in Lord Aylesford's affair in consequence of this threat. . . ."[40]

The following day, Lord Hardwicke appeared at Marlborough House and announced that Sporting Joe, "not wishing to create a public scandal and mischief," had decided not to divorce Edith. In effect, society itself had exerted so much pressure on Sporting Joe that he had to back down. There was to be no divorce, but the following year, 1877, the Aylesfords agreed to a formal separation.

The threatened divorce might have been averted, but the Aylesford scandal still caused considerable collateral damage for both families. Unable to marry Lord Blandford, Edith had to resign herself to remaining as his mistress. The couple traveled in Europe as "Mr. and Mrs. Spencer" and in 1881, Edith gave birth to a son, Guy Bertrand Spencer, in Paris.[41] Guy was not permitted to succeed to the Aylesford title, as Sporting Joe was clearly not his father. Instead, Guy spent much of his boyhood at Blenheim, "a mysterious wraith in that great dumping ground for children."[42]

In the Churchill camp, Randolph's efforts to suppress the divorce ruined his relationship with his brother, Lord Blandford, but at least

Jennie stood by Randolph, telling him that she thought his brother was "worthless."[43] The couple left England and went to stay with Jennie's father in America, where Randolph was forced to sign an apology to Bertie, appropriately enough in Saratoga, New York, where British General John Burgoyne had surrendered to the Americans in 1777.

When Jennie and Randolph Churchill returned to England in the winter of 1876, it was to discover that Bertie had effectively banned them from society. While Queen Victoria was still prepared to entertain the Churchills, the Prince and Princess of Wales threatened to boycott any house that they entered, and only two people disobeyed: Louisa, Duchess of Manchester, who told Bertie to his face that "I hold friendship higher than snobbery," and John Delacour, a close friend of Randolph, who declared, "I allow no man to choose my friends."[44]

There were also repercussions for Randolph's parents, the Duke and Duchess of Marlborough, whose name had inevitably been tainted by the Aylesford scandal. The wily old prime minister, Benjamin Disraeli, smoothly removed the Churchills from public view by offering the Duke of Marlborough the post of viceroy of Ireland. Marlborough had no choice but to accept and agree to what Disraeli referred to as "the dignified withdrawal of the family from metropolitan and English life."[45] In order to take up the appointment, which involved lavish and expensive entertaining, the duke was forced to raise funds by selling off many art treasures from Blenheim, a painful experience. When the queen met the Duke and Duchess of Marlborough at Windsor, she wrote that she "pitied them. They looked so *distressed, wretched,* and the poor Dss [duchess] especially, who could scarcely restrain her tears."[46] Randolph took on the unpaid role of private secretary to his father, duties that would not conflict with his interests as a member of Parliament but would enable him to beat a strategic retreat to Ireland. It was to be eight years before Bertie spoke to the Churchills again. In the meantime, Bertie consoled himself with the fiery Irish beauty Patsy Cornwallis-West, the latest in his long line of conquests, and one of the first "Professional Beauties" whose photographs were sold as postcards.

Having lost Edith, Sporting Joe decided to start a new life in America and took a 22,000-acre ranch in Texas. Known as "Judge" by his cowboys, on account of his firm but fair manner, Sporting Joe needed no excuse to open a bottle of whiskey for any man who dropped in. "He doesn't stop at one, neither," wrote one cowboy. "I've been to the ranch many a time to stay all night, and woke up in the morning to find the bottles lying around thick as fleas, the boys two deep on the floor snorin' like mad buffaloes and the Judge with a bottle in each hand over in the corner."[47] The whiskey did for Sporting Joe in the end. He died of drink in 1885, aged just thirty-six.

The death of Sporting Joe and Goosie's eventual divorce from Lord Blandford should, perhaps, have left the way open for Edith to become Lady Blandford, and then the next Duchess of Marlborough when Lord Blandford succeeded to the title in 1883. But it was too late. By now, Lord Blandford had married Lily Price Hamersley, a rich American widow. There was to be no happy ending for Edith. Exiled from society for her affair with Lord Blandford, she died in Paris in 1897. Collateral damage once again: some of Edith's woes were undoubtedly caused by her relationship with Bertie, and an attempt to use his letters as a bargaining tool. Did Edith's relationship with Bertie go beyond the bounds of friendship? Queen Victoria, we know, was prepared to give Bertie the benefit of the doubt, despite her knowledge of her son's incorrigible weakness for women. Although even Queen Victoria was forced to admit, to her private secretary, Sir Henry Ponsonby, "Tho' I never believed it, some people said it was Lady A the Pce admired—as Lord A was too great a fool to be really agreeable to the Prince of Wales."[48] Perhaps, while Sporting Joe was reluctantly prepared to share Edith with the Prince of Wales, losing his wife to Lord Blandford was a step too far.

Chapter Seven

THE JERSEY TOMBOY

I learned to steady my nerves, control my tears, and
see things from a boy's point of view.
—LILLIE LANGTRY

The woman who would become Bertie's most famous mistress, Lillie Langtry, was born in Jersey on October 13, 1853, a long way from the glittering world of London society. Lillie was born Emilie Charlotte Le Breton, the sixth of seven children and the only daughter of the Reverend William Corbet Le Breton, Dean of Jersey, and his wife, Emilie. Five brothers preceded Lillie: Francis, William, Trevor, Maurice, and Clement. Reggie, to whom Lillie was closest, was the last child, born a year after Lillie. "I was nicknamed 'Lillie' very early in life," Lillie wrote in her memoirs, "perhaps on account of my skin being unusually white, and that soubriquet has clung to me ever since."[1] "Lillie" was the way the young Lillie with a childish lisp pronounced her own name, and the pet name stuck. Lillie's mother, Emilie, had been a beauty in her day, "petite and lovely, with blue eyes, curling auburn hair and perfect skin,"[2] according to Lillie, growing up in Chelsea on the same street as the young Charles Kingsley, author of *The Water-Babies*, and his brother Henry, both of whom were madly in love with her. Charles tells us that Emilie was "the most bewitchingly beautiful creature he had ever seen."[3] Charles and Henry Kingsley had both wanted to marry Emilie, but, instead, Emilie chose the dashing and handsome Reverend Le Breton, a blue-eyed six-footer with an athletic physique and distinctive, prematurely white hair. According to Lillie, her father was "a remarkably handsome man, and widely adored for his gentility and charm of disposition." Born in Jersey to an old distinguished family, and educated at Winchester College and Pembroke College, Oxford, Reverend Le Breton was considered something of a catch. But he also possessed a character weakness that would lead to the humiliation of his wife and daughter and to his own spectacular downfall. It is no surprise that Lillie, a mistress of spin, omitted all mention of this in her narrative.

But this was all in the future. After coming down from Oxford, Reverend Le Breton had accepted a living at St. Olave's, Southwark, the church once frequented by the noted diarist Samuel Pepys. This was something of a surprise posting for an Oxford-educated public schoolboy, but Lillie tells us that her father rejected the position of dean of Jersey in favor of this insalubrious district as a matter of principle. As with so many of Lillie's comments, this has to be taken with a large spoonful of salt. Eventually, Reverend Le Breton accepted the offer of dean and returned home to Jersey with his wife and sons, and it was here that Lillie was born. In her memoir, Lillie described Jersey in lushly sentimental terms:

> *Jersey enjoys the benefits of the Gulf Stream, and therefore the climate is so mild that ixias, camellias, palms and geraniums flourish in the open air throughout the winter. The sky is intensely blue and the sea more violet than the Mediterranean. Indeed, with its indented shores fashioned by nature into numberless small and beautiful bays with their stretches of golden sand, its country lanes with their high hedges topped by green aisles of arching trees, its apple orchards, its soft-eyed cattle browsing knee-deep in cool green valleys through which brooklets of clear water wander, and the comely milkmaids in native costume, the little Isle is certainly most attractive.*[4]

Lillie's antecedents were portrayed in similarly glowing tones, the better to enhance her claims to nobility. Buying into family myth, Lillie boasted that her Jersey ancestors were seigneurs, or "lords of the manor," who dated back to the days of William the Conqueror. One particular forebear apparently fought at the Battle of Hastings and was recorded on the Bayeux tapestry. Such tales, poured into Lillie's ears by her father at an impressionable age, no doubt convinced Lillie that she was more than just the daughter of a rural dean. Other precursors included a bishop and a judge. And, since we all have black sheep in the family, there was a "shameful Le Breton who helped to murder Thomas a Becket," and Raoul Le Breton, "insultingly referred to in French histories as "The Channel Islands Pirate."[5]

On the face of it, life at the old rectory of St. Saviour's, known as "the Deanery," was idyllic. The Deanery, dating back to 1100, was built of gray granite, and "almost entirely covered with climbing roses—red, white, pink, blush" and, to Lillie, "me most beautiful of all) the single damask."[6] Surrounding the Deanery were ancient cherry and pear trees, a walled garden, an orchard, and a vegetable patch that the children all helped to weed. One entrance to the rectory was covered by a glass portico filled with flowering plants, a testament to Mrs. Le Breton's love of gardening; it was her only consolation. After seven pregnancies and an unhappy marriage Mrs. Le Breton had gone from Titian-haired beauty to a depressed invalid who had withdrawn into a world of plants and pet animals. The Le Bretons saw to it that their children were educated: the boys attended Victory College, a minor public school, during the day, and Lillie was taught at home by a French governess. But for the rest of the time the Le Breton brood ran wild, terrorizing the neighborhood with high jinks and practical jokes; any form of mischief in the vicinity was inevitably blamed on "the dean's children," and Lillie joined in enthusiastically, enjoying all their games and escapades and sharing in their punishments. Lillie had already learned a vital life lesson: her brothers had told her "what a miserable handicap it was to be a girl" and she had promptly decided that if she was going to join in, she would have to "steady my nerves, control my tears, and look at things from a boy's point of view."[7] This would prove to be valuable. Becoming "an incorrigible tomboy,"[8] Lillie learned to ride, swim, and sail, climbing trees and vaulting fences with her brothers and sharing in their practical jokes. Escapades including patrolling the churchyard of St. Saviour's at midnight, wearing stilts and draped in sheets, and terrifying late passersby.[9] This continued until someone wrote to the local paper threatening the "ghosts of St. Saviour's" with a dose of cold lead if they appeared again. The Le Breton children also had a passion for stealing door knockers, braving threats, dogs, enraged householders, and even shotguns to obtain one.[10]

One target was an old man called Wilkins, a retired tradesman who lived with his two unmarried daughters at the top of Deanery Lane. Although patient and long-suffering, sometimes he was exasperated beyond endurance by the exploits of the Deanery children, and complained to their father. One evening, having already relieved the poor man of his door knocker, the children tied a strong rope to his bell and tied the other end around a stone, which they threw over a wall opposite. The result of this was that everyone who passed by, whether on foot or on a horse, struck the chord, causing the old man's bell to ring furiously.[11]

Every time this happened, Mr. Wilkins emerged like a cuckoo from a clock striking the hour and hurled abuse at the innocent passersby. The children's laughter gave them away, and they were subsequently hauled up before their indignant father as he stifled his own laughter.[12]

Lillie's lifelong passion for horses began early and she learned to ride bareback, often mistaken for a boy as she galloped her horse along the sands. When she was thirteen, she and her younger brother, Reggie, bought a "weedy English mare"[13] at the Jersey cattle market.

They named the mare "Flirt" and nursed her back to health. Lillie and Reggie took turns to exercise Flirt, and at one point Lillie suffered a serious accident when she fell off. The following year, they entered Flirt in a race with Reggie in the saddle and won. The dean knew nothing of this escapade until it appeared in the local paper.[14]

A year later, as a young woman of fourteen, Lillie realized that it was time to take up her position in Jersey high society. She had already had a taste of official duties, substituting for her mother in visiting the sick, presenting prizes at school, and other island functions.[15] "I dare say thus being put forward a little prominently had the effect of making me rather precocious."[16]

Lillie had something of a high profile in Jersey, her unusual combination of good looks and high spirits ensuring that she attracted the attention of the gossips. And it had become evident that this mischievous tomboy was also becoming a beauty, with golden auburn hair and huge violet eyes. Jealous mothers and envious daughters who regarded Lillie as competition for the limited supply of eligible young men ensured that Lillie was soon notorious, "half witch and half hoyden."[17] It was said that Lillie had run naked up Deanery Lane for a dare; that she rolled naked in the dew of the Deanery meadow at dawn, and wore meat face-packs to achieve her incredible complexion.[18] The gossip failed to deter Lillie's suitors, and by the time she was fifteen she had already had her first proposal, from an officer named Arthur Longley, son of the archbishop of Canterbury, who was garrisoned on Jersey. But poor Longley did not appeal to Lillie, despite the fact that he went to the dean first and asked his permission to marry Lillie.[19] The dean declined, on the grounds that Lillie was too young.

It was already clear that Lillie would never be short of admirers. When she was introduced to Charles Harbord, 5th Baron Suffield (1830–1914), at a picnic, Lord Suffield commented: "Do you know, Miss Le Breton, that you are very, very beautiful? You ought to have a season in London."[20] Lord Suffield was a member of the royal household who often spent his summers in Jersey. His official role was lord of the bedchamber to the Prince of Wales; his unofficial role was that of talent scout, and he had doubtless spotted Lillie's potential as a potential mistress for the prince. Perhaps with a royal introduction in mind, Lord Suffield suggested that Lillie must come to dinner whenever she found herself in London.

This invitation appealed to Lillie, who had already conquered Jersey, and found no man there who could prove a worthy husband. For all her tomboyish ways, Lillie was fascinated by London society, with the true provincial's conviction that it was only in London that she would find her heart's desire. If she could reach London, the capital would fall under her spell, just as the men of Jersey had done. In years to come, Lillie would see the capital at her feet. But her first visit to London, when she was just sixteen, was far from satisfactory.

There was another reason Lillie needed to leave Jersey for a while. Lillie's admirers were numerous, but now another, more serious suitor had emerged from the ranks of available menfolk. This man's name remains unknown to this day, but he was described as a young fisherman, a blue-eyed boy a year or so younger than Lillie, from a modest background. At this point, the Le Breton household had been thrown into turmoil by the death of its third son, Trevor Alexander Le Breton. A lieutenant in the Royal Marine Light Infantry, Trevor had been killed in action in Toronto at the age of twenty-five, fighting against American forces.[21] Preoccupied by grief, the Le Bretons left Lillie to her own devices. And Lillie clearly found some consolation in the arms of her handsome blue-eyed swain, as she announced plans to formalize the relationship, even if the boy was not her social equal. At which point, Dean Le Breton pulled himself together, sat Lillie down, and gently told his daughter that their match could never be permitted. When Lillie demanded why, the dean admitted that the boy was his illegitimate son.

This shocking news revealed the true extent of the dean's philandering. In the past, Dean Le Breton's weakness for the opposite sex had been something of a joke. A popular anecdote describes the dean emerging from his own church with a local beauty on each arm. One was a Mrs. Knatchbull, the other a Lady Saumerez. At the sight of the notoriously lecherous dean, the irate husbands who had been waiting outside the church set about him with their walking sticks. The dean, experienced in extricating himself from jealous husbands, managed to slip away, leaving his would-be assailants to carry on the fight—against each other.[22]

In the past, Lillie had dismissed the gossip about her father as nothing more than tittle-tattle. But now, here was the evidence of her father's weakness in the form of an illegitimate son, rumored to be one of many. So all those stories Lillie had overheard, that no servant girl or flower seller was safe alone with her father, must be true. This was the real explanation for her mother's retreat into invalidism. Lillie herself referred only briefly to this event in her memoirs, viewing it from the perspective of fifty years. Male biographers have seized on Lillie's dismissive account of the incident as evidence of a calculating nature, an episode that "provides the key to the puzzle of that implacable coldness of heart which no man subsequently ever warmed."[23] There is a darker nuance to this story. Many years later, in a muttered aside, Lillie's verdict on her father was that "He was a damned nuisance. He couldn't be trusted with any woman, anywhere."[24] Was this comment evidence of a more disturbing relationship between Lillie and her father?

At this point, Lillie's mother came to her rescue. Despite her desperate unhappiness at the death of her son, and her chronic depression, Mrs. Le Breton planned a visit to London. Although Lillie could not be presented at court as a debutante, she could at least take up Lord Suffield on that invitation to dinner. Sadly, the first trip to London was a disaster. Years later, Lillie admitted: "When I walked into the ballroom, I felt like a clumsy peasant. My one 'party gown,' which had been made for me in St Helier, made me look like one of the serving maids. I had never waltzed, and could follow the leads of none of my dancing partners. The food was strange and never have I seen so many forks and spoons at one's supper place. I had no idea which to use. I disgraced myself so often I could scarcely wait until the evening came to its abysmal end."[25] The visit dragged past in a misery of social unease, but once safely back in Jersey, Lillie learned from her mistakes and undertook a frenzy of self-improvement: "Between the ages of sixteen and twenty, I learned the magic of words, the beauty and excitement of poetic imagery. I learned there was something in life other than horses, the sea and the long Jersey tides."[26]

In June 1872 the Le Breton family suffered another terrible blow when their oldest son, Francis Corbet Le Breton, of the Bengal Pilot Service, died in Calcutta aged twenty-nine. This second tragedy, combined with the revelation of her father's true character, tore Lillie's world apart. The comfort and security of childhood ebbed away, to reveal a new and frightening world.

In November 1873, the oldest surviving brother, William Inglis Le Breton, came home on leave from the Indian Army to marry local girl Elizabeth Price. Due to the prominence of the dean's family and their two recent tragedies, this event was the equivalent of a royal wedding on Jersey. The local paper described a commotion at St. Saviour's Church so great that "one woman was carried to the wall, where her face collided and where the multitude kept her; she came away minus her chignon, another woman had her earrings dragged from her ears; one man lost his boots and several women had their dresses torn."[27] At her brother's wedding, Lillie witnessed scenes of mass hysteria for the first time, and started to plan her escape. "I began to dream of the real Prince Charming who would one day appear."[28] Lillie's salvation appeared in the form of Edward Langtry, a widower from Belfast in his early thirties. "Ned" Langtry had been married to Elizabeth Price's sister, Jane, a local beauty who had died from tuberculosis a year earlier.

As part of the wedding festivities, Ned Langtry, "who was well known in the Islands, and who had a large and luxurious yacht called the *Red Gauntlet*,"[29] gave a lavish ball at the Jersey Yacht Club. "It was a far more elaborate and extravagant affair than anything I had hitherto witnessed," Lillie wrote, "and it electrified me. The walls were hung with quantities of flags; the supper was less sketchy than I had been accustomed to, and, to crown all, the hall and staircase were lined with sailors in their spotless white suits . . . it was simply dazzling, an Arabian Nights' Entertainment, and its donor instantly became in my eyes a wonder!"[30]

In her desperation to get off the island, Lillie was prepared to overlook the fact that Ned was a pudgy chap with a weak mouth and a walrus mustache. The scion of a wealthy Belfast shipbuilding family, Ned claimed to have studied law at Oxford but showed no incentive to work and had no interests apart from sailing and fishing. But to Lillie, in serious danger of being left on the shelf at the age of twenty, Ned Langtry was the original knight in shining armor. Ned took Lillie sailing on the *Red Gauntlet*, with her father as chaperone, and Lillie soon convinced herself that she was "desperately in love."[31] Langtry beguiled Lillie with tales of an Elizabethan house overlooking Southampton Water, a string of racehorses, and society friends. This was enough to ensure that Lillie threw herself at Ned; for once he was a winner in life's lottery. Following a six-week whirlwind courtship, Ned proposed, but it was several months before Lillie's parents could bring themselves to grant consent, or, in Lillie's words, "being the only daughter, my elation was not shared warmly by my mother and father."[32] This was something of an understatement. The Le Bretons had seen straight through Ned Langtry and feared that he was not a fit husband for their daughter. This suspicion was confirmed after Lillie's brother Clement Le Breton, now a qualified solicitor, investigated Langtry's financial affairs. Clement shared his suspicions with the dean, while Lillie's adoring little brother, Reggie, opposed the match bitterly.

But as usual Lillie got her way and the dean eventually married the couple on March 19, 1874, at St. Saviour's, surrounded by the tombstones of Lillie's ancestors. In the last vestiges of her tomboy persona, Lillie rejected the idea of a big wedding and conventional bridal array and chose to be married in her traveling gown. Apart from the dean, who performed the ceremony, Clement was the only other family member to attend. Reggie refused to go to the wedding and went out riding instead, along his favorite clifftop path, reigniting the old gossip about an "unnaturally" close bond between him and Lillie.

Chapter Eight

TAKING LONDON BY STORM

*A most beautiful creature, quite unknown, very poor, and
they say has but one black dress.*
—LORD RANDOLPH CHURCHILL

Immediately after the Langtrys' wedding, the couple sailed away to Cliffe Lodge, Ned's "yachting *pied á terre*" on Southampton Water, where disillusion rapidly set in.[1] Lillie later hinted that Ned had been an unsatisfactory lover; she also realized that Ned was far from the man of property he claimed to be. Cliffe Lodge was rented, not owned, and Ned's connections in society extended only to a bunch of sailing cronies. Far from being a millionaire playboy, Ned Langtry was living beyond his means on a dwindling inheritance. Although Lillie enjoyed winning the International Yacht Race at Havre in a gale, "the excitement of that race, crowding on sail to the verge of danger, with a swirling spray drenching us to the skin,"[2] the dreary reality of sailing was another matter. "Yacht racing could be dull in the extreme. To roll about becalmed for hours, whistling for a breath of wind, was deadly."[3] Lillie's marriage was swiftly becalmed in the same fashion.

Lillie became increasingly isolated in an English coastal town with no friends and dwindling prospects. Within a year, Ned was forced to sell his beloved yachts and began drinking heavily. Early in 1875 Lillie fell ill, her normally strong constitution weakened by homesickness and boredom. Ned, the eternal optimist, informed her family that Lillie was pregnant. Lillie's doctor had a very different prognosis: Lillie had contracted typhoid and was unlikely to survive. As Ned faced the prospect of losing his second wife within a year of marriage, Lillie lay close to death and unvisited by a single member of her family. After weeks of serious illness, Lillie eventually pulled through, and the question of convalescence was raised. When Lillie begged to go to London, her doctor was appalled and suggested returning to Jersey as the best course of action. London, dirty, disease-ridden, and noisy, was the last place to recover from a life-threatening illness. Lillie, with her characteristic will of iron, insisted that London, with its pleasures and its distractions, was just the place she needed to recover. "I have no idea what led us to select the great, smoky city as a sanatorium, but we leave for London early in December," Lillie wrote to her mother. "After stopping at an hotel for a day or two we shall take suitable apartments."[4]

The Langtrys moved into a small house in Eaton Place, Belgravia, the most expensive district of London, and Lillie began to plan her campaign to enter society. This was in spite of the fact that her acquaintances could be listed on the fingers of one hand and consisted of three well-connected peers who wintered in Jersey.[5] These were Lord Suffield, who had suggested Lillie's original trip to London; Lord Thellusson, 5th Baron Rendlesham (1840–1911), and Lord Ranelagh (1812–1885), a raffish character fond of art, artists, and indeed artists' models. The Pre-Raphaelite painter William Holman Hunt, who lost a woman to Ranelagh, once described him as a "notorious rake."[6] Lacking any means of contacting these three peers directly, even Lillie was forced to confess that "it seemed unlikely that the 'long arm of coincidence' would bring us into contact with any of these."[7] The Langtrys were reduced to celebrity spotting, passing their time like country cousins, walking in Hyde Park waiting for royalty to pass. During the season, "the Park" was the place to be seen. The Park was, of course, Hyde Park, any other park being regarded as insufferably common. "There was only *one* Park, called Hyde," recalled Daisy, Countess of Warwick, many years later.

> *We knew dimly of Regent's Park as a place where the Zoo existed . . .*
> *St James's and the Green Park were a short cut to the House of Lords,*
> *but when we spoke of "The Park" it was always Hyde Park near the*
> *Corner. If you entered by the Albert Memorial or Marble Arch, you*
> *were certain to be making for that select spot lying between Albert and*
> *Grosvenor Gates. Here the small circle of Society with the big "S"*
> *was sure of meeting all its members on a morning ride or drive, or in*
> *the late afternoon between tea and dinner in what was practically a*
> *daily Society Garden Party!*[8]
>
> *Late afternoon in Hyde Park meant state carriages and barouches*
> *with beautifully dressed occupants pulled up under the trees . . . then*
> *there would be the clatter of faster horses, and down this mile of drive*
> *came the well-known Royal carriage with the beautiful Alexandra,*
> *Princess of Wales, bowing right and left as only she could bow, and*
> *hats were raised and knees curtsied before seats were resumed and in-*
> *terrupted chatter continued.*[9]

Despite these regular outings, with her face pressed up against the shopwindow of London society, Lillie failed to spot the titled man who had first suggested she visit London. By the end of December, she had failed to make any inroads into society. Then, a year later, in December 1876, devastating news arrived. Lillie received a telegram from Jersey, telling her that Reggie, her youngest brother, had fallen from his horse while out riding on the cliffs. In her memoir, Lillie says that Reggie had already died by the time she received the telegram. "Crushed by the young mare he was riding, he fought against his injuries for three days, only to succumb at last. And I didn't even know of the accident."[10] In fact, Lillie delayed her return to Jersey, either unaware of the extent of her brother's injuries or reluctant to leave London. By the time Lillie set out for Jersey on December 17,

Reggie was dead. There were rumors that Reggie had ridden over the cliffs in a suicide bid,[11] further fueling local speculation that there had been something incestuous about their relationship.

Lillie spent that winter on Jersey, grieving with her parents, and felt that "life was over."[12] She returned to London in a state of deep depression, "caring little for anything."[13] But it was in London, in April 1877, that the "long arm of coincidence" finally operated in Lillie's favor. On one of the Langtrys' regular trawls around London, "the Finger of Fate pointed the way to the Aquarium at Westminster," a popular attraction, and it was here that Lillie spotted Lord Ranelagh and his two daughters, with whom Lillie had been friends on Jersey.[14] This meeting completely changed the current of Lillie's life.[15] Lord Ranelagh invited the Langtrys to his house in Fulham, which in those days was a rural retreat, five miles west of London. Lord Ranelagh occupied "a delightful creeper-covered mansion with a mossy, tree-shaded lawn sloping down to the river,"[16] inhabited by "interesting" people: dancers, artists' models, and amateur actors.[17] It was one of these thespians who was to prove Lillie's salvation. Soon after the trip to Fulham, Lillie received an invitation from Lady Georgina Sebright, an enthusiastic amateur actress, fond of literature and art, who "loved to gather together men and women conspicuous in both callings" for Sunday evening at-homes.[18] As these at-homes were held at Lady Sebright's mansion at 23 Lowndes Square, Lillie accepted without hesitation. Finally, her moment had come. Despite the fact that Lowndes Square was just eight minutes' walk from their house in Eaton Place, the Langtrys "rattled up" to Lady Sebright's house in a humble coach and four.[19] Lillie, still in mourning for her brother, wore a simple black gown, made by Madame Nicolle in Jersey, with her radiant auburn hair twisted into a knot at the nape of her neck. She wore no jewelry, since she possessed none.[20] Slowly, shyly, Lillie made her way into the crowded drawing room and sat in a corner, feeling "very un-smart and countrified."[21] But Lillie was not alone for long. Indeed, she soon realized that she was the star attraction, and some of the most famous men in London had been invited to meet her. Lillie swiftly became the center of attention, with one distinguished guest after another led across the room by Lady Sebright, eager to make her acquaintance. These distinguished guests included two of London's most eminent painters, John Everett Millais and James McNeill Whistler; a lesser-known young artist, Frank Miles; the actor Henry Irving; William Yardley, a famous cricketer; and Lord Wharncliffe, a Yorkshire landowner whose fortunes had soared with the discovery of coal on his estate outside Barnsley, allowing him to become a generous patron of the arts. A "rush of cavaliers" offered to take Lillie in to supper,[22] and victory went to Millais. A handsome Jerseyman, clearly as at home on the grouse moor as he was in his studio, Millais appeared reassuringly familiar. When Millais invited Lillie to sit for him, so that he could record her "classic features," she immediately agreed.[23] Lillie returned home in a state of euphoria, confident that her first night in London society had been a great success. This joy was intensified the following afternoon, when Lillie and Ned returned from a walk to find the hall table heaped with invitations from people they had heard about but never met. From that moment on, invitations poured into Eaton Place at such speed that the Langtrys' landlady was compelled to hire an extra servant to deal with the stream of bewigged footmen knocking at the door. "A complete transformation seemed to have taken place in my life overnight," Lillie tells us. "Invitations to receptions and balls were so numerous that we were mostly obliged to attend two or three of each in an evening. Whatever my husband said and felt, I absolutely revelled in the novelty of it all . . . there was scarcely a great house in London that I did not visit during my first season. . . . I met practically all the well-born and well-known men and women of the day."[24] In fact, Ned Langtry did not say much about it at all. Obliged as he was to escort his wife to these daily events during her meteoric rise, Ned retreated into silence and drink. "We are always afflicted with Mr Langtry, who is nothing," commented Lady Wilton later that year.[25] One cannot help feeling a little sorry for him. London society in full swing was a long way from the wild wet moors and trout streams of Northern Ireland.

Lillie's first invitation following Lady Sebright's at-home was a dinner engagement with the Earl and Countess of Wharncliffe at their house in Curzon Street. As aristocratic landowners, the Wharncliffes had their links with the court, but their vivacious party-giving and interest in the arts placed them firmly in the category of "upper bohemia." To Lillie's shock and amazement Lady Wharncliffe had dyed blond hair and chain-smoked all through dinner.[26] The Wharncliffes, who loved to surround themselves with artists, were well aware that Lillie would provide a considerable "draw" to other guests, and that Lillie's allure was far more important than any conventional notions about her breeding and lineage. The guests that night included Sir Edward Poynter, later president of the Royal Academy, Madge Robertson, a leading actress, and Lord Randolph Churchill, who wrote to his wife, Jennie, that "I took in to dinner a Mrs Langtry, a most beautiful creature, quite unknown, very poor, and they say has but one black dress."[27] Banned from the Marlborough House set for his role in the Aylesford scandal, Randolph remained popular with the rakish Wharncliffes. In retrospect, these three guests prefigure the significant elements of Lillie's life: the art world, the stage, and the British aristocracy. But at this point, it was the artists who would be the making of her. And among these the most influential was the least known: Frank Miles, an illustrator who worked only in monochrome as he was color-blind. That very night, Miles was the first to sketch Lillie.

Concepts of physical attractiveness vary from generation to generation, but Lillie arrived in London at a time when her features represented the apotheosis of female beauty. Her violet eyes and red hair,[28] her "pillared throat and nobly chiselled mouth"[29] appealed to the Pre-Raphaelites, while Oscar Wilde and the aesthetes claimed her for their own as "a pale distraught lady with . . . dark auburn hair, falling in masses over the brow [and] . . . eyes full of love-lorne languor. . . ."[30]

Lillie swiftly fell into a routine of sitting for artists every day, but she was no mere artists' model. Posing for painters had a dual function: the opportunity for effortless self-promotion, as one famous artist after another queued up to record her charms, and the chance to spend time away from Ned Langtry.

Frank Miles occupied a "ghostly mansion, with antique staircases and twisting passages" off the Strand,[31] where a jaw-dropping cross section of London society and high bohemia dropped in for tea. These luminaries included the actress Ellen Terry; the artists Dante Gabriel Rossetti and William Morris; Lady Constance Grosvenor, Duchess of Westminster, wife of the richest landowner in the country after the queen; the poet Algernon Swinburne; the Oxford don and founder of the Aesthetics movement, Walter Pater; and his protégé, the young Oscar Wilde, who had already resolved to become famous, or if not famous, notorious. Of all these, it was the painters who made Lillie's reputation. Within months their canvases would be admired in the capital and reproductions circulated around the world. Millais, Whistler, Lord Leighton, Edward Burne-Jones, and Sir Fredrick Watts were all eager to record Lillie's charms for posterity. Further fame beckoned through the newly emerging medium of photography. One of the most significant technical developments of the day, photography had become increasingly popular, as many famous people posed for photographic portraits, from royalty and statesmen to all the "pretty women in society" who "rushed pell-mell to be photographed in every imaginable pose."[32] Photography led to the popularity of the so-called Professional Beauties, beguiling society women whose portraits appeared in magazines and were sold as postcards. As Lillie recalled, "some smothered themselves in furs to brave photographic snowstorms; some sat in swings; some lolled dreamily in hammocks; others carried huge bunches of flowers and one was actually reproduced gazing at a dead fish!"[33] The fashion for photography at this period was even lampooned in a music hall song:

> *I have been photographed like this,*
> *I have been photographed like that,*
> *But I never have been photoed [sic]*
> *As a raving Maniac.*[34]

Lillie claimed to have sat only once for a photographer during this period, "who reproduced me with a dead bird in my hand and an expression of grief on my face, designed to touch the heart of the sentimental public."[35]

It was not long before a chance encounter at Miles's studio brought Lillie yet another dinner invitation. Frances Maynard, the thirteen-year-old heiress affectionately known as "Daisy," had been sitting for Miles while he sketched her portrait. Having heard about Lillie, Frances was eager to see this phenomenon for herself and descended on the studio with her stepfather in tow. Frances was absolutely astonished by what she saw.

> *In the studio I found the loveliest woman I have ever seen. And how can any words of mine convey that beauty? I may say that she had dewy, violet eyes. A complexion like a peach, and a mass of lovely hair drawn back in a soft knot at the nape of her classic head. But how can words convey the vitality, the glow, the amazing charm that made this fascinating woman the centre of any group she entered? She was in the freshness of her young beauty that day in the studio. She was poor and wore a dowdy black dress, but my stepfather lost his heart to her, and invited her there and then to dine with us next evening at Grafton Street.*[36]

"My stepfather" was Robert Francis St. Clair-Erskine, 4th Earl of Rosslyn (1833–1890), and Daisy, the impressionable young girl who was so captivated by Lillie's beauty, was destined to become the Countess of Warwick. In time, Lillie and Daisy would be great friends, and rivals, too.

The invitation to Grafton Street represented a substantial step up the social ladder for Lillie. For most women, such an event would have provided the ideal excuse to acquire a new gown. But Lillie had already spent enough time among the artists to understand the importance of making an impression and remained steadfastly devoted to her dowdy black dress. This garment defined Lillie, so that she could be clearly identified across a room, surrounded by a sea of colorful silks and satins. With her simple black gown and air of magnificent bereavement, Lillie resembled nothing so much as a beautiful young widow. Such a shame that she had to drag the complaining Ned Langtry along in her wake. As Daisy Maynard wrote: "She came, accompanied by an uninteresting fat man—Mr Langtry—whose unnecessary presence took nothing from his wife's social triumph."[37]

After Lillie's appearance at Grafton Street, the snowstorm of invitations intensified to a blizzard. The tributes of besotted aristocrats reached their zenith on the evening Lillie attended a political reception given by the Marquis of Hartington at Devonshire House, the family mansion in Piccadilly. On Lillie's arrival, Harty-Tarty abandoned the ranks of important dignitaries and took Lillie around Devonshire House, showing her the magnificent rooms and pointing out a few treasures.[38] The tour culminated in an extraordinary scene after Lillie admired the water lilies growing in marble pools in the conservatory. In full evening dress, Harty-Tarty plunged into the water and dragged out bunches of lilies, which he thrust dripping into the liveried arms of his footmen, telling them to fill Lillie's carriage with the soaking wet flowers. Less than impressed, Ned spent the short journey home throwing the lilies out of the window.[39]

Lillie's appeal was such that she even earned a mention in the society journal *Vanity Fair*: "All male London is going wild about the Beautiful Lady who has come to us from the Channel Islands. She is certainly the most splendid creature that has ever risen upon London from an unknown horizon, and so far beyond the pretty with which we are usually more than content, that it is as though some newer and more perfect creature had risen, like Aphrodite, from the sea. She has a husband to make her happy, but still awaits a poet to make her known" (May 19, 1877).[40]

Little did that husband know that his troubles were about to become a whole lot worse. Regardless of her marital status, which served to protect her from the most outrageous speculation, Lillie had begun to acquire a reputation. In the relaxed, postprandial hour, after the ladies had risen from the table and the port and brandy circulated freely, London's gentlemen gossiped over their cigars. In between the racing chat and dirty jokes, the attractions of the latest fillies were discussed in the same terms as thoroughbred mares. It was said that Lillie, who, after all, was an artists' model, was something of a coquette. There were tales that on inviting a gentleman into her drawing room, she would gaze at him with her ravishing violet eyes and fall in a faint, forcing the visitor to catch her in his arms. And then there was the fact that under the simple black dress, Lillie wore no corsets. This was on account of "my dislike of the 'fitting' process,"[41] but it was also taken as a sure sign of a loose woman in the days when tight corsets and layers of undergarments deterred all but the most determined attempts at casual sex. It was known that Lillie entertained gentleman callers, although no man could precisely be identified as her lover. So it was clear that Lillie had a welcoming attitude toward exceptional members of the opposite sex. It was, therefore, no surprise when the sons of the royal family began to take an interest in this flirtatious young beauty.

Prince Leopold, the younger brother of the Prince of Wales, was already one of Lillie's greatest fans. The first of Queen Victoria's sons to respond to Lillie's appeal, Prince Leopold had purchased Frank Miles's sketch of her and hung it above his bed at Buckingham Palace.[42] Queen Victoria did not approve. "I was told she then and there took it down," Lillie wrote, "standing on a chair to do so."[43] This attitude did nothing to deter young Leopold, who soon became one of Lillie's gentlemen callers, visiting the Langtrys' home in Eaton Place. This development could not have pleased Ned Langtry, but he had little choice in the matter. As a social climber of Alpine proportions, Lillie would have scarcely refused the attentions of the young prince. In return for stepping back, Ned accompanied Lillie when she was invited to sail on Prince Leopold's yacht. Perhaps this proved some compensation for Ned, who must have missed his sailing. Visits to the yacht were limited to the occasions when it was moored in Cowes, on the Isle of Wight, as the queen kept Leopold on a short rein. Indeed, Queen Victoria's disapproval of Lillie was so great that the Langtrys were obliged to hide belowdecks "until we got out of range of the Osborne House telescopes."[44]

Lillie's friendship with Prince Leopold would, one would think, have been sufficient to guarantee an introduction to the Prince of Wales. What better way for Lillie to showcase herself than flushed with excitement, drenched to the skin by sea spray as she reveled in the elements on Prince Leopold's yacht? But there was a strict protocol to these matters, and so it fell to Sir Allen Young, the explorer, to effect an introduction between Bertie and the latest beauty, just two months after Lillie had made her debut in London society.

Sir Allen, known to his friends as "Alleno," was a wealthy bachelor who had devoted much of his time and money attempting to find the remains of Captain Sir John Franklin, an arctic explorer who had set out to navigate the Northwest Passage in 1845 and never returned. Lillie found Sir Allen to be "a fidgety creature, already in the forties," with the faraway gaze and monosyllabic speech of the explorer.[45] But despite his lack of small talk, Sir Allen was a loyal and considerate host, and so an invitation to dine at his home, Stratford House, was something of a coup. Even so, Lillie and Ned, along with eight other guests, were somewhat surprised when dinner was delayed and they were asked to remain in the drawing room. Who could they be waiting for? Lillie wondered.

And then came a flurry of activity, followed by an expectant hush, and Sir Allen made a swift exit to deal with the slight commotion outside. After a moment or two, Lillie heard a deep, cheerful voice saying, "I am afraid I am a little late," and looked up to see the Prince of Wales, "whose face had been previously unfamiliar to me except through photographs," appear at the doorway and walk into the room.[46]

Bertie had clearly come from a previous function, and glittered importantly, with medals and the blue ribbon of the Garter over his white tie and tails. At thirty-six, Bertie was still handsome in a substantial, Victorian fashion, slightly overweight but not yet defined by the heavy jowls and obesity that would characterize his middle age. With a twinkle in his blue eyes and undoubted charisma, Bertie became the focus of every eye in the room. The women in particular pressed forward to curtesy to him, while their husbands bowed in a resigned fashion, aware that if Bertie hadn't already slept with their wives, it was only a matter of time. Bertie observed these social niceties and then he turned his attention to the only newcomers in the room: Mr. and Mrs. Edward Langtry.

Chapter Nine

THE REAL PRINCE CHARMING

*I had gone from being an absolute "nobody" to what the Scotch
so aptly describe as a "person."*
—LILLIE LANGTRY

Lillie Langtry later admitted that meeting the Prince of Wales for the first time had filled her with utter terror. "I was panic-stricken, and for one bewildered moment really considered the advisability of climbing the chimney to escape."[1] But the resilient Mrs. Langtry held her nerve, stood her ground, and made her curtsey, confessing that "for various reasons I greatly enjoyed watching my husband go rather stammeringly through a similar ordeal."[2] Sir Allen had arranged that Lillie would be seated next to Bertie at dinner, but Lillie was so overcome by the royal presence that she could only respond to the prince's inquiries with monosyllables, finding him good-natured but slightly aloof. While he complimented the servants and obviously worked hard to make the evening enjoyable, "it would have been a brave man who, even at this little *intime* supper-party attempted a familiarity with him."[3] Some years later, Lillie told the actor Alfred Lunt that she had always been a little afraid of Bertie, and that "he always smelt so *very strongly of cigars*."[4] Given Lillie's physical courage and strong personality, this was an unusual confession. Perhaps Lillie realized, even at that first meeting, that this was one man she must keep on the right side of.

Within weeks of this introduction, Lillie became Bertie's mistress. Although Lillie's memoirs do not reveal exactly how the affair began, Bertie had a fixed modus operandi when it came to married women. At some point in the proceedings, perhaps on the very night that they were introduced, Bertie would have asked Lillie discreetly whether he could call on her at home one afternoon. The meaning of this would have been clear to Lillie: she had, after all, entertained a number of admirers in this fashion, including Bertie's younger brother, Prince Leopold. On the rare occasion that a young woman resisted Bertie's advances, he would retreat graciously and never trouble her again. Once Lillie had consented to Bertie's request, the gentle inquiry would be followed up with a letter, hand-delivered by a royal footman, asking if the prince could call upon a specific afternoon.

Bertie's reputation preceded him and there was a royal protocol to his afternoon visits. When the Prince of Wales came to call, the master of the house was required to make himself scarce. Just as with every other aspect of social intercourse, there was a fixed code of practice regarding adultery if the man in question was the Prince of Wales. In a typically English fashion, this sanctioned cuckoldry revolved around the golden hour of teatime. Long before the discreet royal carriage appeared at the door, the gentleman of the house would have taken himself off to his Pall Mall club, where he would remain until dinner, when it was safe to return home. Or the gentleman in question might very well have gone to visit a mistress of his own. Among the upper classes it was not unusual for a wealthy man to support two households, one for his wife and family and a separate establishment for his mistress. Poor Ned Langtry, being something of a social outcast, had no club to retire to. Instead, he had the choice of spending the afternoon in a public house or walking the streets until their royal visitor had left. Whatever his belief in allowing his wife to do her patriotic duty by sleeping with their future king, Ned must have been appalled by the prospect of Lillie betraying him with Bertie.

Once the tea tray had been taken in to the drawing room, the parlor maid, trying not to stare at Bertie, would withdraw, leaving Lillie alone with the royal visitor. As Lillie hated corsets, she was doubtless already prepared for the occasion, in her loose black dress or a long, floating tea gown. More formal dress presented formidable obstacles to sexual congress: all those layers of corsets and petticoats, elaborate coiffures and jewelry. As one commentator said, seduction in day dress seemed like "an enterprise which would have to be organised like a household furniture removal."[5]

We shall never know whether their mutual captivation was consummated on Bertie's first visit, or the second, or the third. But as Bertie was a fast worker and Lillie was already notorious for her habit of swooning into the arms of a gentleman caller, it is fair to assume that the relationship was established quickly. Lillie was so determined to make her way in society that it is entirely likely she initiated full sex then and there, in the drawing room of Eaton Place, as her landlady and the maid waited expectantly in the basement kitchen, ears cocked for the hurly-burly of the chaise longue or the collateral damage of a smashed teacup.

If Lillie had held out for something more romantic than a quickie on the sofa, she and Bertie would have spent their first night together in the congenial surroundings of a stately home, at a safe distance from Princess Alexandra, who loathed weekending and refused all invitations.[6] Lillie and Bertie's amorous pursuits would have passed without comment in the round of aristocratic wife swapping that characterized country house weekends. But one factor swiftly became evident: Bertie was completely smitten with Lillie and she was more than just another affair. Previously discreet, Bertie was soon parading Lillie in public as his first official mistress. And, given their shared love of horses, what better place to show off this marvelous young filly than riding along Rotten Row in Hyde Park?

Lillie owned a beautiful chestnut gelding called Redskin, presented to her by a young admirer named Morton Frewen before he departed for America. Redskin came with a wonderful testimonial saying that he had "the nuances and devotion of your favourite dog."[7] The horse, or possibly Lillie, was later described by Margot Asquith, who as a child watched Lillie out riding, as "a chestnut thoroughbred of conspicuous action."[8]

For Lillie, riding along Rotten Row with the Prince of Wales meant her wildest dreams had come true. Here she was, the dean's daughter from Jersey, poised on her high-stepping chestnut, next to the heir to the British throne. Lillie cut a magnificent figure in her beautifully cut, skin-tight riding habit, while Bertie, despite his increasing weight, was still a keen rider, and the red browbands of the Prince of Wales and his equerries never failed to create a commotion on the Row.[9] In the mornings, Bertie rode out with "the Liver Brigade," a cohort intent on "shaking up" their sluggish livers with a spot of vigorous trotting, including Sir Allen Young, Christopher Sykes, and the mischievous Beresford brothers. Accompanying these luminaries were the royal equerries, and officers from the Prince of Wales's regiments, the "Blues," the Royal Horse Guards, and the "Royals," the 10th Royal Hussars. Magnificent in its way, Bertie's appearance was reminiscent of the royal progresses of his ancestors, who themselves had once ridden through London, to the general awe of their subjects.

Bertie also liked to ride through the Park late in the afternoons, between lunch and dinner engagements. The closest Lillie came to acknowledging the significance of their relationship is this story:

The latter hour [seven o'clock in the evening] caused dinner to be a very late meal, seldom commencing before nine o'clock. I remember that, on one occasion, when riding with the Prince, it was past that hour when I left the Row, as etiquette demanded that I should ride on so long as His Royal Highness elected to do so. Mr Langtry and I were, as usual, dining out, and when I arrived home I found him impatiently waiting on the doorstep, watch in hand, and in all the paraphernalia of evening dress. After a scrambling toilette we eventually arrived at the Clark-Thornhills', in Eaton Square, where we were due, to find it nearly ten o'clock. Everyone was waiting, of course, but before I could apologise, my hostess greeted me pleasantly, saying: "Sir Claude Champion de Crespigny on his way here saw you riding in the Park, and, as we knew you couldn't get away, we postponed dinner indefinitely." After the very natural grumbling of my husband, these words served as balm to any troubled soul. It is so difficult to please everyone.[10]

Lillie pleased the prince, and that was all that mattered. In the giddy weeks that followed, Lillie began to appear in public with Bertie and realized that she had at last entered the world for which she had been intended. It soon became evident to any hostess that she could not invite the Prince of Wales without inviting Lillie. "There was nothing clandestine about their affair. Lillie became an openly acknowledged and apparently permanent feature of the Prince's life. She became, in short, his first official mistress."[11]

Now Lillie had Bertie, and London, at her feet. But there was another aspect to her conquest, and one that would, over the coming months, become unendurable. Lillie was famous. The simple country girl with a tragic past, dressed in a plain black gown, had become public property, a state for which she was not fully prepared. From the satisfying experience of being celebrated within the safe confines of London society, where the most alarming thing that could happen to her was the fellow guests at a reception standing on chairs to get a better view, Lillie was now experiencing the reality of life as a celebrity.

Thanks to the artists and photographers who had circulated her image around the country, Lillie was forced to forgo the simple amusements of the past. She could not pop out to a shop without drawing a crowd and having to leave through the back door. If she attempted to go for a quiet walk in Hyde Park, she was stalked and swiftly surrounded by adoring fans. When she took Redskin out for a canter on Rotten Row, Lillie had to ensure that the stable gates were closed before she mounted her horse, so that the crowds could not surge in and block her way. When a young girl bearing a slight resemblance to Lillie was spotted in the Park, there was such a stampede that she was almost crushed to death and had to be taken away in an ambulance.[12]

"It is easy to imagine the marvel of it all to a country girl like me, who had not been allowed by my band of brothers to think much of myself in any way."[13] Lillie had changed, in the course of a few weeks, "from being an absolute 'nobody' to what the Scotch so aptly describe as a 'person.'[14] "Surely," Lillie concluded, "London has gone mad."[15]

There was one other "person" who had become distinctly troubled by Lillie's transformation. While Lillie was prepared to sacrifice her privacy and her reputation in order to promote her social ambitions, the same was not true of Ned Langtry. According to Lillie, her husband had grown increasingly more irritated by Lillie's status as a "species of phenomenon" to the extent that he was "sometimes losing his temper and blaming *me!*"[16] Ned's temper would continue to deteriorate, along with his behavior, on an exponential level as Lillie's fame increased.

But as far as Lillie was concerned, she had arrived. She had only to fasten her hair in a loose knot at the base of her neck for the style to be dubbed the "Langtry."[17] When she twisted a band of black velvet around her head and secured it in place with a feather for an afternoon's racing at Sandown Park, milliners swiftly copied the look and marketed it as "the Langtry Hat."[18] So famous, indeed, had Lillie become that she began to dispense with her original persona and change her distinctive appearance.

In June 1877, Lillie was invited to "a magnificent ball given at Dudley House for some visiting royalty."[19] Lady Dudley had tactfully requested Lillie to discard her mourning for the evening, as Lord Dudley hated black, to the extent of banning his wife from wearing it, "so strangely that he could not bear the idea of anyone appearing at his house in that sombre hue."[20] Lillie tells us that the poverty of her wardrobe was not only the result of her own lack of funds and her dislike of the fitting process but "my absolute indifference at the time to elaborate frocks."[21] This, like everything else about Lillie, was soon to change. Deciding that the Dudley House ball was important enough to undergo the ordeal, Lillie commissioned "a fashionable London dressmaker,"[22] Mrs. Stratton, to create a "white velvet gown, severely cut, embroidered with pearls."[23] The gown and its wearer caused a sensation. As Lillie entered the ballroom, the other dancers stopped dead and crowded around her, and then parted like the waves of the Red Sea as she proceeded toward her hostess.[24] And the fantastic white velvet gown did not cost Lillie a penny. Lillie had become so famous that Mrs. Stratton offered unlimited credit, knowing that Lillie would serve as a great advertisement for her skills. This gesture, welcomed at the time, heralded the beginning of a line of credit that would almost destroy Lillie.

Lillie remained Bertie's close companion until the end of the season, which concluded in London with a magnificent ball at Marlborough House, such a significant event that no other hostess in London would dare to throw a party the same night. The following Monday, Lillie and Ned accompanied the Prince of Wales to Goodwood, for the most fashionable race meeting of the season, and joined Bertie at an exclusive house party thrown by Lord Ferdinand Rothschild, who had rented a house near the course. As soon as Goodwood was over, it was off to the Royal Yacht Squadron on the Isle of Wight for Cowes Week. But this was the last engagement of the season, and it was here that Lillie and Bertie must part. For even Bertie could not overthrow royal protocol and delay his visit to the royal family's Scottish retreat at Balmoral, where Queen Victoria demanded his presence. Lillie must have been grateful that she had a standing invitation to go and stay with Frances "Daisy" Maynard at Easton Lodge, the family estate in Essex. Daisy remembered the visit with pleasure.

"Soon we had the most beautiful woman of the day down at Easton, and my sisters and myself were all her admiring slaves. We taught her to ride on a fat cob, we bought hats at the only milliner's shop in the country town of Dunmow, and trimmed them for our idol, and my own infatuation, for it was a little less, for lovely Lillie Langtry, continued for many a day."[25] No doubt for her own reasons, Lillie concealed her riding skills from Daisy, who was her equal as a horsewoman. But Lillie clearly enjoyed the time she spent at Easton, saying that the visit stood out in her memory, and "I think I felt more at home there than anywhere else, galloping about the park with their nice daughters, and enjoying myself thoroughly."[26]

Lillie and Bertie were reunited in the autumn when Bertie invited Lillie to a number of country house parties with Ned Langtry invited along, too, for appearances' sake. And so that they could spend time alone together, Bertie built Lillie a home by the sea at East Cliff in the fashionable resort of Bournemouth, away from prying eyes and away from Ned Langtry. In the past, Bertie had showered his mistresses with jewelry. But those mistresses had houses of their own, and complaisant husbands who were only too happy to be cuckolded by the Prince of Wales. Lillie had nowhere to receive him apart from her rented house in Eaton Place, and so Bertie, for the first time, decided to build his mistress a home of her own. "The Red House," built on land acquired from Lord Derby's estate, overlooked the sea; on a clear day, one could see the outline of Jersey. The Red House was very much Lillie's from the beginning: we can see her taste and style in it. Dispensing with any claims to aesthetics, it is an overgrown suburban villa, all leaded lights and inglenooks, with stained-glass windows and a minstrels' gallery in which the smoke from Bertie's cigars might disperse. The prince had a room of his own with a massive bed, discreetly connected with Lillie's apartments by means of a passageway. Lillie made it her own from the first, with a foundation stone reading "1877 E L L" and her initials scratched on a windowpane with a diamond. As for Ned Langtry, he never visited and it is unlikely he even knew that the Red House existed.[27]

At Christmas 1878 the Langtrys made a triumphant return to Jersey, sailing in on Bertie's yacht, *Hildegarde.* Lillie reveled in the attention, and in seeing her photograph for sale on dozens of postcards in the local shops, alongside the other Professional Beauties. Lillie was no longer just the dean's daughter. She renewed her acquaintance with a childhood friend, Arthur Jones, who would later play a major role in her life, and, as an acknowledgment of her status, Lillie was invited to dinner at Government House. Even in her new role Lillie must have realized what a tremendous honor this was. When she paused to check her reflection in the ladies' room before making her entrance, Lillie was surprised to hear a childish giggle. Pulling aside the skirts of the dressing table, she found two little girls who were eager to see the beautiful Lillie for themselves. One of these little girls, with her red hair, green eyes, and pale skin, was Elinor Glyn, the future romantic novelist.[28]

Back in London, the Langtrys and Dominique, Lillie's faithful maid, moved into a new house in February 1879. According to Lillie, 17 Norfolk Street, off Park Lane and Oxford Street, was not particularly extravagant, "a modest, blushing, red-brick abode"[29] but with ten rooms it could scarcely be described as modest. Lillie decorated Norfolk Place with the help of the American artist James McNeill Whistler, who arrived one morning with a pot of gold paint and some palm leaves. They used the palm leaves as stencils, painted two birds on the ceiling, and emerged later spattered with gold and with gold paint glittering on their eyelashes.[30] Lillie, who became easy prey of so-called antique dealers,[31] furnished the house with distressed furniture and worm-eaten oak, a set of prints from Lord Malmsbury, and a stuffed peacock, a gift from the Earl of Warwick. Peacocks were the signature bird of the aesthetic movement. They were also, as Lillie would learn, considered to be unlucky.

Funereal, pretentious, and a constant drain on the Langtrys' resources, 17 Norfolk Street was said to be haunted by the victims of the notorious Tyburn gallows,[32] which had stood nearby. Mysterious incidents included doors bursting open at embarrassing moments and an unaccountably eerie atmosphere. The butler complained of being woken by the ghosts of Tyburn victims rolling over him with their heads in their hands or swaying from gibbets at the bottom of his bed. Lillie, who attributed these terrifying experiences and his haggard features to whiskey, remained sternly indifferent to the butler's plight and he resigned. Months later, when a reliable housemaid complained that the ghost of a cavalier had barred her way downstairs one morning in broad daylight, Lillie conceded that the house might be haunted after all.[33]

In the spring of 1879 it was agreed that Lillie should be presented at court. This ceremony ensured that Lillie could take her rightful place in society and enjoy the coming season as an insider. It was unusual for a married woman to be presented at court, and the fact that Lillie was presented at all was down to the intervention of Bertie. As Lillie's own mother, Mrs. Le Breton, had not been a debutante, protocol required that Lillie have a "presenter." Lillie found one in the form of Lady Jane Churchill, née Conyngham, who had an official position in the queen's household.[34]

Lillie's mother and aunt arrived from Jersey and reveled in helping Lillie prepare for her big day. The excitement of their own Lillie taking her place at the heart of society more than compensated for that dreadful false start when Lillie first came to London, and made up for the dismal wedding to Ned. Now, on an occasion where "no mere maid was to be trusted," Lillie was eased into an ivory brocade gown with a long "court train" made of the same material pinned to her shoulders. Both gown and veil were garlanded with Maréchal

Niel roses, golden yellow with a strong tea rose scent, and the train was lined in the same golden yellow as the flowers. On the orders of the lord chamberlain, debutantes were expected to wear large feathers, as the queen had complained that the feathers used in the ceremony were getting too small. To be on the safe side, Lillie had obtained three of the longest white ostrich plumes she could find, and had great difficulty in keeping them balanced on her head, as she still wore her hair low, coiled on her neck.[35]

"Courts" were held at three in the afternoon, with debutantes driven along the Mall toward Buckingham Palace and then lined up in St. James's Park, seated in their state coaches with their bewigged footman in livery standing at the back. It was a magnificent sight: dozens of the daughters of England's most eminent families, in superb gowns and glittering with jewelry, waiting their turn, while the band of the Household Cavalry roared away and the Beefeaters stood guard in their magnificent red costumes.[36] Then the girls were sent to wait in the crush-room, penned in like so many sheep, with their heavy trains over their arms.[37] Among these young daughters of the nobility sat Lillie, with low neckline and bare arms, in full sunlight on a hot May afternoon, starving as she had been too nervous to eat, and clutching a huge bunch of Maréchal Niel roses sent by Bertie.[38]

As if Lillie wasn't nervous enough, there was another shock to come before she was beckoned into the chamber. Lillie had been told that Princess Alexandra would be "receiving" the debutantes, which she was pleased about, as she was understandably scared of Queen Victoria, the monarch herself who had stood on a chair to remove Lillie's portrait from Prince Leopold's bedroom wall. To Lillie's horror, she heard the lord chamberlain declare: "Mrs Langtry comes next, Your Majesty!"[39]

Lillie was ushered into the royal presence in a state of turmoil. There sat Queen Victoria herself, a petite woman but the very embodiment of majesty, dressed in black, with a small diamond crown and tulle veil with black feathers, ropes of pearls glimmering around her neck and the blue ribbon of the Garter across her ample bodice. Lillie smiled and curtseyed nervously, while the queen stared straight through her and extended her hand in a perfunctory manner. "There was not even the flicker of a smile on her face," Lillie recalled, "and she looked grave and tired."[40]

The most difficult aspect of being presented at court that every debutante had to learn was the trick of catching her train over her left arm as it was thrown to her by the pages after her presentation. This called for some physical dexterity, as one was simultaneously catching the train and backing out of the royal presence. And it all had to be done without looking back over one's shoulder, a sure sign of being a gauche country girl. There were awful tales of debutantes failing to accomplish this feat and dropping their trains or, worse, falling over. Mercifully, Lillie managed to achieve this sleight of hand and retreat gracefully from the throne room.[41]

That evening, at a ball at Marlborough House, Lillie told Bertie that she had been surprised to see Queen Victoria receiving the debutantes. Bertie explained that his mother had been overcome with curiosity and had deliberately taken the opportunity to see Lillie for herself. The queen had been annoyed, Bertie said, because Lillie was one of the last to appear. Lillie replied that she hoped that her ostrich feathers had lived up to the queen's strict specifications.[42]

Chapter Ten

ROYAL MISTRESS

A highly sensational divorce case, in which a well-known
beauty will play a prominent part!
—TOWN TALK

Once Lillie was "out" as a fully fledged member of society, she threw herself into "the orgy of convivial gatherings, balls, dinners, receptions, concerts, opera, which at first seemed to me a dream, a delight, a wild excitement, and I concentrated on the pursuit of amusement with the wholeheartedness that is characteristic of me, flying from one diversion to another from dawn to dawn."[1] Now that she had been presented, Lillie was automatically invited to a succession of grand events at court. While uniform or court dress was de rigueur among the men, the women wore their most resplendent clothes and family jewels, creating a brilliant carnival of color.[2] Scarlet-coated footmen scurried around the supper table, which blazed with gold plate, tazzas (shallow ornamental wine cups), and fruit and flowers from the royal gardens at Frogmore. "These balls at Buckingham Palace completely realised my girlish dreams of fairyland," she recalled.[3]

Lillie had reached the social pinnacle and mingled with "bejewelled and beautifully clad women who changed their gowns as a kaleidoscope changes its patterns."[4] In her capacity as mistress of the Prince of Wales, Lillie was required to do likewise. "For the first time in my life I became intoxicated with the idea of arraying myself as gorgeously as the Queen of Sheba, and, being accorded unlimited credit by the dressmakers, who enjoyed designing original 'creations' for me, I began to pile up bills at all their establishments."[5] Just as Lillie's previous role had hinted at that of tragic young widow, she now adopted a new persona. She had come a long way from the days when just day dresses and an evening gown were sufficient, and began, as she admitted, to engage in a life of "colossal extravagance."[6]

"The days of mourning for my brother being past, the simple black or white that had made dressing economically and becomingly an easy matter was henceforward thrust aside, and I indulged unrestrainedly in a riot of coloured garments. . . ."[7] Lillie required a new outfit for every occasion and became increasingly reckless, allowing "insidious saleswomen to line negligees with ermine or border gowns with silver fox without inquiring the cost."[8]

One of Lillie's most memorable dresses was a yellow tulle gown, draped with golden net under which preserved butterflies of every size and hue were held in glittering captivity.[9] Lillie wore this eccentric costume to a ball at Marlborough House and afterward Bertie told her that he spent the following morning picking dead butterflies up off the ballroom floor.[10]

These astonishing costumes were somewhat at variance with the portrait of Lillie displayed in June 1878 at the Royal Academy. Millais's portrait of Lillie, entitled *A Jersey Lily*, caused such a sensation it had to be roped off for its own protection, although Lillie herself had been somewhat disappointed at its content.

"I was surprised, and certainly disappointed, to find that it was [Millais's] intention to paint me in my plain black gown. . . . I had hoped to be draped in classic robes or sumptuous mediaeval garments, in which I should be beautiful and quite transformed."[11] Instead, Lillie was depicted in the sober black dress that had attracted so much attention on her first night out in London, and a demure white lace collar, to which was pinned a white gardenia. The black and white acted as a perfect foil for Lillie's creamy white skin, dark red hair, and "Grecian" features as she stared out into mid-distance, suggesting, if not exactly tragedy, then a nuance of regret: homesickness, perhaps, nostalgia. In one hand, Lillie clutched the Jersey lily that Millais, in a spirit of inquiry, had sent for. Millais was a little disappointed to find the flower was little more than an amaryllis, *Nerine sarniensis*. But it was this picture that communicated, to the outside world, just how significant Lillie's role had become. Depicting the woman whom everybody knew to be the mistress of the Prince of Wales, Millais's portrait immortalized her as "A Jersey Lillie."[12]

If Lillie had thought that being presented at court and "received" into royal circles would protect her from press intrusion, she could not have been more wrong. By June 1878, the press had begun to speculate about not only Lillie's relationship with Bertie, but the future of the Langtrys as a couple.

When Lillie was newly arrived in London, the gossip magazine *Vanity Fair* had written tantalizingly about "the Beautiful Lady who has come to us from the Channel Islands."[13] Now *Vanity Fair* had subtly changed its tone: remarking that Lillie had appeared at a Buckingham Palace ball "dressed gorgeously" in white and gold and with no jewelry at all, it reproached her for her choice of gown. "I have seen a woman who when dressed plainly and simply shone among her fellows as a bright particular star . . . now competing with all London, not in beauty only but in dress . . . she did not reflect that her chief charm lay precisely in that modest simplicity which she was so anxious to abandon for rich trappings."[14]

Later in the season, *Vanity Fair* again remarked on the change that had come over Lillie since the days when she was "observed to be extremely modest in dress, very quiet and unassuming in her manner, and discreet in all her actions."[15] Now Lillie had "a house in Norfolk Street and she rides in the Park on a highly trained walking chestnut, on which indeed she looks admirable. . . ."[16] The implication was that Lillie could not afford these luxuries herself, and that she was being bankrolled by a rich and influential protector. The reader was left to make the connection between the suddenly wealthy Lillie and her friendship with the Prince of Wales, insinuating that Lillie was a kept woman. In defense of Bertie, other men were contributing to Lillie's upkeep: Lord Wharncliffe, the sympathetic older man; Morton Frewen, who had bequeathed the chestnut Redskin before departing for America; and now Crown Prince Rudolph of Austria (1858–1889), described by Lillie herself as "a callow youth who burst upon the horizon of London one spring . . . tall, fair but not handsome, with deep-set grey eyes and the prominent Hapsburg lip."[17] Accompanied by his tutor, Prince Rudolph was determined to make the most of being freed from the rigid etiquette of the Viennese court.

Baron "Ferdy" de Rothschild decided to throw a dance in Prince Rudolph's honor at his Louis XVI–decorated house in Piccadilly, at which Bertie would be present. Since the distinctive white ballroom at the baron's house was "a searching background for doubtfully clean gowns,"[18] Ferdy invited his female guests to lunch a week before and offered them all new dresses from Jacques Doucet, a leading French designer noted for his flimsy, translucent, pastel-colored gowns. Lillie's own dress was a pale pink creation of clinging crepe de chine, heavily fringed.[19] At the ball Prince Rudolph insisted on dancing with Lillie after supper until he was hot and sweaty, and the imprint of his hands showed up on Lillie's dress. When Lillie asked the prince to put on his gloves so that he did not damage her gown, he replied rudely: *"C'est vous qui suez, madame!"* ("It is you who are perspiring!")[20] Lillie's response is not recorded, but it did not appear to put him off. Prince Rudolph laid siege to Lillie in a series of regular visits to Norfolk Street, on one occasion arriving at eight o'clock in the morning after overturning his carriage. Lillie continued to resist the prince's advances, even after he offered her a magnificent emerald ring. Lillie threw the ring into the fireplace in disgust, but swiftly retrieved it as soon as Prince Rudolph had left.[21]

As if the allegations that Lillie was nothing more than a courtesan were not enough, the man *Vanity Fair* referred to as "a husband to make her happy" was anything but. According to the same publication, in December 1878, "A lady well-known in society is said to have been seen with two black eyes, *not* the result of self-embellishment. The question asked is, who, or rather which, gave them?"[22] Meanwhile, the scurrilous *Town Talk* voiced its suspicion that Ned was surplus to requirements. "I wonder how the husbands of the 'beauties of Society' like their wives to be shown about in a 'visitors-are-requested-not-to-touch' sort of way. I don't believe they are husbands at all— only dummies. Some of the beauties, I'm afraid, have too many husbands."[23]

Town Talk was a cheeky weekly, produced in an alley off Fleet Street. Its editor was twenty-seven-year-old Adolphus Rosenberg from Brixton, who was essentially continuing the tradition of slanderous gossip dating back to the eighteenth century. Such journals had flourished forty years earlier but had been suppressed. Now they were reemerging with titles such as *Peter Pry, Puck,* and *Tomahawk,* providing lurid gossip for scandal-hungry readers and mercilessly pillorying the eminent men who were their targets.[24]

Editing such titles was not a career for the fainthearted. When *Town Talk*'s competitor, *The Queen's Messenger,* ran a series of articles criticizing Lord Carrington for his affair with Nellie Clifden, Carrington lay in wait for the editor, Greville Murray, and challenged him to a duel. When Murray simply smiled at him, Carrington horsewhipped Murray, and then successfully sued him for libel.[25]

Teasingly, *Town Talk* asked its readers if they had heard rumors of "a highly sensational divorce case, in which a well-known beauty will play a prominent part? And is it also true that someone occupying a very high position in society will be called upon as a witness?"[26]

Legally, Rosenberg was on a slippery slope by insinuating that Mr. Langtry was about to cite as correspondent the highest in the land: none other but the Prince of Wales himself. A more prudent editor might have thought twice before including such an item. But not this one. The titillating whiff of a scandal ensured a spike in circulation. Two months later, Rosenberg told his readers that: "About the warmest divorce case which ever came before a judge may shortly be expected to come off. The respondent was a reigning beauty not many centuries ago, and the co-respondents—and they are numerous— are big 'pots.' The poor husband is almost frantic. 'Darn this country,' he says, 'nothing belongs to a fellow here. Even his wife is everybody's property.' Oh that woman! I myself loved her. I bought her portrait . . . in thirty-five different positions, and wept over it in the silent hours of the night. And I am not even a co-respondent."[27] It is easy for the modern reader, accustomed to more blatant terminology, to miss the obscene subtext in this paragraph; "weeping" was Victorian slang for ejaculation.

Town Talk's insinuations must have put the fear of God into Bertie. Once again, the Prince of Wales faced the prospect of public exposure. Worse still, he might have to attend court, not just as a witness but as the correspondent in a divorce case. If there was any truth in this rumor, Bertie would need to keep his solicitor, George Lewis, close at hand. Meanwhile, Lillie experienced "tall poppy syndrome," as the newspapermen who had made her famous shredded her reputation in the interests of sales. Ned Langtry, after months of being publicly cuckolded by Lillie's string of lovers, finally decided he had had enough and resolved to sue the editor of *Town Talk,* not without "considerable opposition" from Lillie, who had "a great horror of being dragged before the public."[28] The "atrocious statements" circulated in *Town Talk* had left her unable to leave the house. "I became so morbidly sensitive that I dared not walk in the street & I am still utterly miserable."[29]

In response, Adolphus Rosenberg, *Town Talk*'s editor, reported:

"I am informed that Mr Langtry has announced his intention of breaking my neck. Now, if the brave gentleman wants to go in for neck-breaking, surely he can find plenty of his friends (?) who have injured him more than I have."[30]

Following this came an official retraction from Rosenberg, suggesting that he had been threatened with legal action. "There has been lately a rumour that Mrs Langtry was about to appear in the divorce court, with more than one illustrious correspondent. The rumour is, like many others, without the least foundation."[31]

This had a double purpose: it got Rosenberg off the hook, or so he believed, and it served to keep the budding scandal high in the news agenda.

The wild rumors circulating about the Langtry divorce case placed Lillie's relationship with Bertie under pressure. Lillie knew that it was only a matter of time before Bertie tired of her and sought consolation elsewhere. The prospect of Bertie being summonsed as the correspondent in Lillie's divorce case put their relationship under intolerable strain, and the reputational damage Lillie suffered made itself manifest in other ways. The dressmakers who had offered Lillie an unlimited line of credit started to bill her for all those extravagant gowns. The blue pencil hovered over Lillie's name on the grandest of guest lists. Lillie might have been the mistress of the Prince of Wales, but the rumors grew that she was also the mistress of several other men. The running costs of 17 Norfolk Street and keeping Redskin and a coach and horses at the livery stables were eating up Ned's limited income.

"I knew little about his income except that what remained of it was mainly derived from inherited Irish land,"[32] Lillie confided in her memoirs. "Still, I gathered from ominous signs that the tenants thereon paid less rent and demanded more outlay every year. Indeed, the tales of woe wafted from Ireland to the absent landlord were so staggering that they made me wonder how these unhappy tenants existed at all. Roofs fell in; pigs died; farms were inundated, and cottages became uninhabitable . . . that at last my husband buckled on his armour and went to the Green Isle to investigate the cause in person. But, money, seeming scarcer than ever after that rash expedition, I suspected the good-natured happy-go-lucky Irishman of refilling the pigsties and rebuilding the entire village of Parkgate."[33]

Driven to distraction by financial anxieties and the attentions of the gutter press, Lillie decided to beat a strategic retreat to the Red House in Bournemouth, emerging only for short trips to London. It was on one of these excursions that Lillie encountered the woman who was to become her rival for Bertie's affections: Sarah Bernhardt.

From the moment that Sarah Bernhardt set foot on English soil, the French actress was treated like a celebrity. Oscar Wilde took the train down to Folkestone so that he could be among the first to greet Sarah as she stepped off the boat, laying a bouquet of lilies at her feet. Lord Dudley displayed Sarah in his open carriage as they drove around Hyde Park. Others were not quite so enthusiastic. Lady Cavendish thundered that: "London has gone mad over Sarah Bernhardt—a woman of notorious, shameless character. . . . Not content with being run after on the stage, this woman is asked to respectable people's houses to act, and even to luncheon and dinner; and all the world goes. It is an outrageous scandal."[34] This did nothing to diminish Sarah's reputation. On the contrary, she flourished on outrageous scandal. The world knew that Sarah's mother had been a courtesan, and Sarah did nothing to dispel rumors that she, too, had undertaken a little light whoring as a starving young drama student at the conservatoire. Sarah had an illegitimate son, Maurice, a string of lovers, some female, was addicted to opium, and slept in a coffin. All this simply enhanced her myth; unlike poor Lillie, Sarah could not be torn apart by gossip columnists and cheap rumormongers because she had a bohemian disregard for social convention. Sarah had come into the world with nothing apart from her outstanding talent. Illegitimate, Jewish, female, Sarah was a born outsider, with nothing to declare but her genius. Inevitably, Bertie found Sarah completely irresistible.

Sarah and Bertie were old friends, having already encountered each other in Paris. So it came as no surprise that, when Sarah arrived in London, Bertie took a box at the Gaiety Theatre for the entire tour of the *Comédie-Française.* The company's repertoire consisted of two comedies by Moliére, *Le Misanthrope* and *Les Précieuses ridicules,* in which Sarah did not figure, and one act from Racine's tragedy *Phèdre,* in which Sarah finally appeared, long after ten o'clock at night. Bertie led the applause as Sarah reappeared for her curtain call, so exhausted by her performance that she was almost too weak to stand and had to be supported by her leading man.

As the critics raved that there had been no one like Sarah since the late Rachel, the French actress who had London at her feet a generation earlier, Sarah was borne away to her rented house in Chester Square, where she spent the night vomiting blood. Sarah's doctor, summoned from Paris, immediately banned her from all future performances. The following day, self-medicated with opium, Sarah threw on her cloak and ran off to the theater. Unfortunately, due to the side effects of the opium, audience and cast alike appeared to be shrouded in a luminous mist.

According to Sarah, "The opium that I had taken in my potion made my head rather heavy. I arrived on the stage in a semiconscious state, delighted with the applause I received. I walked along as though I were in a dream. . . . My feet glided along on the carpet without any effort, and my voice sounded to me far away. . . . I was in that delicious stupor that one experiences after chloroform, morphine, opium, or hasheesh."[35]

Sarah also cut two hundred lines from her script without informing her fellow actor, who collapsed in shock.[36] This episode did much to enhance Sarah's personal myth, as did the fact that she kept a menagerie. Sarah's animals included a cheetah, a wolfhound, and seven chameleons, which she wore like brooches on her shoulder, the chameleons changing color to fit in with her gowns. Sarah also had four dogs, a parrot, and a caged monkey named Darwin.

Much to Sarah's amusement, Bertie swiftly became her stage-door Johnny. Unlike Lillie, Sarah was never afraid of Bertie and even told him off when he entered her dressing room without removing his hat.[37] In terms of appearance, Sarah Bernhardt was certainly not Bertie's usual type. Bertie favored curvaceous women, while Sarah embodied the decadent ideal with her ethereal looks and druggie stare. But Sarah, like Lillie, was a character: sexy, clever, funny. She possessed tremendous spirit and for that Bertie was prepared to overlook such minor eccentricities as opium addiction, pet cheetahs, and sleeping in a coffin. Indeed, such was Sarah's hold over Bertie that, in years to come, she would persuade the prince to appear live on stage with her. Sarah was performing in *Fedora,* a melodrama about Russian Nihilists, when Bertie confirmed something that Sarah had always suspected: he said that he would have loved to have been an actor. Sarah promptly dressed Bertie in the costume of Vladimir, Fedora's husband, whose corpse is returned to her in an early scene. So Bertie finally made his theatrical debut lying in a coffin on stage at the Vaudeville Theatre.[38]

Soon after arriving in London, Sarah began to visit Marlborough House at Bertie's request. After one such visit, she wrote a scribbled apology to Edmond Got, director of the Comédie-Française: "I've just come back from the PoW. It is twenty past one. I can't rehearse any more at this hour. The P has kept me since eleven . . . I'll make myself forgiven tomorrow by knowing my part."[39]

It would have been understandable if Lillie had regarded Sarah as a threat. But Lillie seems to have become as infatuated with Sarah as all her other admirers. Lillie was introduced to Sarah at a breakfast party hosted for the Comédie-Française by Sir Algernon Borthwick, editor of the *Morning Post* and a great patron of the drama. The vision that was Sarah appeared in one of her trademark embroidered white robes, with a large tulle bow tied around her slender neck, her fluffy auburn hair a nimbus of curls around her pale white face, her eyes rimmed with kohl.

According to Lillie, "the Divine Sarah" was almost too individual, too exotic, to be completely understood "all at once." Lillie praised Sarah's "superb diction, her lovely silken voice, her natural acting, her passionate temperament, her fire—in a word, transcendent genius," and reflected that "Bernhardt's personality was so striking, so singular, that, to everyday people, she seemed eccentric; she filled the imagination as a great poet might do."[40]

Lillie's generosity extended to her rival's appearance, so very different from Lillie's own. "Her beauty, frankly, was not understood by the masses. It was a period of tiny waists, large shoulders, larger hips; and this remarkable woman, who possessed the beautiful, supple uncorseted figure—the long lines we all admire today—was called a skeleton."[41]

Oscar Wilde, as besotted as everyone else, dragged Lillie off to the British Museum to hunt for Sarah's profile on coins and vases, upon some of which they found almost exact replicas of her symmetrical Latin features. It must have been difficult to share Oscar with Sarah, having already lost Bertie, but Lillie remained magisterial in her tolerance. "Like all great beauty however, it did not blaze upon one's vision, but grew upon acquaintance. And hers, being a combination of intelligence, of feature and of soul, remained with her until the end of her life."[42] Lillie's generous attitude toward her rival would later pay dividends. Sarah proved a source of inspiration for Lillie when she herself decided to take to the stage. There is a photograph of both women, taken in New York, when they were touring in different shows. In this picture, Lillie bears an astonished expression, and Sarah a mischievous glint, having pinched Lillie's arm at the critical moment.

But however friendly with Sarah Lillie became, she must have felt hurt by Bertie's latest craze and realized that she was slowly and surely losing him. One incident in particular would have left Lillie in no doubt.

Lillie before Langtry: the young Lillie Le Breton, c. 1872.

Just married: the Langtrys, 1874.

Lillie Langtry, in one of her many soap commercials, 1880.

"Bertie" in Paris, c. 1895.

"Daisy" Warwick, mistress of Prince Edward VII, as Marie Antoinette, 1894. (V&A Images)

The wedding of "Daisy," future Countess of Warwick, 1881.

Bertie as seen from
France (a criticism of
Britain's position over the
Boer War), 1901. (Mary
Evans Picture Agency)

L'Impudique Albion

The King as he will appear in Coronation Robes.

Colm r' Starch

Coleman's starch
advertisement showing
the coronation of King
Edward VII, 1902. (Mary
Evans Picture Agency)

King Edward VII with his dog, Caesar, c. 1903. (Mary Evans Picture Agency)

King Edward VII at Rufford Abbey, Nottinghamshire, with Alice Keppel, standing, fourth from left, 1905. (Mary Evans Picture Agency)

Lillie as Lady de Bathe, with Sir Walter and Lady de Frece, c. 1928.

At the end of July 1879, Lillie and Sarah both attended a fundraiser held at the Royal Albert Hall to raise money for the French hospital in Leicester Square. The money would guarantee a bed for any French actor who needed treatment while in London. Sarah sold her own sculpture and paintings, and some of her animals. Lillie, in a brocade dress and yellow bonnet, was stationed at the refreshment stall run by the Countess de Bulow, wife of a German diplomat, selling flowers and cups of tea. According to *Vanity Fair* magazine, a cup of tea with milk and sugar was priced at five shillings, or a guinea (one pound, one shilling) if Lillie took the first sip. When Bertie arrived, with Princess Alexandra and two of their daughters, two policemen had to part the crowds so that Bertie could buy a box of bonbons.[43] Bertie moved on to Sarah Bernhardt's stall, and purchased one portrait and commissioned another, while Alix bought two white kittens with blue eyes. At the end of the afternoon, it emerged that Sarah's stall had made £256, more money than anybody else's. From Sarah's stall, Bertie returned to Lillie and asked for a cup of tea. Lillie poured out the tea, then lifted the cup to her lips. Bertie did not touch it. Instead, he merely said: "I should like a clean cup, please." Her cheeks burning, Lillie served tea in a fresh cup. Bertie gave her two gold sovereigns and walked away.[44]

Well might Lillie blush. She had been blatantly indiscreet by alluding to their relationship in front of Princess Alexandra. The matter was quite simple: Bertie might, if he wished, indicate that Lillie was his mistress. Indeed, he left people in little doubt about the matter. However, for Lillie to do so, in public, in front of his wife and daughters, was quite another matter, particularly as the rumors swirled thicker than Scots mist that Bertie was about to be cited as a correspondent in the divorce courts. Lillie had overstepped the mark. Not only was Bertie losing patience with her: Lillie was becoming an embarrassment.[45]

In August, an invitation to Scotland from Sir William Cunliffe Brooks allowed Lillie some respite. A self-made man and Conservative

MP, Sir William had recently secured his place in society by acquiring the estate of Glen Tanar, Aberdeenshire, in close proximity to Balmoral. One afternoon two of Sir William's guests, Hugh Rose, Lord Strathnairn, and Lady Errol, decided to drive over to Balmoral to look at the extraordinary castle fondly referred to by Queen Victoria as "my dear paradise in the Highlands."[46] While "dropping in" on Queen Victoria would have been a dreadful breach of protocol, taking a look at the castle was a legitimate activity. When the visitors had finished their tour and it was time to write in the visitors' book, Lillie had some reservations. But her companions persuaded Lillie that, since she had now been presented at court, she must inscribe her name or risk offending the queen. Lillie duly wrote in the book and left the castle. Twenty minutes after the party had left, Queen Victoria appeared and glanced with curiosity at the book. "I should have liked to have seen Mrs Langtry," the queen said to Lady Ely, one of her ladies-in-waiting. A servant was sent off on a horse to try to overtake Lillie, but he was too late. Lillie later confessed that she had not enjoyed what she had seen of Balmoral, finding the castle "bleak and unappealing."[47]

Chapter Eleven

THE WHEEL OF FORTUNE

A petition has been filed in the Divorce Court by Mr Langtry. HRH the Prince of Wales and two other gentlemen are mentioned as co-respondents.
—TOWN TALK

On his allegorical painting *The Wheel of Fortune* (1875–1883), Edward Burne-Jones memorably depicted Lillie as Dame Fortune, "clad in grey draperies, a tall, very tall figure, with resolute and pitiless face, turning a huge wheel on which kings, princes, statesmen, millionaires, and others rise, reach the top, and then fall, to be crushed by the ever-revolving wheel of Fate."[1] This vision of Lillie crushing men beneath her pitiless wheel was a typical Victorian conceit. It was also an inaccurate prediction of Lillie's own destiny. Far from crushing the life out of lesser mortals, Lillie endured her own struggle with Dame Fortune, emerging at intervals triumphant but by no means unbroken. Lillie's protracted battle with *Town Talk* was a case in point.

Society might have retreated to its Highland castles and country estates for the summer of 1879, but at the meager offices of *Town Talk*, Adolphus Rosenberg had no intention of taking a break. On August 30, 1879, Rosenberg returned to his attack on the Langtrys, with the announcement in *Town Talk* that: "A petition has been filed in the Divorce Court by Mr Langtry. HRH the Prince of Wales, and two other gentlemen, whose names we have not enabled to learn, are mentioned as co-respondents."[2]

There followed a vicious article entitled "Who Is Mrs Langtry?" which accused Lillie of posing for photographers in "suggestive attitudes," enabling any passerby to make indecent remarks about her and disgusting "all respectable thinking women at the public exhibition she makes of her charms."[3] When this verbal assault failed to produce the popular outcry that Rosenberg was anticipating, he took it one step further: "No attempt has been made to contradict the statement published in these columns last week as to the Langtry divorce case, and my readers may be assured that it was no invention."[4] Announcing that the Langtry divorce case would be one of the first trials when the court reopened in November, Rosenberg added that "it has been finally decided to try the case in camera and so scandalmongers will be deprived of a fine opportunity."[5] Stating that he believed Lillie had denied the adultery, Rosenberg continued that the case was of such grave national importance that the home secretary, Viscount Cross, had ordered music hall proprietors to ban references to the case during comedy routines.[6]

But by October 4, the situation appeared to have changed, and Rosenberg told his readers that Ned Langtry had withdrawn his divorce petition. "The case of Langtry v Langtry and others is therefore finally disposed of, and we have probably heard the last of it. It is useless for the sixpenny twaddlers to deny that Mr Langtry ever filed a petition. He did, and as I have said before, an application was made to Sir James Hannen to hear it privately, and he consented."[7] Rosenberg added that "Mr Langtry will shortly be appointed to some diplomatic post abroad."[8] The Langtry divorce case appeared to have been laid mercifully to rest, in return, Rosenberg insinuated, for Ned's diplomatic posting.

In the same edition of *Town Talk* Rosenberg turned his attentions to another glamorous society figure and mistress of the Prince of

Wales, Patsy Cornwallis-West. Rosenberg ran a story mocking Patsy Cornwallis-West's fascination with photography, alleging that she charged photographers commission for taking her picture and personally drove from shop to shop collecting the fees for the sale of her photographs.[9] In attempting to lambast Patsy, Rosenberg had made a grave error of judgment. While Ned Langtry might be apparently powerless in the face of defamation, Patsy's husband had an entirely different attitude and took out a lawsuit against Rosenberg.[10] At his first hearing before the Guildhall magistrates, Rosenberg was horrified to see another lawyer rise to present a further, unrelated charge against him: that six issues of *Town Talk* magazine had libeled Mr. and Mrs. Langtry.[11] There was to be a Langtry trial after all, but it was not the one that Rosenberg had anticipated.

When the case was heard at the Old Bailey on October 25, 1879, Adolphus Rosenberg found himself up against the Langtrys' high-powered legal team, while the trial judge was the notoriously vindictive Mr. Justice Hawkins, who had a reputation as a "hanging judge." In another shocking development, the Earl of Londesborough, who had also taken out a libel action against Rosenberg, was in court that day, permitted to sit on the bench alongside the judge. The *Town Talk* libel case had become a cause célèbre and the court was packed, with an overflowing public gallery and a regiment of newspaper reporters.[12]

The Langtrys' team was led by John Humffreys Parry, who held the ancient legal rank of "Sergeant at Law," and had defended Whistler in his suit against John Ruskin.[13] Rosenberg's own counsel consisted of a Mr. Willis, QC, and his junior, Mr. Grain. Rosenberg's printers, William Head and Henry Mark, were also charged with libel. They were defended by Mr. Horace Avory, later to become another merciless "hanging judge." Rosenberg's defense consisted of claiming that he had been misled by a source whom he wanted to name but was forbidden to. His counsel was reduced to pleading in mitigation that Rosenberg was a hardworking man of good character, who had a wife and family to support at his home in Brixton Hill. But this approach proved futile.

Members of the public who had hoped to see Lillie put in the witness box were disappointed. Lillie was not required to appear in court, and unusual as it was for Lillie to shun the limelight, she made the right decision by staying away. While she might have played a blinder in the witness box by appearing compellingly innocent, a thorough cross-examination by Rosenberg's counsel could have presented her in an unflattering manner. But Ned was there, unusually spruce and sober. When asked if there was any truth in the rumor that he was planning divorce, Ned replied, "not a single word."[14]

Was there any truth in the rumor that Langtry had been offered a diplomatic assignment?

"Not a word," replied Ned.

"I am very glad to hear that," replied Avory, somewhat ambiguously.

Ned had never, he said, filed for divorce, and was still living "on terms of affection with my wife at Norfolk Street."[15]

Rosenberg's counsel took a different approach. Mr. and Mrs. Langtry might have been "content to rely upon their own consciousness of perfect purity and upon the domestic happiness which they continued to enjoy," began Mr. Willis. "Far be it from me to suppose that the Prince of Wales could for a moment depart from that morality which it is his duty to exhibit. . . . But have not men in high stations fallen before now? Has a luxurious age not sometimes corrupted men placed in an exalted position? Is it the case that such a thing as this could not possibly happen? I leave out the Prince of Wales, but has no peer of the realm been before now co-respondent in the Divorce Court?"[16]

Summing up, Mr. Justice Hawkins declared that it was not for the jury to decide whether or not Mr. and Mrs. Langtry could have stood on their own reputation, without taking action against their libeler. The jury's verdict was swift. Rosenberg was found guilty without the jury even retiring. He was sentenced to eighteen months in jail, with Mr. Justice Hawkins wistfully regretting that he lacked the power to sentence him to hard labor.[17] Rosenberg had been made into a terrible example, one to discourage other journalists from lurid speculation. From this point on, every newspaper in the country was compelled to be circumspect in its references to Lillie Langtry.

Rosenberg was already in prison by the time that *Town Talk* published its final remarks on the case, in the form of a reference to the recent death of Sergeant Parry, who "did not long survive his exceptionally vindictive speech against Mr Rosenberg. . . . The amount of forensic ammunition which this portly advocate wasted on that occasion was noticed even by persons unfriendly to Mr Rosenberg. But I never forget the ancient aphorism, *De mortuis nil nisi bonum,* and instead of saying anything further of that *cause célèbre,* I simply inscribe on the late Sergeant's tomb RIP."[18]

The legal battle with *Town Talk* had been won, but Lillie's future had become increasingly uncertain. Not only had her relationship with Bertie been damaged by the impact of the libel trial, but her marriage to Ned continued to deteriorate, mainly as a result of their appalling financial problems.

"By now our waning income had almost touched vanishing-point and . . . Mr Langtry also enjoyed the pastime of quiet squandering, so that, as time went on, we began to find ourselves unpleasantly dunned by long suffering tradesmen. . . ."[19] When bailiffs appeared at the door, Lillie would gamely pass it off as a joke, while her maid, Dominique, resorted to cramming Lillie's jewelry and trinkets into the pockets of anyone who came to visit. "In this way some very distinguished friends departed from the beleaguered house with their pockets full, all unconscious that they were evading the law."[20]

In another cruel twist of fate, Lillie's father, Dean Le Breton, had been forced to leave Jersey with his reputation in tatters after his philandering had become public knowledge. The sole consolation for

Lillie's mother was the fact that she could spend more time in London with Lillie. This moral support was doubtless welcome at the most difficult time of Lillie's life.

One glimmer of hope had appeared in the form of Bertie's nephew, Prince Louis of Battenberg, a handsome young naval officer. After being introduced by Bertie, Lillie and Louis had taken an instant liking to each other, and soon fell passionately in love. Bertie, who was losing interest in Lillie, tolerated Louis's visits to Norfolk Street, while Lillie believed that Louis represented a better, more secure future. True, she would have to divorce Ned to marry Louis, and no divorced commoner had yet married into the British royal family, but ever-confident Lillie set her sights on marrying Louis. Their assignations were conducted with discretion, but the love affair was an open secret among their closest friends. On one occasion, during Cowes Week, Lillie and Prince Louis were invited aboard HMS *Thunderer,* commanded by admiral-in-waiting Charlie Beresford, one of Bertie's court jesters.

"All the cabins being below the water line, it was necessary to supply them with oxygen artificially, through air-shafts," Lillie recalled. "One afternoon, while Lord Charles' small cabin was being inspected by royalty and others, his love of mischief caused him to switch off the supply of air and to watch the effect of his practical joke with great delight. Very soon our faces became scarlet, our breathing grew difficult, and we began to go through the uncomfortable sensation which must be experienced by a fish out of water. Fortunately, Lord Charles did not go beyond the frightening-limit, or the Beresford joke might have developed into a Beresford tragedy."[21]

Alongside her relationship with Prince Louis, for which she had every hope of a positive outcome, Lillie was already busy reinventing herself. Since meeting Sarah Bernhardt, Lillie had begun to toy with the idea of a stage career. Lillie had seen how "the Divine Sarah" had entranced Bertie, and, as her power over him was slowly weakening, perhaps Lillie wanted to captivate him a similar way. Lillie had also come to realize that her notoriety, at first so painful, had its own consolations. Thousands would pay to see her beauty, framed by a proscenium arch, for themselves. Lillie describes the process as a dawning awareness that her future lay elsewhere:

> *Finally, one night, at a ball given by the Duchess of Westminster at Grosvenor House, I remembered feeling that I must forthwith cut adrift from this life, which we could no longer afford to enjoy, and, prostrating myself in admiration before the wonderful portrait of Sarah Siddons, I recalled the fact that the artist had signed his name on the hem of her gown and had declared himself satisfied to go down to posterity that way. Then from the Siddons portrait I passed on to other great works of art, and became filled with the desire to become a "worker" too. Impulsive as I was in those days, I did not wait for my carriage, but, pushing my way through the throng of footmen clustering round the hall door, I walked, in spite of my white satin slippers, through the wet and muddy streets to my house, happily not far distant, eagerly considering how to remodel my life.[22]*

This decision came not a moment too soon. At last, after the patience of the Langtrys' creditors had been tested to the limit, the crisis arrived. The little Norfolk Street house was invaded by bailiffs, while Ned went off fishing and left Lillie to deal with the intruders as best she could.[23] Lillie and her mother fled to Bournemouth, leaving "the carpet flag" hanging from the drawing-room window, the traditional method of indicating that the house had been repossessed. The contents of "the poor little red-faced house," as Lillie referred to it in her memoirs, were auctioned off, with souvenir hunters snapping up every item of furniture, even the gilded fans that Lillie and Whistler had painted together in happier times. Lillie's stuffed black bear, a little tea table with Lillie's initials on it, and even her skates were all sold. The peacock, a gift from the Earl of Warwick, was rescued by

Lady Lonsdale, who kept it for Lillie, but Lillie, believing the bird to be unlucky, sent it to Oscar Wilde following a tiff. Oscar's friend Frank Miles, unable to believe that Lillie would have sent Oscar such a valuable item after a quarrel, assumed the peacock was meant for him, and took ownership of it. Perhaps the peacock was unlucky: Frank Miles immediately suffered a series of disasters, ranging from the sudden death of his father to arrest on pedophilia charges, before a descent into madness from which he never recovered.[24]

There was another reason for Lillie's swift departure from Norfolk Street. One Sunday evening in early 1880, Lillie had been dining with Bertie and Princess Alexandra when she suddenly turned pale and almost fainted. Alix showed immediate concern and sent Lillie home, instructing Bertie's own physician, Dr. Francis Laking, to examine her. The following afternoon, Alix arrived at Norfolk Street, full of concern. There could only be one topic of conversation between the two women: Dr. Laking had confirmed the fact that Lillie was pregnant. But, given the complexity of Lillie's relationships, who was the father?

And it is here we must leave Lillie for the time being. Although Bertie would continue to support Lillie during her pregnancy, he could not afford to be seen with her in public. Besides which, Bertie was otherwise engaged, renewing his friendship with an old flame, Jennie Churchill.

Chapter Twelve

JENNIE AND RANDOLPH

More of the panther than of the woman in her look.
—SIR EDGAR VINCENT, VISCOUNT D'ABERNON

Banished to Ireland as a result of Randolph's part in the Aylesford scandal, the Churchills had thrived in exile. Jennie remembered Ireland with fondness for the rest of her life, developing a real affection for the magnificent landscapes and friendly people. Jennie was also genuinely shocked at the dire poverty that persisted decades after the famines of 1846–47, and Randolph developed a sympathy for the Republican cause. And both Jennie and Randolph enjoyed the hunting, which became their ruling passion.[1] Jennie would "beg, borrow or steal"[2] any horse she could get her hands on, with little regard for her own safety. On one occasion, after her mare had sailed over an iron bedstead used as a gate, Jennie had to crawl out of the ditch she had fallen into, and was hoisted into the saddle by farm boys, screaming with laughter.[3] Years later, Winston Churchill remembered his mother "in a riding habit fitted like a skin, and often beautifully spotted with mud; she and my father hunted continually on their large horses; and sometimes there were scares because one or the other did not come back for many hours after they were expected."[4] But, however wonderful the hunting was in Ireland, this was not the future that Jennie had envisaged. Ireland was even more remote than Blenheim Palace. When the Duke of Marlborough, Randolph's father, retired as viceroy of Ireland in 1880, Randolph and Jennie came back to London and Jennie resumed her duties supporting Randolph's political career. Returned to Parliament in 1880, Randolph positioned himself as a "radical Tory" scourge of the Tory frontbench and outspoken critic of the prime minister, Lord Salisbury. Clearly intent on becoming prime minister himself, Randolph set out to create a "Fourth Party," a new form of "Tory Democracy" appealing to working-class men. He even campaigned in the radical citadel of Birmingham, a Liberal stronghold. With his charismatic personality, Randolph could work a crowd, cramming halls full of "boisterous working men"[5] who were captivated by his oratory. A born actor, Randolph knew how to manipulate a scene in the always lively Commons debates. On one occasion, he even threw an offending pamphlet to the floor of the House and stamped on it.[6] Randolph's mood swings became the stuff of legend: he vacillated between euphoria and gloom, and could be viciously rude to those he considered his inferiors, particularly women. Despite increasingly ill health, which colleagues attributed to the burdens of office, Randolph continued to be a committed and ambitious MP. When the second Salisbury administration was formed after the general election of 1886, Randolph became chancellor of the exchequer and leader of the House of Commons, a role in which he was uncharacteristically tactful and discreet.

Spoken of as a rising star, widely tipped to be prime minister someday, Randolph Churchill "stalked elegantly through [the] London of the 'Eighties" although as "a febrile being without heart,"[7] he had inherited the Marlborough disdain for affection. Jennie's sister, Leonie, by now married to Sir John Leslie, an Irish baronet, noticed that Randolph would shoo away his little sons with his newspaper when they were brought down to say good morning to him. "The two pairs of round eyes, peeping around the screen, longed for a kind word."[8] This *froideur* extended to Jennie, who confided in her sisters that Randolph had ceased to visit her bed after 1881.[9] Jennie suspected that Randolph had become involved with Lady de Grey, a society beauty, although she had no evidence of this. Puzzled and hurt by Randolph's neglect, Jennie attempted to "keep her mortification to herself."[10] Jennie also embarked on a string of affairs; it was widely believed that her second son, John, was actually the son of Viscount Falmouth. As is so often the case with politician's marriages, Randolph's floundered as his career flourished. The Liberal MP Henry Labouchere noted that "though [Randolph] gets on pretty well with his wife when they are together he is always rather glad to be away from her,"[11] while the writer Frank Harris witnessed this scene between the couple:

> *The door opened and Jennie walked in. Out of courtesy, Harris stood up as Jennie entered the room, but Randolph remained seated.*
>
> *"Randolph!" said Jennie. Randolph did not reply and in spite of his ominous silence, she came across to him. "Randolph, I want to talk to you!"*
>
> *"Don't you see," he retorted, "that I've come here to be undisturbed!"*
>
> *"But I want you," she repeated tactlessly.*
>
> *He sprang to his feet. "Can't I have a moment's peace from you anywhere?" he barked. "Get out and leave me alone!"*
>
> *At once she turned and walked out of the room.[12]*

Frank Harris also knew something that Jennie did not: Randolph had been to visit several doctors, convinced that he had contracted syphilis. This had been one of the reasons for breaking off relations with Jennie, for fear that he infect her. The frequent visits to Paris, which had made Jennie so suspicious, may have been trips to see specialists in venereal disease. Before the discovery of antibiotics, the only treatment for syphilis was mercury and potassium iodide,[13] a poisonous combination. Even if Randolph had not been syphilitic, and his symptoms were due to a brain tumor, the side effects of the treatment would have been the explanation for his mood swings, nervous irritability, tremors, lethargy, and cognitive impairment. There was something else Jennie did not know: Randolph spent time with a secret homosexual coterie known as the Uranians, a group that included Lord Rosebery, John Addington Symonds, and Lord Drumlanrig, elder brother of Oscar Wilde's lover "Bosie" Douglas.[14] If Randolph had been homosexual this would have added to his stress. As well as the demands of a political career and a failing marriage, he would have had to endure the constant fear of blackmail and exposure.

As Randolph spent increasingly more time at his club, the Carlton, and traveling abroad with male friends, Jennie could at least distract herself with the world of the "Court and Social," as *The Times* of London described it. In November 1885, Jennie was invited to Windsor, where the queen wished to confer the Order of the Crown of India upon her. Jennie wore a black velvet dress, so thickly embroidered with jet beads that "the pin could find no hold and, unwittingly, the Queen stuck it straight into me."[15] Jennie met the queen once again the following spring. On March 6, 1886, Jennie was presented to her in a variation of the debutante ceremony. As a married woman, Jennie was permitted to appear in a colored gown, and wore a magnificent golden dress made by Monsieur Worth to Jennie's own design. "Diamonds flashed in her ears, on her throat and arms and her dress glistened like a glass of golden wine held to the sunlight"[16] gushed one besotted journalist.

Jennie also had the consolation of her close friendship with Bertie, which she had renewed over the past two years. Following Randolph's political success, Jennie had persuaded Bertie to forgive and forget, and Bertie had joined the couple for dinner in 1884. A more formal reconciliation took place in May 1886, when Bertie joined the prime minister, Mr. Gladstone, and his wife as guests of the Churchills at Connaught Place. It could have been an awkward evening, particularly when the electricity generator broke down and the house was plunged into a blackout,[17] but Jennie handled it perfectly. Since then, their friendship had blossomed. Jennie and Randolph were invited to dine at Windsor Castle, where Queen Victoria noted that "Lady Randolph (an American) is very handsome and very dark."[18] The couple were also invited to stay at Sandringham, the royal family's country house in Norfolk, the details of which Jennie noted like an anthropologist writing about a strange tribe, from the enormous meals, including a long leisurely breakfast,[19] a picnic lunch in a tent for the shooting party, and a huge afternoon tea, to the horrors of the actual shoot itself. Although a keen fox-hunter, Jennie loathed shooting, particularly when indulged in by women. "Crash, Bang! And the glorious creature became a maimed and tortured thing . . . if these things must be done, how can a woman bring herself to do them?"[20] Jennie did at least have the opportunity to demonstrate her musical skills, playing duets with Princess Alexandra, who was particularly fond of Brahms's Hungarian Dances, or struggling with a Schumann piano concerto in Princess Victoria's sitting room. "The pace set was terrific, and I was rather glad there was no audience."[21]

Then came the delightful evenings, heralded by the sound of the dressing gong. "Off came the tea-gowns and on came the low-necked, tightly-laced evening dresses. The gentlemen wore full dress with decorations though never uniform, and the Prince of Wales led each lady in turn into dinner."[22] After dinner, there was an hour or so of whist before the princess took the ladies off to bed. "Occasionally, Princess Alix would invite one into her dressing room, which was crowded with objects and souvenirs of all kinds. On a perch in the center of the room was an old and somewhat ferocious parrot. At other times, rather alarmingly, Princess Alix might surprise you by coming into your room, ostensibly 'to see if you have everything you want' but in reality to offer a few words of advice, or her sympathy if she thought you needed any."[23]

Plenty of friends and acquaintances were prepared to believe that Jennie and Bertie were having an affair, but Jennie was too clever to leave any explicit clues about the relationship. Notes from Bertie to Jennie are models of discretion, while Jennie's own letters remain under lock and key at the royal archives in Windsor, and are likely to be as discreet as Bertie's. After all, Jennie had learned the value of discretion after witnessing the fate of Lady Aylesford and others like her. Bertie's carriage was often to be seen outside the Churchills' house at Connaught Place, while Jennie received him alone. Notes such as "Would it be very indiscreet if I proposed myself for luncheon?"[24] or "I have to sit on a Royal Commission from 12–4 tomorrow but if I can get away by 3 I will call with pleasure on the chance of seeing you?"[25] certainly fit Bertie's modus operandi for lovemaking.

Did Jennie become another of Bertie's sexual conquests? Given her sexual promiscuity—she was rumored to have had over two hundred lovers—her unhappy marriage, and starstruck attitude to royalty, it would scarcely have been surprising. Bertie's friendship, whatever form it took, must have been a great consolation as Randolph's behavior became increasingly erratic. Despite this, Jennie's positive attitude shone through. On December 22, 1886, Jennie entertained Bertie at lunch at Connaught Place, while Randolph lunched at the Carlton Club with the minister for war. Jennie and Bertie discussed plans for the New Year, and the boys, Winston and Jack, were home for the Christmas holidays, which they intended to spend in London. Jennie had everything to look forward to.

That evening, Jennie and Randolph went to see *School for Scandal* and Jennie noticed that Randolph was unusually preoccupied. Randolph left their box after the intermission, saying he was going to his club, but this was not out of character, and Jennie returned home, unconcerned. The following morning, as usual, a copy of *The Times* was sent up with her tray of early-morning tea. The front-page news consisted of Randolph's resignation from the government.

White and shaking, Jennie went down to breakfast, to discover Randolph calmly smiling. "Quite a surprise for you!" he commented.[26]

"He went into no explanation and I felt too utterly crushed and miserable to ask for any or even to remonstrate."[27] Mr. Moore, permanent under-secretary at the Treasury, who had hero-worshipped Randolph, rushed into the room and told Jennie: "He has thrown himself from the top of the ladder and will never reach it again."[28]

Randolph's shock announcement rocked the cabinet. Most MPs were at home in their country houses, preparing for Christmas. Nobody had suspected that a dispute of this magnitude had been brewing. The prime minister, Lord Salisbury, who had received a copy of Randolph's letter the previous evening, wearily asked his wife to find him *The Times*. "Randolph resigned in the middle of the night and if I know my man, it will be in *The Times* this morning."[29] Queen Victoria was furious at having to learn about the resignation of her chancellor from *The Times*. A misprint in an Irish newspaper announcing that "Lord Randolph has burnt his boots"[30] elicited a little strained laughter in the Churchill household, but Jennie, who had spent so much time and energy supporting her husband's meteoric rise to power, was completely crushed. As Bertie tried to comfort her, Jennie could only write that "When I looked back at the preceding months which seemed so triumphant and full of promise, the debacle appeared all the greater. I had made sure that Randolph would enjoy the fruits of office for years to come, and apart from the honour and glory, I regretted these same 'fruits.'"[31]

Many explanations have been offered for Randolph's resignation from the cabinet, but the most obvious one is that he believed that his resignation would bring down Lord Salisbury's minority government, and that he would be invited back to form a new one on his own terms, with himself as prime minister. Randolph had often said that politics was the most exciting form of gambling, but this gesture was a throw of the dice gone wrong. Lord Salisbury reshuffled the cabinet and placed George Goschen, a financier, in the role of chancellor of the exchequer. Devastated by these developments, Stafford Henry Northcote, Lord Iddsleigh, who had hoped to become chancellor himself, collapsed and died suddenly at 10 Downing Street.

After a few halfhearted attempts to get back into the cabinet, and in increasingly poor health, Randolph switched his attention to horse racing. He proved far more successful at this activity than he had been at politics, and his mare, L'Abbesse de Jouarre, won the Epsom Derby.

L'Abbesse, named after a book Jennie had been reading by Henry Renan, was a beautiful black mare with a heart bigger than her body. Randolph loved all his horses, but especially L'Abbesse. Randolph's friend, the Hon. George Lambton, recalled that whenever Randolph went around the stables, his pockets were always stuffed with apples and sugar. On one occasion he was talking to Lambton when they heard a tremendous kicking and squealing and neighing in a box farther down the yard.[32] When they opened the door of the box, L'Abbesse rushed at Randolph like a dog, trying to stick her nose into his pockets to get at the sugar and apples. Randolph was so overcome with emotion at the sight of his old mare that tears rolled down his cheeks.[33] With this anecdote, a rare glimpse of Randolph's human side emerges, inspired by a horse. Like many Englishmen, Randolph could express his emotions to an animal, but not to another human being.

Randolph's health went into steep decline after he quit the cabinet, and he died in 1894. Jennie went on to marry Captain George Cornwallis-West, younger than Jennie by twenty years, much to the dismay of her sons. When this marriage failed, Jennie married Montagu Phippen Porch, a member of the British Civil Service in Nigeria. Born too early for a political career of her own, Jennie never fulfilled her promise as a beauty with brains and spirit. Margot Asquith paid her a typically backhanded compliment when she commented that "had Lady Randolph Churchill been like her face, she would have governed the world."[34]

Chapter Thirteen

MY DARLING DAISY

As rare as any oiseau bleu, *a great heiress and a great beauty.*
—DAISY, COUNTESS OF WARWICK

rances Maynard was born in Berkeley Square on December 10, 1861, during a black and gloomy winter that saw London hung with mourning for the recently deceased Prince Albert.[1] "Daisy," as she was known from her earliest years on account of her white skin and bright eyes, had illustrious forebears, including Nell Gwyn, mistress of King Charles II, and the Duke of St. Albans. Daisy's father was the wild and headstrong Charles Maynard, son of Henry Maynard, 3rd Viscount Maynard. Charles Maynard, tall, red-haired, with blazing blue eyes, was a famous athlete, and many of his exploits when colonel of the Blues had become legendary. Charles was such an accomplished rider that he could jump his favorite horse over the mess table without disturbing a single wineglass, and he had once interrupted a bullfight in Spain and ridden the animal around the ring by the horns, much to the consternation and anger of the onlookers.[2] Charles had met Daisy's mother, Blanche, while visiting his family's estate in Northamptonshire, and, although the marriage between a humble vicar's daughter and an extroverted aristocrat twenty years her senior seems unconventional, the match brought Blanche great wealth and Easton Lodge, the sprawling gothic mansion near Dunmow, Essex.

Three years after Daisy's birth, tragedy struck. Charles Maynard died suddenly at the house in Berkeley Square and left Blanche a widow, alone in the world with Daisy and her little sister, Blanchie. After Charles had been buried in the family vault at Little Easton church, old Viscount Maynard invited Blanche to visit Easton Lodge, and bring the children with her. All that Daisy could remember was her grandfather "as an old man, being dragged round uncarpeted rooms at Easton in a bath chair, and feeling the thrill of his wonderful eyes as he gazed on me."[3] The old viscount died, just two months later. But Daisy had made an impression. Blanche was once again summoned to Easton Lodge, this time to hear the family solicitor read out Viscount Maynard's last will and testament in the breakfast room. It was commonly supposed that, following young Charles's sudden death, the bulk of Viscount Maynard's estate would be inherited by the Capel boys, two cousins who had been brought up at Easton Lodge. To Blanche's astonishment, the old viscount had other ideas. After meeting young Daisy, Viscount Maynard had altered his will, making the little girl his heir, and leaving the estate to her.[4]

This made some members of the family so angry that they threw pats of butter at the viscount's portrait, despite the fact that he had provided "amply for all of them."[5] Thus, the Maynards went from genteel poverty to a life of luxury, moving immediately to Easton Lodge. Years later, Daisy recalled "the long drive from the station on a wet night, the plop-plop of the horses' hoofs, and the swaying motion of the heavy closed brougham which made me physically sick."[6] Family feeling over the inheritance was so strong that Blanche feared for Daisy's safety, and the children were accompanied at all times by a bodyguard whenever they ventured farther than the gardens.[7]

Easton Lodge, with its rolling ten thousand acres of estate, gentle parkland, and elegant gardens, formed the ideal backdrop to an idyllic childhood. Originally the Manor of Estaines, Easton Lodge had once been the property of the Crown. According to Daisy, the manor was "full of historic memories. There are even fragments of Roman remains in the foundations of the old house . . . there are reminiscences of monastic occupation. . . . "[8] And Elizabeth Woodville, wife of Edward IV, had spent her honeymoon at the old manor house.[9] A century later, Queen Elizabeth I granted the manor to Henry Maynard as a reward for his duties to Lord Burghley, Elizabeth's private secretary. Henry Maynard demolished a hunting lodge on the land known as Easton Lodge and commissioned a vast Elizabethan mansion, similar in appearance to Blickling Hall in Norfolk. From the seventeenth century, Easton Hall became noted for its formal gardens, while the house was regarded as a masterpiece of Tudor architecture until the terrible night in 1847 when the hall was almost entirely destroyed by fire. Easton Lodge was rebuilt at a cost of £12,000 to a design by Thomas Hopper, who specialized in the Victorian gothic style. A watercolor of the Victorian incarnation of Easton Lodge reveals a gothic monstrosity in glowing redbrick of little aesthetic value, with heavy casement windows, and an ungainly turret topped with battlements.[10]

But to a child, such aesthetic considerations were meaningless. As far as Daisy was concerned, Easton Lodge was a wonderful place to grow up and run wild. For Daisy was a tomboy who loved "climbing, running, jumping, and challenging all the rules."[11] She could climb trees "like any sailor lad"[12] and loved animals, birds, and even watching an ants' nest for hours on end. "Birds, kittens, rabbits, dogs, even toads and frogs were our pets."[13] But Daisy's greatest love was horses. "I had my first pony when I was five, I can scarcely remember when I could not ride."[14] When Daisy's mother married the Earl of Rosslyn, a famous racehorse trainer, horses proved a great bond between Daisy and her new stepfather. The Earl of Rosslyn built new stables at Easton Lodge, and "my stepfather had such confidence in our fearlessness that he used to let us children ride his young thoroughbreds that were unfit to race and showed temper. It was excellent practice for us, as the horses were often unbroken, and few of them had natural good manners."[15] Daisy even took out a beautiful horse named Crust, who had bucked off Lord Ribblesdale, the Liberal peer, in front of Easton Lodge. Ribblesdale warned Lord Rosslyn that Crust was unfit for any girl to ride, and would savage anyone he could throw, but Daisy leaped determinedly on the horse's back. "I knew that I must stick on at any price!"[16]

Blanche Maynard proceeded to have five more children with the Earl of Rosslyn, two sons and three daughters, and soon there were seven children growing up at Easton Lodge. Their life was a secluded one, without parties or social entertainment outside the family, but they had the consolation of living "in a beautiful country place" with "ponies to ride and animals to caress."[17]

The girls were educated at home by a devoted tutor and a governess who took a genuine interest in their education, and from an early age, Daisy learned the importance of noblesse oblige. Daisy would accompany her mother on visits to the sick and elderly, with blankets and provisions. She developed a social conscience, and understood that to be a landowner was to be responsible for all who lived upon one's estate, however lowly. This gave Daisy "a passionate sympathy with the under-dog; a troubled awareness that life for all the world was not as it was in the garden of Easton."[18]

By the age of fourteen, Daisy was a beauty in waiting. Even being forced to dress in her mother's castoffs merely served to offset Daisy's dazzling ash blond hair and deep blue eyes. The earl was duly instructed to take Daisy to have her looks recorded by Frank Miles at his studio off the Strand, and it was here that Daisy met Lillie Langtry for the first time, and the earl invited Lillie to visit to the Rosslyns' London mansion. Lillie's arrival the following evening was watched by Daisy and her little sister, Blanchie, peeping through the banisters as Lillie and Ned arrived in the magnificent entrance hall.

By the following year, Daisy's nascent loveliness was beginning to captivate admirers, much to the surprise and delight of this self-confessed gawky tomboy, who found "in men's eyes an unfailing tribute to a beauty I myself had not been able to discern."[19] Such was Daisy's appeal that her parents knew she could make a match of the highest order. And so it was that at the age of seventeen, before Daisy had been officially launched into society, she found herself at the theater one evening alongside former prime minister Benjamin Disraeli, now sitting in the House of Lords as Lord Beaconsfield.

Seated at the Lyceum Theatre, in a box that had been lent for the occasion by Baroness Burdett Coutts, Daisy and Disraeli made an odd couple. Here was Daisy, a tall girl in a white muslin frock with a blue sash,[20] alongside her distinguished companion of seventy-three, a regular guest at Easton Lodge. Very few young women could boast of being taken on a "date" by a former prime minister. Daisy stared around her at the glittering audience, the men in evening dress and the ladies bejewelled and dazzling in beautiful gowns. For once, the pearls of wisdom from the lips of the legendary politician and author fell on deaf ears. Daisy had come here to worship Ellen Terry, appearing that night in *Romeo and Juliet*. The performance made such an impression on Daisy that she begged her stepfather for a volume of Shakespeare, and eventually received an "expurgated" volume of his plays, learning *Hamlet* by heart.

While marriages across the generations were not unusual by Victorian standards, even Daisy's mother might have balked at the age difference between her beautiful young daughter and the ancient Lord Beaconsfield. But, while Disraeli had been widowed four years previously, marriage was not on the agenda. Daisy's visit to the theater had been an audition. Queen Victoria herself had instructed Disraeli to spend the evening in Daisy's company and see for himself what sort of a wife she might make for Prince Leopold. The youngest son of Queen Victoria had become a frequent visitor to Easton Lodge and had expressed an interest in Daisy. It was true that they had nothing in common. Daisy was a horse-mad tomboy, full of high spirits, while Prince Leopold was a lifelong invalid, a hemophiliac "too delicate in health to ride or to take part in any sport."[21]

Disraeli's report was clearly a glowing one, for soon there came a request for a photograph of Daisy. There was just one drawback. Whenever Prince Leopold came to visit Daisy, he was always accompanied by his equerry, Lord Brooke. Eight years older than Daisy, Francis Greville, heir to the Earl of Warwick, or "Brookie" to his friends, was Daisy's match in temperament. After leaving Christ Church, Oxford, without taking his degree, Brookie had obtained a post as aide-de-camp to Robert Bulwer Lytton, viceroy of India, and traveled in the East before returning to England. Intent on a political career, Brookie had been selected as Tory candidate for the safe seat of Somerset East, and would become a member of Parliament at the next election. Brookie's people were genuine aristocrats, of ancient lineage, but not particularly wealthy. As far as Daisy's family was concerned, Brookie could not compete with a prince of the royal blood. But Daisy's parents, it appeared, were no match for true love. "In Lord Brooke's eyes I had recognised something that told me, in mute appeal, that his happiness and destiny were inseparably linked with mine."[22]

Just before Daisy's eighteenth birthday, she was summoned to Windsor Castle, "that I might be inspected as a future daughter-in-law."[23] This was an alarming prospect for even the most sophisticated young ladies, with a dismal protocol that dictated that the guests spend three-quarters of an hour shivering in a drafty corridor before dinner at eight-thirty. Dinner was "served with hot haste" as Lord Rosslyn, a favorite of the queen, did his best to amuse her.[24] The dinner was also significant for another reason. It was here that Daisy first encountered Bertie, her senior by twenty years. Daisy said nothing of this first meeting in her memoir, apart from the fact that Bertie had inherited his mother's "ingenuous, charming smile."[25] After dinner, Queen Victoria, who reminded Daisy of her old nurse, came over to talk. "How did I like the idea of coming out? Was I fond of music or of drawing?"[26] This interview was an ordeal, as the agonizingly shy Daisy struggled to respond to the queen's questions, despite the fact that these were softened by the gleam of the rare smile.

In December 1879, Daisy celebrated her eighteenth birthday with a magnificent ball at Easton Lodge. Daisy would not, of course, be officially "out" in society until she had been presented at court, but this lavish occasion would mark her debut as one of the most beautiful and sought-after heiresses of the day. The ball was so magnificent that a top hairdresser was brought down from Knightsbridge, London, to attend to the wigs of the footmen.[27]

The following February, Daisy was invited to visit Prince Leopold at Claremont, his country estate, in the hope that the meeting might lead to the longed-for proposal. And indeed, "one afternoon, the Prince opened his heart to me," Daisy breathlessly confides. But the prince did not say the words that Daisy had expected to hear. Instead, Prince Leopold confessed that he was in love with someone else, and that he had guessed how Brookie felt about Daisy, and indeed how Daisy felt about Brookie. It emerged that Prince Leopold had fallen in love with the German Princess Helena of Waldeck-Pyrmont, a kindly young woman celebrated for her warm heart, keen intelligence, and charitable work.[28] Prince Leopold offered to explain this all to his mother, the queen, and to ensure that Daisy would be able to marry Brookie. Daisy and the prince talked for hours, telling the footman who attempted to come in to pull down the blinds and light the lamps to come back in ten minutes. The poor footman was left to come and go for over an hour while Daisy and Leopold made their plans.[29]

The following day, although it poured with rain, Daisy and Brookie went out for a walk together. "Under a large umbrella, on the muddy road between Claremont and Esher, he proposed to me" wrote Daisy. "And I accepted."[30] When they returned to the house, Prince Leopold was waiting at the front door, full of genuine delight at their happiness. There was just one problem: as it was considered inappropriate for young ladies to become engaged before "coming out," the engagement must remain secret.

In March 1880, Daisy was presented at court in a gown of silver tissue.[31] Daisy was that rare thing, "as rare as any *oiseau bleu* a great heiress and a great beauty. Only those who were alive then know the magic that word held for the period. I was physically fit, unspoilt, and I adored dancing."[32] Daisy's parents rented 7 Carlton Gardens (now part of the Carlton Club) and Daisy was fêted, feasted, courted, and adored, in one continual round of gaiety. Daisy attended balls thrown in her honor where she floated through "fairy palaces, where lovely beings in diaphanous frou-frous of tulle or chiffon swayed in the grace of the rhythmic waltz . . . [which] never failed to make me thrill and pulsate in an abandonment of young ecstasy."[33]

At this point, Queen Victoria believed that Daisy was still potential daughter-in-law material. So did Disraeli, Lord Beaconsfield. But in May 1880, against the wishes of her mother, Daisy officially rejected Prince Leopold as a potential suitor. When Daisy's engagement to Brookie was announced the following month, the queen was angered by the news, as indeed was Disraeli, disappointed to see his matchmaking thwarted. But Prince Leopold also got his own way. He married Princess Helena in 1881 and they enjoyed a brief but happy marriage before Leopold's untimely death in 1884.

When Daisy developed measles that summer of 1880, the wedding was postponed until the following April. On a day welcomed by one guest who declared that "Henceforth, this beautiful Daisy will flourish by a brook-side"[34] the couple were married at Westminster Abbey. The streets leading from 7 Carlton Gardens to the abbey were lined with hundreds of well-wishers, celebrating "the most brilliant wedding of a dozen seasons."[35] Guests, including the Prince of Wales and Prince Leopold, who had volunteered to be Brookie's best man, crushed into the abbey from the choir to the door. Daisy had no less than twelve bridesmaids, whose names read like a digested version of Burke's Peerage.

A day later, the bride and groom were commanded to dine with the queen at Windsor Castle, and, as was the custom at that period, Daisy was required to wear her wedding dress, "orange blossom and all!"[36] for her first official dinner as a married lady. The shy bride was already mortified with self-consciousness by the time the queen asked if she could take a spray of orange blossom from Daisy's corsage as a souvenir.[37] But Queen Victoria went out of her way to be kind to the young newlywed, saying "many charming things about the beauty of my frock."[38] Indeed, so charmed was the queen that she asked Daisy to have a photograph taken of herself wearing her wedding dress.[39] Daisy had clearly made an excellent impression on the queen, despite her refusal to marry Prince Leopold.

However, this genuine goodwill on the part of the queen was severely tested the following year. Daisy and Brookie were invited to dinner and to spend the night at Windsor Castle. Headstrong Daisy, who planned to go hunting, tried to postpone the engagement, reminding the queen that Brookie would be away fishing in Ireland. Daisy's objection was batted away as the excuse it so obviously was, and Daisy was instructed to attend the dinner on her own. Daisy was furious, as she had a horse running in the Essex Hunt races the following day, and she had planned a morning's fox hunting first. The train times between Windsor Castle and Essex were prohibitive, and it seemed impossible to get away from Windsor in time to attend the hunt meet at eight o'clock in the morning.[40]

Carefully, Daisy made her plans. The dinner at Windsor was to be a quiet affair, just six guests with the queen and Princess Beatrice. The custom was that the following morning, guests would depart from Windsor on a specific train, with a lord-in-waiting to see them off. As this train would leave too late to allow Daisy to arrive at the hunt meet in time, Daisy rose early and put on her hunting clothes, including her coat of "pink," "a fashion innovation of my own."[41] Hunting "pink," the distinctive red jacket worn on the hunting field, was reserved for men. Women habitually wore black, with a black top hat. By dressing in a coat normally worn only by male riders, Daisy revealed a characteristic streak of vulgarity. She had ordered a carriage to take her to the station to catch an earlier train, much to the irritation of the lord-in-waiting, "Lord C," who stumped downstairs yawning to see her off, scandalized by this breach of protocol and Daisy's pink hunt coat. Daisy caught her train on time and had a "splendid day's hunting" before heading off to the Essex races, where her horse won the cup.[42] But Daisy's escapade had not gone unnoticed. The queen, always an early riser, had glanced out of her window that morning to see Daisy clamber into her carriage in her bright pink coat. The queen was less than impressed. "How fast! How very fast!" she muttered to her lady-in-waiting.[43] The queen's verdict was prescient.

As the hunting jacket reveals, Daisy was not the sort of wife to bow to convention. Strong-willed, beautiful, impulsive, Daisy had only one person to please in her life, and that was herself, and she soon took up her place in what she referred to as "the social pageant" in a characteristically lavish and flamboyant manner. In 1882, Daisy and Brookie settled at Easton Lodge, as its attractions rivaled those of Brookie's more modest Warwick Castle. At Easton, "we entertained shooting-parties and friends . . . my husband was one of the best shots of the day."[44] The couple also rented a furnished house in London for the season. Daisy moved with ease between the two main groups of society, the court set and the less conventional world of high bohemia. At Lord Wharncliffe's house in Curzon Street Daisy socialized with Lord Leighton and Edward Burne-Jones, Millais, Watts, and Whistler.[45] At Lady St. Helier's literary salon Daisy met the poets Tennyson, Browning, and Matthew Arnold. Sarah Bernhardt became a friend and was invited to perform *Hamlet* at Warwick Castle, while another new acquaintance was Lady Florence Dixie, née Douglas, daughter of the 8th Marquis of Queensbury. A headstrong and intelligent woman, Florence enjoyed walking her pet jaguar in Kensington Gardens and later served as a war correspondent during the Boer War, one of the first women to embrace this dangerous occupation. Daisy had moved into a world where the normal rules of social behavior did not seem to apply, but this was something of an illusion. Many of those who were drawn, mothlike, to the glittering world of society had their wings burned, and Daisy would be no exception.

Chapter Fourteen

THE HEART HAS ITS REASONS

He looked at me in a way all women understand.
—Daisy, Countess of Warwick

From the start of her married life, Daisy regularly witnessed the courtly dance of romantic affairs played out against the backdrops of grand country houses, and longed to be part of it, regardless of Brookie's feelings. There seems to have been a certain acceptance on Brookie's part that Daisy was a force of nature who made her own rules. Brookie's real passions were hunting, shooting, and fishing,[1] although given the opportunity, he possessed a keen eye for the ladies. Daisy loved hunting, too, but she found shooting and fishing desperately dull. However, being married to a sporting man was not without its advantages. Brookie's love of field sports meant that the couple were invited to numerous shooting parties at remote country houses.

It was in this milieu, as a married woman, that Daisy saw exactly how her contemporaries conducted their affairs. Indeed, it appeared to Daisy that an affair was almost de rigueur, as long as both parties remained discreet. Unfortunately, discretion was one quality of which Daisy was almost entirely devoid.

Determined to have a little fun of her own, and realizing that country house weekends were the ideal opportunities to bag a lover,

Daisy began to cast around for a suitable man for the role. But finding the right individual proved to be more difficult than Daisy expected. On one occasion, Daisy experienced the thrill of "a certain Lord X" professing undying love for her,[2] and was very much attracted to him in her turn. But one night at a party Daisy overheard Lord X address Lillie Langtry as "my darling" as he draped her cloak around her shoulders, following the gesture with a request for an assignation. Utterly furious, Daisy resolved that she would never look at Lord X again.[3] However tedious the country house circuit might be, Daisy had her standards.

The Prince of Wales himself should have met Daisy's exacting criteria in these early days of Daisy's marriage. Bertie had already made one visit to Easton Lodge, and Bertie and Daisy met again at Eastwell Manor, Kent, home of Bertie's brother, the Duke of Edinburgh, at a ball thrown in Bertie's honor. Daisy wore "a ruby velvet dress, *en princesse,* which was much admired,"[4] she recalled, although in hindsight she admitted that it might have been a little dowdy. "The Prince asked me to dance, and sat out a long time talking with me in a corridor, but he doubtless found me shy or stupid, for he spent most of the evening with Mrs Cornwallis-West, then in the zenith of her beauty."[5] Patsy Cornwallis-West was also in the zenith of her affair with Bertie, which is perhaps why Bertie did not trouble Daisy with his advances.

Having provided Brookie with three children, Daisy succeeded in sticking to her marriage vows, despite her headstrong and impulsive character, until the fateful day when she met Lord Charles Beresford. A close friend of the Prince of Wales, Charlie Beresford was the practical joker who had turned off the oxygen in Louis Battenberg's cabin while he was belowdecks "inspecting the facilities" with Lillie Langtry.[6]

Despite his catastrophic impact, Charlie Beresford appears only once in Daisy's memoirs. Daisy recalled an incident when she was sitting at Easton Lodge in a large tent that Charlie Beresford had brought back from the Sudan. Daisy's guest was Sir Donald Mackenzie Wallace, a distinguished linguist and foreign correspondent with *The Times,* and Daisy had asked if he could translate the writing on the tent walls. Sir Donald shook his head and replied: "You would not sit long in this tent if you knew what is written on these embroideries. I cannot possibly tell it. I might tell it later on to your husband and a few men; I cannot translate it here and now." Daisy never did get to find out what the embroidery on the tent said. Apparently the text was "too obscene."[7] This brief reference gives no indication of the role played by Charlie Beresford in Daisy's life.

Lord Charles Beresford (1846–1919) was Bertie's former naval aide-de-camp, a decorated war hero, and fourth lord of the admiralty. The son of an Anglo-Irish marquis, Beresford was hugely popular with the British public, who referred to him as "Charlie B" and "John Bull" on account of his pet bulldog. By the age of thirty-seven, Charlie Beresford was as outrageous as ever, much to the discomfort of his long-suffering wife, Mina. Older than Charlie, and physically unprepossessing, Mina had resorted to cosmetics to improve her appearance. This included false eyelashes, one of which was ripped off by a small child who mistook it for a butterfly.[8] Exposing a nasty streak, Daisy took great pleasure in humiliating Mina. Daisy loved to recount the terrible occasion when she and Mina drove out in an open carriage and a gust of wind blew off Mina's hat, taking with it her wig.[9]

Charlie Beresford had been a frequent visitor to Easton Lodge from the early months of Daisy's marriage. London gossips claimed that Charlie Beresford was "positively 'bewitched' by" Daisy within weeks of their meeting,[10] while Daisy seemed equally smitten with Charlie. Within three years of Daisy's marriage, they were lovers, much to poor Mina's consternation.

Daisy had fallen spectacularly in love, despite the fact that Charlie was fifteen years older. Charlie Beresford was a celebrity, with his irrepressible high spirits, his war record, and the charm that preceded him into the room: it was said you heard the voice before you saw the man. Their affair unfolded with the momentum of an Elinor Glyn story, and with a conclusion more astonishing than anything that the romantic novelist could have imagined.

As we have seen, Daisy was accustomed to getting her own way. So it was that one morning, while the Beresfords were staying at Easton Lodge, Daisy strode into Mina's bedroom and told her that she was planning to desert Brookie, abandon their three children, and elope with Charlie.[11] Mina's response to this extraordinary disclosure was measured. Mustering all the hauteur of which she was capable, Mina retorted that "the circumstances of the affair" were already well known in society,[12] and that she had no intention of relinquishing her husband. More significantly, Mina said that she was not prepared to sacrifice her husband's career on such an insane scheme and she was taking Charlie home immediately.

If Daisy was devastated by this outcome, it came as something of a relief to Charlie Beresford. Charlie's infatuation with Daisy was fading fast, and any lingering sentiments he may have had were destroyed by Mina's allegations that Daisy was "not content with his attentions alone."[13] Charlie seemed anxious to move on and consign his relationship with Daisy to the past.

But not so Daisy. Upon hearing, in 1886, that Mina was pregnant, Daisy flew into a rage. There could be no possibility that the father was anyone but Charlie. Betrayed by her lover, and with his own wife! With insane disregard for her own reputation, Daisy sent Charlie a furious letter, demanding that he leave Mina and join her on the Riviera. In addition, Daisy claimed that Charlie was the father of her oldest daughter, Marjorie, and that he had no right to father a child with his wife.[14] This behavior was scarcely calculated to win Charlie back, but as far as Daisy was concerned, Charlie belonged to her, and not to Mina Beresford.

In a twist of fate, it was not Charlie who opened the letter when it arrived. As Charlie Beresford was away at sea, his mail was opened by a trusted member of the household: Mina.[15] Once again Mina demonstrated an impressive level of composure. She immediately passed the letter on to George Lewis, the top London solicitor who was so skilled at keeping controversial cases out of court. Lewis was the obvious choice for a woman of Mina's social standing. Mina Beresford instructed Lewis to write to Daisy, informing her that the letter was now in Lady Beresford's possession, and warning her to cease and desist from any further contact with his client. Daisy's response was predictable; she penned a furious reply to Lewis, claiming that the letter was hers and demanding it back. Lewis responded that, legally, the letter belonged to Charlie Beresford, to whom it had been addressed. Lord Beresford had surrendered the letter to his wife, who had now lodged it with her solicitor, George Lewis.[16]

Infuriated by the machinations of these irritating wives and pettifogging lawyers who stood in her way, and facing the prospect of ruin if the matter became public, Daisy realized that there was only one person she could turn to. Only one man had the power, the contacts, and the chivalry to come to the aid of this damsel in distress: Bertie, the Prince of Wales.[17] Daisy was by now on good terms with Bertie, dined regularly with him, and had met him at Ascot and Goodwood. More significantly, Daisy was aware that Bertie was sympathetic and wise concerning affairs of the heart. Confident that Bertie would act on her behalf, Daisy wrote to the prince and asked if he would see her.

Bertie responded immediately, and summoned Daisy to Marlborough House. It was late in the evening, and he received her in his oak-paneled study, a snug, masculine room dominated by an enormous desk littered with books and documents. Daisy, her deep blue eyes brimming with tears, confessed her affair with Charlie Beresford and her impulsive letter to Mina and begged Bertie to come to her aid.

Bertie, all concern, listened patiently as Daisy unburdened her heart. "He was charmingly courteous to me," Daisy said later, "and at length he told me he hoped his friendship would make up in part, at least, for my sailor-lover's loss. He was more than kind."[18] Indeed he was. Daisy must have realized that there would be a price to be paid for Bertie's assistance. As she sat in front of his desk, Daisy found that Bertie was looking at her "in a way all women understand."[19]

After Daisy had left, Bertie summoned his carriage and paid a late night visit to George Lewis. As far as Lewis was concerned, the inconvenience of being dragged out of bed in the small hours was more than compensated for by the arrival of the Prince of Wales. The men were on good terms, as Lewis had been Bertie's guest at an event to celebrate one of Lillie Langtry's stage successes. In fact, Lewis was so impressed by Bertie's visit that he even agreed to show him the letter from Daisy. This was highly unprofessional behavior on Lewis's part, but he no doubt felt outmaneuvered by the Prince of Wales. After reading the letter, Bertie ordered Lewis to destroy it.

Even Lewis was unwilling to go this far. He refused, deferentially explaining to the Prince of Wales that he could not destroy the letter without the consent of his client, Mina Beresford. Bertie's response was simple. He would ask her himself.[20] And with that, Bertie went to call on Mina at her London home. Bertie ordered Mina to do the decent thing and destroy the letter, arguing that it could cause nothing but harm. But, unlike George Lewis, Mina was not overawed by the Prince of Wales and flatly refused to destroy Daisy's letter. Bertie left the house, furious, only to return later to try again. This time, he begged Mina to be charitable and told her that Daisy had been spoken to and would never cause her trouble again. But Mina still refused to destroy the letter, arguing that it constituted her only defense against Daisy and her machinations. Again, Bertie left in a mood of anger and frustration. And then, through George Lewis, Mina Beresford proposed a different solution. Mina offered to destroy the letter on one condition and on one condition only: that Daisy was banned from London for the entire season.[21]

When Daisy learned about this draconian request, she was horrified. It was perfectly barbaric. How could Daisy be expected to endure social ostracism? Daisy went to see Bertie and pleaded for help, and Bertie, by now falling for Daisy, agreed to see what he could do. Once more, Bertie visited Mina Beresford, and pleaded with her to change her mind and destroy the letter. But the obstinate Mina stuck to her own terms of engagement, insisting that Daisy be banned from London for the entire season. It was then that Bertie unleashed his broadside. If Mina was not prepared to hand over the letter, said Bertie, she would forfeit her own position in society. In other words, if Mina refused to destroy Daisy's letter, it would be Mina, and not Daisy, who suffered. As Mina later recalled, the threat was that her "position in Society!! Would become injured!!!"[22] But Mina refused to change her mind on the matter.

Inevitably, after Bertie looked at Daisy "the way all women understand," the pair became lovers. In December 1889, Bertie had been invited to Easton Lodge to attend Daisy's birthday celebrations, at which point it appears that the affair was consummated. Writing to Daisy a decade later, Bertie observed, "how well I remember spending your birthday with you just 10 years ago at your old home," and referred to the "very warm feelings" they had shared then.[23]

We have not yet heard Charlie Beresford's reaction to these sensational events. As might be expected, Charlie had done his best to persuade Mina to surrender Daisy's letter. As one of the offending parties, Charlie had kept a low profile, hoping that the problem would just resolve itself. But now, upon hearing rumors that Bertie had stolen Daisy away from him, Charlie cast aside all attempts at diplomacy. Due to set sail on the HMS *Undaunted*, Charlie demanded to see Bertie immediately, and have the matter out once and for all.

Charlie had already started shouting at Bertie before he stormed into Bertie's study at Marlborough House. In tones of thunder, Charlie declared that intimidating George Lewis into showing him Daisy's letter had been the act of a blackguard. Bertie retorted that Charlie was the blackguard, whereupon Charlie replied that there was only one blackguard in this case, and that was Bertie, for daring to interfere in a private quarrel. Bertie waspishly informed Charlie that it was time he controlled both his women: he must silence Mina and renounce Daisy. If he failed to do so, the Beresfords would suffer the same fate as the Churchills before them: they would become social outcasts and their names would be obliterated from every guest list in the land. Furiously, Charlie vowed that he would never give up Daisy.

"You're not her lover!" shouted Bertie.

"Yes I am," replied Charlie, "and I'm not going to stop!"[24]

At this point, Charlie forgot himself and lunged at Bertie; but before Charlie could hit him, Bertie seized the inkstand off his desk and hurled it at Charlie; it whistled past Charlie's head and crashed into the wall, leaving a huge stain.[25] Shaken, and shocked by his own lese majesty, Charlie retreated. The following day he took command of his ship and sailed for the Mediterranean.

Bertie swiftly proved that his threat was not an idle one.[26] Within a few days of the quarrel with Charlie, Mina paid the price for refusing to comply with Bertie's demands. Bertie ensured that Daisy and Brookie were invited to all the same parties as himself, and if he saw Lord and Lady Beresford's names on a guest list, he crossed them out and substituted those of Lord and Lady Warwick. To her horror, Mina realized that Daisy was being actively promoted. "Wherever [Bertie] went, he desired that she also should be invited, and invited she was, but to the disgust of everyone!"[27]

In a simple word that conveyed a wealth of meaning, the Beresfords had been "dropped." There wasn't a hostess in the land who would risk the disapproval of the Prince of Wales by inviting the Beresfords. While Charlie, probably much to his relief, was posted to the Mediterranean indefinitely, Mina put her London house on the market and went into exile.

One beneficiary of these events was George Lewis, the solicitor who had allowed Bertie to read Daisy's letter. Soon after the affair of the purloined letter, Lewis was spotted as a guest at Sandringham. Two years later, Lewis received a knighthood, presumably for services to the Crown. Daisy also profited from the potential scandal by becoming Bertie's mistress. The intensity of their relationship may be gauged by Bertie's nickname for his new lover: for the rest of his life, Bertie would refer to the Countess of Warwick as "my Darling Daisywife."

Daisy became one of the brightest stars of the Marlborough House set, that fast crowd of the titled and wealthy who wined and dined and danced and hunted and raced with Bertie. The Marlborough House set did not so much follow Bertie as revolve like satellites around his stately body. Even Daisy, the spoiled and beautiful heiress, was overwhelmed.

"Of course, the Marlborough House set had glamour," she recalled in old age. "Indeed, glamour was its particular asset. It created the atmosphere which intrigued the public. I can feel something of the same sense of enchantment, in recalling it, that children experienced when they watched the transformation scene at the pantomime. For them, the girls in their spangles were beautiful fairies, and the scene a glimpse of fairyland."[28]

The highest social honor of all was to be invited to what were known as the "small evenings" at Marlborough House, a dazzling mixture of luxurious partying and high jinks. Young men tobogganed down the stairs on tea trays, and carpets and rugs were pushed aside for dancing. Bertie was a huge fan of slapstick and practical jokes, such as spiking the wine, sliding squares of soap among the cheeses or topping puddings with "whipped cream" made from shaving soap.[29,30] This was a world that Daisy adored, and she played the role of mistress to perfection, accompanying Bertie to balls, receptions, country house parties, and horse racing at Ascot, Goodwood, and Epsom. The correspondent of *The World* magazine, craning her neck to see Daisy at the opera with Bertie, described "a goddess whose fame had penetrated even to the dim recesses of the placid country, her profile was turned away from an inquisitive world, but I made out a rounded figure, diaphanously draped, and a brilliant, haughty, beautiful countenance."[31] The diaphanous fabric became Daisy's signature look, a fittingly classical style to show off her superb figure to its uttermost. Toward the close of the century, women's gowns had become light, fluid, and unstructured, and bustles and puffed sleeves were a thing of the past. This style suited Daisy, who dressed at Worth and Doucet and never spent less than three hundred guineas on a gown, or £30,000 at today's prices. A particular hit was "the gauzy white gown beneath which meandered delicately shaded ribbons" worn to a dinner party with Bertie.[32] On another occasion Daisy appeared in "splendid purple-grape-trimmed robes and a veil of pearls on white," and a "violet velvet gown with two splendid turquoise-and-diamond brooches on her bodice,"[33] which she wore to a hunt ball.

Daisy and Bertie's affair was conducted against the backdrop of London society, and the stately homes of England, particularly Daisy's own Easton Lodge. In London, a certain degree of discretion was required. Daisy and Bertie could meet at Daisy's house in Cavendish Square, or at Marlborough House, or even, and this was a daring choice, at a restaurant. While "respectable" women did not dine in public restaurants, they were permitted to meet a gentleman in a private dining room at Rules, or the Café Royal, or Kettners. These private dining rooms provided a sofa in addition to tables and chairs, and some even featured a double bed.[34] Daisy and Bertie also traveled to Paris, where for the sake of propriety they booked into separate hotels, with Bertie registered as "Baron Renfrew," and visited restaurants and theaters, and race meetings at Longchamps and Auteuil. Life with Bertie was truly, astonishingly glamorous.

The majority of Daisy's liaisons with Bertie were conducted at Easton Lodge, which Daisy had converted from an uncomfortable English country house to a palace fit for a king. Bertie and members of the Marlborough House set had always been regular visitors to Easton Lodge. Now Bertie's visits increased in number and Daisy often chartered a private train down from London, building a small station on her estate where the train could stop and unload the guests and their retinue of servants and mountains of luggage. One particular attraction were the gardens, tributes to the elaborate skills of Victorian horticulturalists, where Daisy would walk with Bertie,[35] delighted to have Bertie all to herself, while Bertie, who liked his women bright, but not intellectual, enjoyed sharing political gossip and discussing foreign affairs. In later life, Daisy looked back fondly on the "Garden of Friendship" where they strolled. "Many of the trees the Prince of Wales planted at Easton serve to remind me how thankfully he threw aside for a few hours the heavy trappings of his state to revel in his love of nature."[36] The gardens, with red deer in the distance beneath the shade of the ancient trees, were a favorite trysting place for Daisy's guests. One of these was young Elinor Glyn, last seen as a little girl on Jersey, hiding under the dressing table at Government House in order to spy on Lillie Langtry. Now a beautiful young woman in her own right, with green eyes and "the most beautiful red hair I have ever seen" Elinor had been taken up by Daisy as something of a fellow spirit.[37] Elinor had recently married one of Daisy's neighbors, an Essex landowner and barrister named Clayton Glyn, and settled in a nearby mansion named Sheerings.[38] As a young beauty, Elinor was receiving the cold shoulder from the ladies of the country set, who "had lost their complexions on the hunting field [and] stared incredulously at her, as though nobody had a right to be as pretty as that."[39] After meeting Elinor at a dismal hunt ball, Daisy immediately befriended her, and invited her and her husband to stay at Easton.

On the very first evening of Elinor's visit to Easton, Daisy's husband, Brookie, invited Elinor to come and inspect "the rosarie," Daisy's newly planted rose garden. Elinor accepted the invitation, but the moment that they were alone Brookie seized her in his arms, embraced her passionately, and told her that she was, by far, the loveliest rose in the garden. Elinor screamed in horror and ran inside to report the incident to her husband. When Elinor told Clayton that their host had made a pass at her, Clayton laughed out loud and exclaimed: "Did he, by Jove! Good old Brookie!"[40]

Elinor later recorded her impressions of Daisy and the astonishing and scandalous world of Easton, a world that would provide inspiration for the sensational romantic novels that were to make Elinor's fortune.

"No one who stayed at Easton ever forgot their hostess and most of the men fell hopelessly in love with her," Elinor recalled.[41] "In my long life, spent in so many different countries, and during which I have seen most of the beautiful and famous women of the world, from film-stars to Queens, I have never seen one who was so completely fascinating as Daisy Brooke. She would sail in from her own wing, carrying her piping bullfinch, her lovely eyes smiling with the merry innocent expression of a Persian kitten that has just tangled a ball of silk. Hers was that supreme personal charm which I later described as 'It,' because it is quite indefinable, and does not depend on beauty or wit, although she possessed both in the highest degree. She was never jealous or spiteful to other women, and if she liked you she was the truest, most understanding friend."[42]

Daisy was almost universally popular. At Easton Lodge, the staff and tenants loved her; she was a generous and responsible landlord, known for her good works and a social conscience, which was becoming more pronounced as the years went by. They were tickled pink when the Prince of Wales himself came up on his special train to call on Daisy; "Her tenants and estate workers—who adored her for her kindness to them—watched goggle-eyed as their own 'Miss Daisy' drove the Prince of Wales up her long avenue."[43] "Their lady had caught a very big fish and they cheered her for it."[44]

Daisy's generosity was legendary. On one occasion a guest borrowed Daisy's favorite hunter, "returned blanched at tea-time to say he had broken its neck. 'How dreadful for *you*,' was all that Daisy said. Only later, alone with [her maid] Olive, did she weep."[45]

But even Daisy had her enemies. Lady Beresford was unlikely to forgive the events that had seen Charlie and herself banned from London society, and was plotting her revenge. And one other person was beginning to tire a little of Daisy's antics: Daisy's own husband, the Earl of Warwick himself, poor dear Brookie.

Chapter Fifteen

SHE STOOPS TO CONQUER

Sing of Mrs Langtry, a lady full of grace,
Four-and-twenty sonnets written to her face;
Now that face is public, and we can also sing,
"Is she not a dainty dame, and worthy of a King!
—HENRY LABOUCHERE

In the spring of 1881, a pregnant Lillie Langtry fled to Paris with her mother. Lillie had spent some time in Jersey with Arthur Jones, but Jersey was no place to conceal a pregnancy and Lillie knew that she would have no privacy once the baby arrived. So Lillie and Mrs. Le Breton headed to Paris, and an apartment Bertie had organized for them on the Champs-Élysées. It was here that Lillie gave birth to her daughter, Jeanne-Marie, on March 18, 1881. On their return to England, Mrs. Le Breton took the baby, with a nurse, down to the Red House in Bournemouth, and Lillie went to recuperate with George Lewis and his wife at Ely Place, Holborn. Lewis had handled the finances and helped keep Lillie's pregnancy secret.

Thanks to positively supernatural crisis management by George Lewis, Ned Langtry appears to have had no idea of what happened. Ned had been kept off the scene by Lewis, who had created a series of meaningless business trips to America and fishing expeditions in Scotland. But gossip about Lillie's baby began to spread, with Bertie as the favorite when it came to potential fathers, accepting the "dubious credit of being the father as flattering to his virility and the reputation he enjoyed of being something of a Casanova."[1] In the May 14 edition of *Town Talk,* Adolphus Rosenberg reprinted the Langtry libel suit and, in his gossip column, stated that: "I am exceedingly gratified to hear that the Hon Miss Tabitha Grimalkin (real name suppressed for obvious reasons) has returned to town quite restored to health. The darling baby girl is also well."[2] It was a vicious little item. Both names are slang terms for cats, while "grimalkin" derives from the French *grimaud,* or "dunce." The following week, Rosenberg teased his readers again with the observation that: "I really don't know why we should blackguard the memory of Harry the Eighth. True, he had a great weakness for the fair sex, but, unless history lies, he *married* all the women he fancied, which is not a bad trait in a prince."[3]

As the gossip spread, Lillie floundered. Ned was a cruel and unreliable husband, her position in society was not what it once was, and she had a child to support. Lillie could, of course, have become the mistress of another rich and influential man. She had all the accomplishments to become a top society mistress, "for there were many victims of her devastating charms, some of them in high circles."[4] In some respects, one wonders why she did not take this easy way out. Some inner prudence, perhaps—the dean's daughter shunning a life of vice—prevented her. It was time to find another way to make a living.

One of Lillie's biographers claims that it was the Prince of Wales himself who suggested a career on the stage. "You are the most beautiful woman in the world," Bertie told Lillie. "I think you ought to show yourself to the world more. You should go on the stage."[5] According to this source, Bertie advised Lillie to exploit her physical attributes and the glittering notoriety she had earned as his mistress. He reminded her of the time, as a practical joke, she had disguised herself as a Piccadilly flower girl and sold violets to mutual friends, unrecognized. The theatrical wig maker, Willy Clarkson, of Wellington Street, had disguised her as a flower seller with makeup and a matted gray wig; she had remembered Clarkson's advice to shuffle, not walk, and adopt a Cockney accent . . . and had succeeded spectacularly.[6]

Rumors had already been circulating about Lillie's theatrical intentions. The previous January, the *Sporting Times*, informally known as the *Pink'Un* because it was printed on pink paper, had written: "Mrs Langtry is well advised to go on the stage. She will thus justify her claim to the title of 'Professional Beauty.' "[7]

> *This beautiful beauty in persona,*
> *By kind permission of her owner,*
> *May now be viewed by every baker*
> *Or butcher who is a ticket-taker,*
> *At a playhouse kept by Mr Baker.*[8]

This was a knowing reference to the fact that Mr. Baker was the licensee of a playhouse known as none other than the Prince of Wales Theatre.[9]

Lillie invited Ellen Terry to visit her, to see if she could help Lillie become a real actress. "Nell Terry came and spent a precious hour of her time, outlining the different aspects of the vocation I was being so persistently advised to follow. The difficulties and disappointments that I might encounter, and what she termed the 'rough side,' seemed to her almost insurmountable for one who had been so petted and spoiled and idle as myself. On the whole, she was discouraging."[10]

In many ways, Ellen Terry was correct. Later in life, Lillie would admit that the day-to-day business of theater bored her. And although Sarah Bernhardt had made a stage career look so easy, it was anything but. At the end of the nineteenth century, actors themselves were regarded as less than respectable, while the word "actress" was synonymous with "prostitute." As an actress, Lillie would become a bohemian, an outsider, and less than respectable. But she could also earn a great deal of money.

Oscar Wilde, who had more faith in Lillie's capacity to fill a theater, introduced Lillie to "Mrs. Labouchere," or Henrietta Hodson, a professional actress with over twenty years of experience on the stage, who had played the West End and endured grueling tours of the provinces with barnstorming Henry Irving. "Mrs. Labouchere" was actually an honorary title, as Henrietta was already married, to a solicitor named Henry Pigeon. Long estranged from Mr. Pigeon, Henrietta now lived with the Liberal MP Henry "Labby" Labouchere. Henrietta, a mannish woman with "a square jaw, short curly grey hair, and a dominating personality"[11] saw possibilities in Lillie. Henrietta was keen to further Labby's political career, and knew that Lillie was on good terms with the prime minister, William Gladstone, who had a soft spot for "fallen women." Lillie herself greatly admired Gladstone, once observing that "one could not be in his company without feeling that goodness emanated from him,"[12] while Gladstone, in turn, had given Lillie a piece of advice: "In your professional career, you will receive attacks, personal and critical, just and unjust. Bear them, never reply, and, above all, never rush into print to explain or defend yourself."[13] It was advice that would prove invaluable in the years to come.

Henrietta wanted to exploit Lillie's links with Gladstone, as her somewhat unrealistic ambition was to see Labby made ambassador to Washington, although he had been thrown out of the diplomatic service years before. But when she met Lillie, Henrietta realized that Lillie herself was a potentially more rewarding project, and took on the role of Lillie's manager.[14] Once again, Lillie had met the right person at the right time. Usually, that person was male; but in Henrietta Hodson Lillie had met someone who was as forthright and assertive as any man. This inevitably sparked rumors of a Sapphic affair. "The scandal-mongers, who let nothing Lillie did escape them, murmured about lesbianism, but that was the wildest kind of conjecture."[15] Lillie, her usual courage and resourcefulness shaken by the combination of financial disaster, the birth of Jeanne-Marie, and separation from her child, allowed Henrietta to dictate her future.

Lillie moved in with the Laboucheres at their Twickenham home, Pope House, a gothic villa on the banks of the Thames originally designed by the poet Alexander Pope. Here, Lillie worked on her lines as Lady Clara in *A Fair Encounter,* "a duel of wits between two women, and, as Henrietta Hodson played the other character, we rehearsed incessantly."[16] Lillie prepared for a fortnight for her first performance, in soaring temperatures, while Labby grumbled that a flock of sheep would have done less damage to his lawn and belittled Lillie's attempts at acting every time she tried a new gesture or a different inflection.

Lillie did not know quite what to make of Labby. As she was a friend of Oscar Wilde and the Rothschilds, she found his rabidly anti-Semitic, antihomosexual views "preposterous" and described him as a "paradox," constantly amusing and given to telling stories against himself.[17] Labby seems to have been one of the rare men who remained indifferent to Lillie's charms; or perhaps suffered a sense of wounded pride on knowing that Lillie had no use for him whatsoever.

Lillie made her stage debut in a charity performance at Twickenham Town Hall. The hall was packed with friends, well-wishers, and the frankly just plain curious, but disaster struck. The moment Lillie set foot on the stage, she "dried," the actors' term for completely forgetting one's lines. Looking across the hastily improvised footlights, "I stood with a forced smile on my lips and a bunch of roses in my arms, without the vestige of an idea of what was going to happen next."[18]

This awkward start didn't seem to do Lillie's reputation any harm. According to the London *World,* Lillie was perfectly at her ease and her voice "full, round and vibrant, filled the large town hall."[19] A

New York gossip columnist noted that if Mrs. Langtry was intending to come to America, "she will be very welcome, especially as it seems that she has talent to back her beauty."[20] The *Whitehall Review* of November 22, 1881, concluded that the critic had gone along, as one of Lillie's million humble admirers, expecting nothing more than a *succès d'estime,* but after seeing her achieve a "remarkable triumph" . . . "we could all imagine the tempest of cheers which would have greeted her had the debut been made at a London theatre, crowded as it would surely have been, by social leaders and that incongruous herd usually lumped together as the representatives of art and literature."[21]

Lillie's next role was that of Kate Hardcastle in *She Stoops to Conquer* at the Haymarket, with a professional cast. Henrietta Hodson had convinced Squire Bancroft and his wife, a successful theatrical couple, to give Lillie the role of Kate Hardcastle in a fund-raiser for the Royal General Theatrical Fund at the Haymarket on December 15. Although casting an amateur in a lead West End role put the Bancrofts in an awkward position, it was a charity performance and Lillie's involvement would guarantee the presence of the Prince of Wales, maximizing ticket sales. Squire Bancroft was sanguine about the prospect. "After all, the extraordinary popularity which has been Mrs Langtry's lot for several London seasons must remove all fear of complete failure, since she has already often and gracefully passed through the ordeal of facing the public."[22]

Lillie would be supported by a professional cast, including such West End luminaries as Kyrle Bellew, Lionel Brough, Arthur Pinero, Charles Brookfield, and Sophie Larkin. All the same, the performance came as something of an ordeal. On the afternoon of the show, as crowds gathered outside the theater long before the pit and the gallery doors opened, Lillie was telling the Bancrofts that "my best friends will be anxious to get as near as possible, and crowd into the front rows of the stalls, all more or less amused, and disinclined to take me seriously."[23] Standing in the wings, Lillie was terrified:

the house was packed to capacity, overflowing with rank, fashion, and celebrity, including Bertie and Alix in the royal box, and Louisa, Duchess of Manchester, with a large party.

Lillie's immediate impulse was to run away. Was it too late to back out, or hand over to her understudy?[24] Then, in the distance, Lillie heard her cue, and somehow managed to get out onto the stage, to be greeted by a tremendous burst of applause, "a willing, eager homage to the far-famed beauty."[25] Abraham Hayward, an elderly lawyer who combined journalism with the bar hailed Lillie's West End debut in *The Times,* and suggested that Lillie's next role should be Lady Teazle, from *School for Scandal.* "It strikes us she possesses all the leading qualifications, and it is a part which only a lady born and bred can play well."[26]

The critic at *Punch* magazine was not so easily impressed. In a withering review, he observed that:

> *Mrs Langtry intended us to suppose by this performance to put herself up for hire to the highest managerial figure in the theatrical market, and therefore we are justified in strongly and honestly reminding her that without positive genius there is no royal road to eminence, even in the histrionic art; and that a novice must stoop to pick up the rudiments and master them before she can conquer its difficulties. Mrs Langtry is of too solid a physique for any skittish movement; her laugh not yet being under control appears forced and painful; and her action is as constrained and mechanical as that of an Eton sixth form boy on speech-day.*[27]

The Pink 'Un reported the event like a race meeting, listed all the members of the nobility present, and reported that there were "howls from the young dukes and earls sitting in the gallery—nothing under a Hon—cries of 'Up with the rag!' and 'Speak hup Lily!' were heard during the performance. Nobody bothers to look at the stage, they have one and all come to see Mrs Langtry. . . ."[28]

Adolphus Rosenberg, the editor of *Town Talk,* took the opportunity to lash out at Lillie in retaliation for his libel conviction the previous year. "I don't like to say nasty things of this lady, but I don't think that she is quite as good looking as she is represented to be. Unless your attention were specially directed to her, she would, popularly speaking, 'pass in a crowd.' As a matter of fact, Mrs Langtry's beauty has been much exaggerated. 'The Life of an Actress, by Her Husband', is the title of a forthcoming book. I think the work will be written in a very acrimonious and pungent style."[29]

Reactions in the interval range from "wretched," "easy," "angular," "a born actress, my boy," to "with about five years hard work may play singing chambermaid." At the end, "there were a number of curtain calls and great applause for Mrs Langtry."[30]

Era, a theatrical journal, took a more jaundiced view, concluding that "Mrs Langtry is a respectable amateur"[31] but her reputation for beauty was not "discoverable behind the footlights."[32] As to her acting abilities, compared with the professional talent of the rest of the cast, she was like "a candle to the sun."[33] Lillie's own verdict, once she was safely back in her dressing room and surrounded by admirers and bouquets of flowers, was that she would have to stop looking at the audience. "I'll have to practice that. I must admit all those familiar smiling faces out in front considerably disconcerted me."[34]

Sustained by mostly favorable reviews, Lillie went on to appear in another Bancroft production, *Ours,* retaining Henrietta as her acting coach. What Lillie lacked in talent she made up for in application, rehearsing tirelessly when her professional colleagues admitted defeat. Hiring Lillie proved no real ordeal for the Bancrofts. Bertie was a regular visitor backstage, and in 1897 recommended Squire Bancroft for a knighthood.

Ours proved to be another triumph, although, as *The Times* admitted, her role was not much of a stretch. All that Lillie was required to do was "fall in love with an officer, faint when he goes to

Russia and play at soldiers in his hut in the Crimea in a number of becoming costumes." This Lillie did, with great success.[35]

Lillie did not think much of *Ours*. One night, entreating her lover not to leave for the Crimea, she fainted away and toppled backward into the ample lap of a lady seated nearby. "I thought the play silly, and old-fashioned; so did the Duchess of Edinburgh, who one night sat in the royal box shaking with suppressed laughter at the absurdity of the Russian scene."[36]

But Lillie did not enjoy theater life. She had never really been star-struck, never felt "the glamour of the stage." Unlike a born actress, who "cannot but feel added zest in the stimulus of emerging from private life, and even obscurity, to become famous on the boards and a figure in the artistic world,"[37] Lillie hated "the dreary rehearsals, hour after hour, day after day, in a cold and darkened theatre. To make matters worse, Henrietta sat in a corner of the stage almost nightly in a highly critical frame of mind, which added to my natural self-consciousness . . ."[38]

Lillie soon grew tired of appearing in the same play every night, "speaking the same words, wearing the same gowns at the same time every evening; it seems a very dull and monotonous existence."[39] She was already accustomed to more than her fair share of publicity. "There's no novelty in facing the crowded audience. I know most of the occupants of the stalls and boxes, and all in the cheaper parts know me."[40] The biggest drawback, as far as Lillie was concerned, was the fact that being on stage every night wrecked her social life. How was one supposed to cope with an existence when one dined at five, before the show, and was not properly free again until eleven?

In May 1882, Lillie embarked on her first tour of the provinces. In something that resembled a royal progress across the country, she opened in *She Stoops to Conquer* at the Prince of Wales Theatre, Birmingham, on May 29, 1882. Lillie also appeared in a play by the dramatist and editor of *Punch,* Tom Taylor, entitled *The Unequal*

Match. There were no cheap seats. Next came the Royal Alexandra Theatre, Liverpool, the Bradford Theatre Royal, and the Princes' Theatre, Manchester, where, after Saturday night's performance, exuberant members of the audience unfastened the horses from Lillie's carriage and dragged her to her hotel themselves.[41] "With that damned steep hill down from the theatre, I got here more rapidly than safely, and at the moment the anxiety outweighed the honour. Still, I'm sure I should feel very proud."[42]

This was certainly not the usual provincial tour as experienced by professional acting companies. At every railway station, there was a top-hatted station master to greet Lillie with a red carpet and a brass band. At the theater, another red carpet ran from her dressing room to the stage, and she did not even appear in the wings until the way had been cleared by her dresser, the stage manager, and the callboy.[43] Lillie herself had called for the red carpets: firsthand experience of royalty had shown Lillie how to make an impression. To be treated like a queen, Lillie knew, one had to behave like a queen.

At Edinburgh, students packed the King's Theatre and protested at any scene of *The Unequal Match* in which Lillie was not present. In an appalling breach of theatrical etiquette, Lillie would walk on stage and greet the audience even if her character was not due to appear in the scene. Henrietta Hodson was horrified by this lack of professionalism, but of course Lillie was delighted and the audience lapped it up. When Henrietta remonstrated with Lillie afterward in the dressing room, Lillie's unimprovable reply was that "it isn't a very good play, so it doesn't much matter!"[44] Lillie was escorted to the station in a torchlight procession and not allowed to depart for Glasgow until she had delivered a speech from the train window. At Glasgow, more students harnessed themselves to her carriage, but, having endured this experience once already in her short and eventful life, Lillie quietly slipped away through the front entrance.[45]

The tour crossed the Irish Sea to Dublin, and then on to Belfast,

Ned's birthplace. Playgoers in the gallery took the opportunity to throw pheasants and hares onto the stage at moments throughout the play, either as a comment on Lillie's acting or as a gesture of sympathy with her husband—it was hard to tell. Lillie splendidly rose above it, adhering to her personal philosophy of "let us not make a fuss" and telling her fellow actors that "at least we shall eat this week!"[46] Belfast University students presented Lillie with a huge cage of doves, tied with blue ribbons.

The tour returned to London in September, where, on September 16, 1882, Lillie appeared in *The Unequal Match* at the Imperial, the same theater that was part of the aquarium where she had had that life-changing encounter with Lord Ranelagh. Lillie followed up this triumph with her own production of *As You Like It* with herself in the role of Rosalind. Inevitably, the prospect of the Prince of Wales's mistress live on stage with her legs on view was box office gold, and Bertie himself was there on opening night. What did it matter that *The Times* declared that Lillie's Rosalind was "entirely lacking in feeling" or that she never "touched the common chord of humanity"?[47] Lillie had arrived. And there were rumors that she was planning another tour: in America!

It had been Henrietta Hodson's idea. An experienced theater professional, Henrietta knew that Lillie's stage career was founded on novelty, and that once the British public had tired of her, that career would be over. Henrietta wired the American impresario Henry Abbey in New York. The charismatic Abbey, dark-eyed and dashing, with his black moustache and charming manners, "though a little flabby of figure, perhaps, to an English eye,"[48] had made Sarah Bernhardt a star in America two years earlier. Knowing that sex sells, Henry had enabled Sarah to make her stateside debut, and both had made an astonishing amount of money out of the venture. As Bernhardt was denounced from the pulpits as a ruthless European courtesan out to corrupt public morals, the box office receipts piled up. The streets outside Booth's Theatre, where she played, were lit up with electric light for her opening night; she was serenaded by ecstatic crowds in the Albermarle Hotel on Madison Square.[49]

Now Henry turned his attention to Lillie, who might not be much of an actress but had one unique selling point: her well-publicized affair with the Prince of Wales. Before Lillie could change her mind, Lillie and Henrietta negotiated a fee with Henry even larger than Sarah's, and Lillie made plans to emigrate. In a debilitated condition, exhausted by a year's performing without a break, Lillie could at least look forward to a relaxing sea voyage. But she confessed she was not "wildly enthusiastic over the prospect."

"The States, at that time, seemed to me to be about as far off as Mars, and nearly as inaccessible . . . my many friends and relations were within easy reach, and to leave them for unknown lands gave me a feeling of utter depression."[50] The Red House in Bournemouth was rented out, and Lillie's mother took little Jeanne-Marie back to Jersey. Henrietta Hodson, intending to accompany Lillie to America, mothballed the villa in Twickenham, covered the furniture with dust-cloths, and dismissed the cook and most of the servants. When Labby protested, Henrietta responded by taking out her anger on Labby's wardrobe and cutting all the buttons off his shirts.[51]

Labby marked the occasion by publishing the following verse in *Truth* magazine:

Sing of Mrs Langtry, a lady full of grace,
Four-and-twenty sonnets written to her face;
Now that face is public, and we can also sing,
"Is she not a dainty dame, and worthy of a King!"[52]

After being seen off by friends at Euston, Lillie sat in the train for Liverpool, where she was due to board the ocean liner the *Arizona*, crying her eyes out and "feeling perfectly miserable."[53] It would be over two years before she saw Bertie again.

Chapter Sixteen

THE UNFORGIVABLE SIN

There are only two unforgiveable sins:
buggery, and cheating at cards.
—CAPTAIN DONALD SHAW, *LONDON IN THE SIXTIES*

G ambling was Bertie's third vice, after women and dining. Indeed, at a time and place where an appetite for
wine, women, and song was regarded as appropriate for a future head
of state, it is scarcely surprising that Bertie indulged in that other
great pastime, gambling. In Bertie's case, horse racing was indeed
the sport of kings, and so were many other games of chance. Having
grown rather portly, Bertie had forsworn dancing after dinner in
favor of more sedentary pursuits, so gaming represented an alternative form of entertainment. Bertie had recently introduced baccarat from the Continent, and although the High Court had declared
it illegal, the game was frequently played at fashionable house parties. Indeed, Bertie enjoyed playing baccarat so much that he traveled with his own set of baccarat counters engraved with the Prince
of Wales's feathers and ranging in denomination from five shillings to
ten pounds. (Ten pounds in 1889 was the equivalent of £250 a
century later, so one can gain some idea of the massive gains and
losses for the winners and losers.[1]) It was baccarat that Bertie chose
to play on the fateful weekend that he went to stay at Tranby Croft.

When Bertie made arrangements to attend Doncaster races in

September 1890, he initially planned to stay with Christopher Sykes at Brantingham Thorpe in the East Riding of Yorkshire. But Sykes, after years of playing the affable stooge who allowed Bertie to pour brandy over him, was bankrupt from entertaining the prince, and Brantingham Thorpe was now in the hands of his creditors.[2]

Bertie then decided to stay at Tranby Croft, home of Arthur Wilson, a wealthy ship manufacturer. Having invited the Prince of Wales, the Wilsons were of course obliged to ask the rest of his entourage, including Daisy and Daisy's husband, Brookie, who always accompanied his wife for appearances' sake. Also on the guest list were the Earl and Countess of Coventry, the banker Reuben Sassoon, General Owen Williams, who had been Bertie's equerry during the Indian tour, Christopher Sykes, Sub-Lieutenant Berkeley Levett, and Lord Edward Somerset and his cousin Arthur. The Wilsons' son Stanley would also be present and their daughter Ethel, with her husband, Edward Lycett Green, master of the York and Ainstey Foxhounds. Daisy was looking forward to the visit, but on September 6 Daisy's beloved stepfather, Lord Rosslyn, died, and she had to cancel the trip.

One guest who did attend, however, was Sir William Alexander Gordon Gordon-Cumming, Lieutenant Colonel of the Scots Guards. Dashing Gordon-Cumming had inherited Gordonstoun castle and a 38,000-acre estate in Scotland, although his family had been on the decline ever since the death of his ancestor, the Red Comyn, at the hands of Robert the Bruce.[3] A friend of Bertie's for over twenty years, Gordon-Cumming was described by Daisy as "the smartest of men about town,"[4] and also one of the most handsome, tall, and strong with his face deeply tanned from army service in Africa and India. Gordon-Cumming was also an incorrigible womanizer, whose stated intention was to "perforate members of the sex."[5] He favored uncomplicated relationships with married women, and his lovers included Lillie Langtry, Sarah Bernhardt, and Lady Randolph Churchill. On one occasion, shortly after Leonie Churchill had married Sir John Leslie, Gordon-Cumming pounced on her in a corridor and when she broke away exclaimed: "You silly little fool, all the married women try me!"[6] Gordon-Cumming fitted into the Prince of Wales's set perfectly.

The guests arrived at Tranby Croft on September 8, and after dinner Bertie suggested a game of baccarat in the library. This caused Bertie's hosts much consternation as the Wilsons did not possess a baccarat table because Arthur Wilson did not approve of the game and did not want to encourage his young sons to play for high stakes.[7] But who could refuse the Prince of Wales? The Wilsons swiftly improvised a baccarat table by putting three small whist tables together and covering them with a strip of tapestry.

Bertie took on the role of bank, seated at the center table, flanked by other players. Other guests who were not playing stood around to watch; drinks were poured, and cigars lit. Reuben Sassoon took charge of the counters and kept a note of which counters the players had received. For the benefit of beginners, Bertie and Gordon-Cumming explained the rules.[8]

Baccarat is a very simple game. Four packs of cards, 208 cards altogether, are shuffled and placed in front of the banker. The banker deals two cards to the player on his right, two to the player on his left, and takes two himself. The object of the players is to make up as nearly as possible the number nine, tens and court cards not counting—perhaps a three and a five, or a four and a five. For this purpose they may ask each other for another card, but in doing so they must not spoil the hand by exceeding the number nine, so it is customary to ask for another card *only* if the first two add up to five or less. Similarly, the banker may also take another card, his decision depending partly on the amount of money that has been staked on one side and on the other. The rest of the players hold no cards but simply bet on those held by the players on either side of the banker.[9]

In this instance, the bank's liability was limited to £100 (around

£9,000 today). An experienced player, Gordon-Cumming had a white sheet of paper in front of him, upon which he marked, with pencil dots, every time the bank won and every time the players won, "trying to match science against chance."[10] He discussed, with his neighbor, young Stanley Wilson, how difficult it was to distinguish the counters against the tapestry table covering. Gordon-Cumming suggested that everyone put their stakes on the white paper, so that they might more clearly be seen. The other players were reluctant to do this, and in the end it was only Gordon-Cumming who placed his stakes on the white paper, where they could clearly be seen.

Most of the guests were playing for small stakes, but Gordon-Cumming was playing a rather more daring game, usually wagering £5 (nearly £500 today) for a coup, and up to £25 (£2,250); his system, known as *coup de trois*, or *masse en avant*, was to leave his stake on, as if he'd won the coup, and add another £5 and his winnings to it for the next coup. When he lost, he handed his stake up to the croupier on the sheet of white paper because the counters could not be raked in, as would be the normal procedure, because the tables were uneven.[11]

At the very beginning of the game, Stanley Wilson noticed a single bright red £5 counter on Gordon-Cumming's sheet of white paper. Then his attention was distracted, and when he looked back again, there were three bright red counters. The cards were favorable, and Gordon-Cumming was paid £15. Stanley Wilson became suspicious. A little later, Stanley was convinced he saw Gordon-Cumming drop three red counters from his hands onto the white paper and add to his stake once the cards had been declared favorable: in a harsh whisper, Stanley turned to the man on the other side of him, his friend Sub-Lieutenant Berkeley Levett, and hissed: "This is too hot! The man next to me is cheating!"[12]

"Impossible," came the reply.

"Well, look for yourself!" Stanley retorted, and Levett, after watching for some minutes, agreed. "This is too hot!"[13]

The game continued for around an hour and a half, and afterward Bertie congratulated Gordon-Cumming on his good luck.

"Why, sir," replied Gordon-Cumming, "I could not help winning with such a tableaux as this," and showed Bertie the record he had kept on the piece of paper.

After the party had broken up for the night, Stanley followed Levett back to his room. Levett threw himself across the bed and exclaimed: "My God! To think of it! Lieutenant-Colonel Sir William Gordon-Cumming caught cheating at cards!"[14]

"What are we going to do?" asked Stanley.

"For God's sake, don't ask me! He's in my regiment and was my own captain for a year and a half! What can I do?"[15]

Stanley replied that he would have a word with his brother-in-law, Edward Lycett Green, in the morning, then went to his mother's dressing room to tell her what had happened. But Mrs. Wilson begged her son to remain silent about the matter. The last thing Mrs. Wilson wanted was a scandal at Tranby Croft.

"I think I can stop him," Stanley replied, and explained that, for tomorrow evening's entertainment, he had asked the butler to provide a long table from the pantry and cover it with green baize.[16]

The following morning, Stanley spoke with his brother-in-law and told him he had seen Gordon-Cumming cheating. Lycett Green was as astonished by this news as Levett had been, unable to believe that a man who held such an elevated position in society would risk his reputation in this way. "It is not possible!" declared Lycett Green. Stanley replied that it was, and that Berkeley Levett had also witnessed Gordon-Cumming cheating.[17]

Later that day, the house party went off to Doncaster races by special train, and was royally entertained at the Wilsons' box in the members' grandstand at Town Moor racecourse. Bertie's two-year-old filly, Pierrette, won the Clumber Stakes, and the party returned happily to Tranby Croft. No mention had been made of Gordon-Cumming's suspect behavior the night before.

After dinner, Bertie once again suggested they play baccarat. A long narrow table covered with green baize had been set up in the billiard room, between the billiard table and the fireplace. Bertie drew a chalk line right around it, about six inches from the edge, behind which the players were supposed to keep their counters when not in play. On the way in, Stanley whispered to Mrs. Wilson that now all would be well, because the players had a proper baccarat table with a chalk line on it.

Once again, Bertie took the bank, and General Williams acted as croupier. When Gordon-Cumming arrived there were only two seats left, and wherever he sat he would be surrounded by members of the Wilson family. Gordon-Cumming sat next to Ethel Lycett Green, and directly opposite him was Berkeley Levett, who had witnessed Gordon-Cumming cheating the night before. The table was still not a proper baccarat table: at only three feet wide, it was too narrow, and it was difficult to keep the counters behind the chalk line and off the edge of the table. Edward Lycett Green had told Stanley that he intended to keep an eye on Gordon-Cumming, and if he saw him cheating he would denounce him then and there, contributing to the atmosphere of suspense.

Half an hour into the game, Lycett Green thought he saw Gordon-Cumming push a blue counter over the line; he became suspicious, but none of the other watchers seemed to notice anything wrong. Then Gordon-Cumming staked a red £5 counter four inches beyond the line. Stanley Wilson thought he also pushed a £10 brown counter just over the line or, as Lycett Green thought, just on the line.

The bank lost, and had to pay out. Gordon-Cumming said to the prince, "There's another tenner, sir, to come here."[18] At which, Bertie told General Williams to give him another tenner, and then told Gordon-Cumming, "I wish you would put your counters so that they can be seen better." Ethel Lycett Green thought Gordon-Cumming pushed the counter forward as he said he had not been paid; then she thought he pushed a counter forward under a piece of paper.[19]

Convinced that he had seen an act of cheating, Lycett Green left the table and went into the smoking room next door. After wondering what to do, he wrote a note to his mother-in-law, Mrs. Wilson, telling her that Gordon-Cumming had been cheating and telling her to stop the game. He gave the note to Mrs. Wilson, who read it, but did not immediately stop the game. Indeed, she, too, thought she had just witnessed an act of cheating, as Gordon-Cumming appeared to push a counter over the line with his pencil. Lycett Green went back to the table and the game continued for the rest of the evening. With Stanley Wilson holding the cards, Lycett Green won five successive coups, winning money for himself and more for Gordon-Cumming, who was betting heavily.

The next morning, news came that Mrs. Wilson's brother had died suddenly. Despite this tragic news, she begged her guests to continue as before, to go and enjoy the racing and then return to Tranby Croft in the evening.

The party did as Mrs. Wilson wished and traveled, as before, by special train to Doncaster races, where they were to watch the most significant race of the meeting, the St. Leger. During the journey, Lycett Green found himself sharing a carriage with fellow guest Lord Edward Somerset and confided his suspicions about Gordon-Cumming. Lord Edward said that he would consult his cousin, Captain Arthur Somerset. Captain Somerset was "dumbfounded" by the allegations but more significantly realized the implications of this news given that the Prince of Wales was not only staying in Tranby Croft but actually taking part in the game. Captain Somerset, in turn, decided to consult another eminent guest, the Earl of Coventry. Described as "a man of the world," Lord Coventry was well known in sporting circles as a top racehorse owner and breeder of foxhounds. If Lord Coventry did not know what to do, then nobody did.[20]

That evening, Edward Lycett Green, Stanley Wilson, Lord

Edward Somerset, and Captain Arthur Somerset visited Lord Coventry's dressing room. Lieutenant Berkeley Levett refused to accompany them on the grounds that Gordon-Cumming had been his captain in the Scots Guards. Edward Lycett Green told Lord Coventry that Gordon-Cumming had been seen cheating at cards. The obvious response to this information would have been to go straight to Arthur Wilson and tell him about the allegations, and the sensitivity of the matter in view of the fact that the Prince of Wales was not only staying at Tranby Croft but had been playing baccarat while Gordon-Cumming was apparently cheating. Instead, Lord Coventry replied that the matter was so serious that he would have to speak to General Williams, because the latter was friendly with both Bertie and Gordon-Cumming, and was really "a man of the world."[21] Yes, he would know what to do!

Lord Coventry fetched General Williams from his room and told him about the allegations against Gordon-Cumming. Without pausing to establish whether or not the allegations were true, General Williams declared that he was "overwhelmed with a sense of calamity."[22] One can understand why. This development threatened to be another Aylesford scandal; the public must never learn that Bertie had been playing baccarat, an illegal game, with cheats and swindlers. Bertie's reputation had to be protected at all costs.[23]

The next difficulty would be persuading Gordon-Cumming to admit to the accusations. The real danger was that he would challenge the allegation that he had been cheating, fall out with the Wilson family, and make the whole episode public knowledge. The only solution was to shame Gordon-Cumming into admitting that he had cheated, and give him the opportunity to leave quietly so that a veil could be drawn over the affair. Edward Lycett Green was adamant that Gordon-Cumming must be confronted. If not, then Lycett Green would publicly denounce him at Doncaster races the following day. "I will not be a party to letting Gordon-Cumming prey on society in future,"[24] Lycett Green declared, with a fervor that makes one wonder whether he was referring to other aspects of Gordon-Cumming's character. Bearing in mind the fact that Lycett Green would not be silenced, General Williams came up with a solution. Gordon-Cumming would be confronted and compelled to sign a statement swearing that he would never play cards again.

Knowing that if they did not tell Bertie what had happened, then Gordon-Cumming would, General Williams and Captain Arthur Somerset went to see the prince. This was a grave tactical mistake: the men had no conclusive evidence against Gordon-Cumming, the five witnesses had all seen different aspects of his apparent "cheating," and they had not questioned Gordon-Cumming himself as to the allegations against him. In blind loyalty to the Prince of Wales, General Williams and Captain Somerset were actually placing him in a very difficult position. It would have been far better if Bertie had questioned the allegations and interviewed Gordon-Cumming himself, as well as the men who had accused him of cheating. But Bertie accepted Edward Lycett Green's version of events and agreed that a document should be drawn up for Gordon-Cumming to sign. Bertie's next task would be to persuade Gordon-Cumming, who still knew nothing of these allegations, to sign it.

They tracked Gordon-Cumming down in the smoking room, where Lord Coventry confronted him. "Some of the people staying here object to the way you play baccarat," he said, explaining that Lycett Green and four other people had accused him of cheating, and that the Prince of Wales had been informed.[25]

Gordon-Cumming seemed as astonished as everyone else at hearing this accusation. He denied the charge as an abominable falsehood, and demanded to know who had accused him. When he was told that the accusers were Lycett Green, Stanley Wilson, Sub-Lieutenant Berkeley Levett, Ethel Lycett Green, and Mrs. Wilson, he became indignant. How could they take the words of these people against his?

At this point the gong was struck for dinner, and proceedings had to be suspended. However serious the allegations against Gordon-Cumming, dinner was more important. The iron discipline imposed upon the Marlborough House set dictated that appearances must be kept up at all times. At the table, Gordon-Cumming attempted to speak to Captain Somerset, but the latter simply turned his head away.

After dinner, there was conversation and music until eleven o'clock, but no game of baccarat. Instead, Bertie went into a small drawing room with Gordon-Cumming's accusers. After speaking to them, he sent for Gordon-Cumming. When Gordon-Cumming arrived, he appealed to Bertie, denying that anything of the sort had taken place, and reminding the prince of his years of loyal service.

"It is very shocking," Bertie replied, "but what can you do against so many? There is only your word against theirs."[26]

Gordon-Cumming retorted that he was going to confront his accusers the following day at Doncaster races. This was immediately dismissed as disastrous: it would bring the scandal out in the open. Gordon-Cumming came up with another suggestion. Perhaps he should appeal to his commanding officer, or to the Duke of Cambridge, commander-in-chief of the British army?[27]

When this proposal was rejected, Gordon-Cumming once again appealed on the basis of his former reputation. What a tragedy this would be, he said, for someone who, for twenty-five years, had attempted to lead the life of an officer and a gentleman.

Gordon-Cumming was dismissed while the document was drawn up. Half an hour later, they sent for him again. Bertie had left the room. Lord Coventry told Gordon-Cumming that the only way to avoid a scandal was for him to sign the document saying he would never play cards again. Gordon-Cumming immediately refused, on the grounds that to do so would be incriminating. But he was told that if he refused to sign, Edward Lycett Green and his friends would expose Gordon-Cumming as a cheat at Doncaster races in the morning. General Williams, speaking as a friend, told Gordon-Cumming that the best thing to do would be to sign the document. Gordon-Cumming was not a stupid man; he could see the benefit of hushing up the allegations. If they went public, the accusation would always haunt him. Innocent or guilty, he would be ruined. But as long as everyone kept quiet, the affair might be forgotten. Once again, the *omertà* of the Marlborough House set reigned supreme.

But Gordon-Cumming made one last attempt to avoid signing, arguing that to do so would immediately cause suspicion. Gordon-Cumming was noted for his card playing; if he signed this document, he would not even be able to play so much as a rubber of whist in the barracks. It was like being sent into the library with a revolver: Gordon-Cumming had no choice but to do the decent thing. He would also be obliged to leave Tranby Croft quietly, early in the morning, an action that would in itself excite comment.

Defeated, Gordon-Cumming signed, and the document was taken to the Prince of Wales for signature.

> *In consideration of the promise made by the gentlemen whose names are subscribed to preserve silence with reference to an accusation which has been made in regard to my conduct at baccarat on the nights of Monday and Tuesday the 8th and 9th of September 1890 at Tranby Croft, I will on my part solemnly undertake never to play cards again as long as I live.*
>
> *Signed, W Gordon-Cumming.*
> *Albert Edward P Coventry.*
> *Owen Williams.*
> *Arthur Wilson.*
> *A C E Somerset.*
> *Edward Somerset.*
> *E Lycett Green.*
> *A Stanley Wilson.*
> *Berkeley Levett.*
> *R D Sassoon*[28]

After the prince and the nine other men had signed the document, Arthur Wilson, the host of Tranby Croft, vowed all present to secrecy.

"This will be no secret, sir," replied Captain Somerset.

"Not when gentlemen have given their word not to divulge it?" asked Bertie.

"It's impossible, sir. Nothing in the world known to ten people was ever kept secret."[29]

The following morning Gordon-Cumming left early, walking to the railway station after leaving a note for Mrs. Wilson saying that he had urgent business in London. He also wrote to General Williams, strongly denying the charges and asking for any money he had won at baccarat to be donated to charity. Bertie also left Tranby Croft, relocating to the 10th Hussars' Mess in York for the last day of the races. This was "a terrible blow to the Wilsons' social aspirations. They realised His Royal Highness would never enter their house again."[30] But while Mrs. Wilson's social climbing had suffered a setback, this was as nothing compared with the collateral damage caused by the disgrace. Arthur Wilson had been correct when he had cast doubt upon the Tranby Croft scandal ever remaining a secret.

Chapter Seventeen

THE TRANBY CROFT TRIAL

Bertie never forgives.
—PRINCESS ALEXANDRA

D espite all attempts to keep the Tranby Croft scandal secret, news of the affair spread like wildfire through the Marlborough House set. Lady Mina Beresford, eager to take revenge on Daisy for her affair with Charlie Beresford, claimed that Daisy Brooke was the source of the leak, and nicknamed Daisy "Babbling Brooke."[1] It was said that Bertie had bumped into Daisy and Brookie at York railway station, where the couple were on their way to Scotland for the Earl of Rosslyn's funeral, and shared the extraordinary tale of Gordon-Cumming with them.[2] Over twenty years later, Daisy took the opportunity to defend herself from these allegations in a letter to *The Times*:

"The subsequent funeral and deep mourning prevented me for a long time joining any social gatherings so that I was among the last to hear of what, at the time, set Society agog."[3]

Mrs. Wilson and her daughter Ethel were another potential source of the leak, although Mrs. Wilson had been at pains to cover up the allegations when first told about Gordon-Cumming's behavior by her son. It was perhaps inevitable that suspicion would rest upon the Wilsons, as Mrs. Wilson and Ethel had not signed the letter.

There were plenty of other people whom Gordon-Cumming had offended who were ready to let the cat out of the bag. Gordon-Cumming had made many enemies over the years, and the list of people who wanted to get their own back was extensive. Examples of Gordon-Cumming's infamous rudeness included this anecdote: "A gentleman whom [Gordon-Cumming] had just met for the first time came up to him and said how delighted he was to have made his acquaintance but might he just mention that his name was Gilette with G soft as in gentleman? Gordon-Cumming replied 'I thought it was hard, as in beggar.' It is not even certain that he said *beggar.*"[4] On another occasion, Gordon-Cumming had just come off guard duty at Buckingham Palace when he encountered a physician who had just attained his life's ambition and been summoned to the royal bedside. "Did you see my brougham at the palace gates?" the doctor proudly asked Gordon-Cumming. "No, really?" Gordon-Cumming replied. "Is one of the servants ill?"[5] Gordon-Cumming's rudeness had extended to Leonie Jerome, Jennie Churchill's little sister, even before her marriage. Spotting Leonie in Hyde Park, Gordon-Cumming had marched up to her and asked, "with a sneer, if Leonie was 'Over here husband-hunting?'"[6]

Queen Victoria responded wearily to yet another scandal with her son at its center. "It is a sad thing Bertie is dragged into it. . . ."[7] The queen was also anxious to make it clear that Bertie was not attempting in any way to shield "this horrid Mr Cumming. On the contrary he is most anxious that he should be punished. The incredible and shameful thing is that others dragged him into it and urged him to sign this paper which of course he never should have done. He is in a dreadful state about it for he has been dreadfully attacked about it."[8]

Queen Victoria believed that the most appropriate course of action was for Gordon-Cumming to undergo a court-martial. Gordon-Cumming himself had offered to retire on half-pay for the duration of the trial, but the army regarded this as unacceptable, and Gordon-

Cumming was immediately suspended pending an investigation. At this point, Gordon-Cumming offered to break off his engagement to the American heiress Florence Garner, but Florence refused, determined to stand by him.

By now, the newspapers were feasting eagerly on the impending scandal. Despite legal threats, the *Echo* claimed that:

> *The Baccarat Scandal is to be hushed up . . . a very comfortable arrangement for all parties immediately concerned, especially for the exulted personage who condescended to act as banker at the Tranby Croft gambling table but it is certainly discreditable . . . the nation has a right to expect that a prince who pitches the key-note to society should recollect that his evil example is tenfold more mischievous than that of the common run of men . . . the spectacle of a prince presiding at a gambling table is far more demoralising than the circulars of betting touts. . . . The sense of justice is shocked when a couple of street urchins are sent to prison for playing pitch-and-toss whose offence in its essence is no wise distinguishable from that or peers and princes. . . .*[9]

As soon as Gordon-Cumming discovered that the secret pact had been broken, he went straight to his solicitors, Messrs Wontner's in St. Paul's Chambers, and instructed them to demand a retraction from everyone who had signed the letter, along with an apology and £5,000 each, otherwise he would bring an action for slander against them all, including the Prince of Wales.

The Wilson family, finding themselves hit with a writ for slander, went straight to George Lewis. Unfortunately, the dispute had gone too far before they called him in. The only course of action was to fight the case. George Lewis's primary objective was to keep Bertie out of court. Both Lewis and Bertie himself knew that Bertie's presence in court would provoke a hostile reaction from the public and the press. The stress of the impending trial began to tell upon Bertie; Captain Somerset, who ran into Bertie leaving the

Marlborough Club, was shocked to see that half of the prince's beard had turned gray.[10]

On May 13 it was announced that the case would be heard on June 1 before the Lord Chief Justice, Lord Coleridge, at the Royal Courts of Justice. The Lord Chief Justice's court was converted into a new courtroom with a raised bench, witness box, and chairs instead of the usual seats. According to *The Times,* admission was by ticket only, with thirty seats reserved for the press, and the remaining seats to go to members of the bar, witnesses, and special guests. Most significant of all, the Prince of Wales would be present.

The clerks were besieged by requests for tickets, as if for an important theater premiere. The Prince of Wales was to be the star attraction; as the showman P. T. Barnum had once told Bertie: "[I]t is you, sir, who will be the greatest show on earth."[11]

On June 1, fashionably dressed people began to queue outside the iron gates of the Royal Courts of Justice in the Strand from nine-thirty in the morning, even though the proceedings were not due to begin until eleven. The clerks stalwartly refused all applications from anyone without a ticket, and by half past ten the courtroom was packed. According to the correspondent of the *Telegraph*: "A bright fine sun streamed through the skylight upon a gallery filled with ladies in the gayest of summer dresses and dainty bonnets, all looking as exactly interested as though they were going to witness a wedding instead of a trial. Many of them had provided themselves with opera glasses, others carried lorgnettes: they amused themselves by spying out the counsel as they arrived."[12] According to the reporter from the *Pall Mall Gazette,* who had squeezed in like a sardine in a can, "the court presented an appearance which, save for the dignity of its own fittings and its rows of learned-looking law books, might have been taken for a theatre at a fashionable matinée."[13] Sir Edward Clarke, attorney general and defense counsel for Gordon-Cumming, recalled later that "the court had a strange appearance," because the judge, Lord Coleridge, had "appropriated half of the public gallery, and had given tickets to his friends."[14] Lady Coleridge, the judge's attractive young wife, arrived wearing a blue fox fur around her shoulders and took her place on the bench alongside her husband, armed with a fan to tap the judge on the arm when he fell asleep. "Close to the footlights,"[15] as Sir Edward Clarke later described it, sat the judge's daughter-in-law, Mrs. Gilbert Coleridge, sketching the chief protagonists of the drama for posterity.

The jury all arrived promptly, a remarkable feat in those days, and every barrister in London not employed elsewhere crowded into the courtroom. This was an exceptional day in legal terms. Apart from Bertie's brief appearance as a witness in the Mordaunt divorce case, no heir to the throne had appeared in court since Prince Hal, the future Henry V and hero of Agincourt, was committed for contempt of court by Judge Gascoigne in 1411.

All eyes were on Bertie, dressed in a somber black frock coat and seated in a red leather chair between the judge and the witness box, with Sir Francis Knollys behind him. One could be forgiven for assuming that it was Bertie himself who was on trial.

The instigator of the proceedings, Gordon-Cumming, sat beside his solicitor, St. John Wontner, as Gordon-Cumming's counsel, Sir Edward Clarke, Attorney General, opened the case for the defense. Clarke focused on Gordon-Cumming's previous good character, his military record, and his long-standing friendship with the Prince of Wales. Why, Clarke demanded, would a man accustomed to such advantages suddenly take to cheating at cards? He also made his views on baccarat clear to the jury by commenting that baccarat was "about the most unintelligent mode of losing your own money, or getting somebody else's, I ever heard of."[16] Calling Gordon-Cumming as a witness, Clarke took him through the events at Tranby Croft, and concluded by asking Gordon-Cumming if he had cheated at cards on that night. Gordon-Cumming replied that he had not.

Clarke also outlined Gordon-Cumming's *coup de trois* system of placing bets, which, he explained, could have been mistaken by the inexperienced players as cheating, rather than a correct method of gambling. After his opening speech, Clarke then questioned Gordon-Cumming, and his approach was to show that Gordon-Cumming "was a man of honour who had been sacrificed to save the courtiers."[17]

After the court had adjourned for lunch, it was time for Gordon-Cumming to be examined by Sir Charles Russell. Sir Charles was a natural choice to represent the Prince of Wales against Gordon-Cumming's libel suit. Flamboyant and stylish, Sir Charles was a member of the Jockey Club, owned a racehorse called Miss Shylock, and never traveled without a pack of cards. He was also a formidable advocate who could tie any witness up in knots.[18]

Russell provided a model of the table used for the game of baccarat and a photograph of the room, and questioned Gordon-Cumming about the bets where cheating had been suspected. Russell also asked him about why he had signed the document agreeing not to play cards: Gordon-Cumming stated that he had "lost my head . . . on that occasion. If I had not lost my head I would not have signed that document."[19] Gordon-Cumming's cross-examination ran into the second day, after which he was then reexamined by Clarke; his time in the witness box lasted until 1 P.M. The *Illustrated London News* concluded that Gordon-Cumming made an admirable witness. "Leaning easily on the rail, his grey-gloved left hand resting easily on the bare right, perfectly dressed, his tones equable, firm, neither over-hurried nor over-deliberate, cool, but not too cool,"[20] while the *Pall Mall Gazette* decided that "Sir William faced the fire of the most deadly cross-examiner in England much as he would have faced his foe on the battle-field . . . knowing that its issue was social life or death."[21]

Bertie followed Gordon-Cumming into the witness box and, according to the *Daily Chronicle,* he appeared to be nervous. "The Prince stood with one hand easily resting on the rail, his head a little down, his attitude free and not undignified. His voice was a little hoarse and rough, and somehow had a queer unfamiliar note

in it; but the replies were given with great readiness, and even rapidly."[22] The reporter for *The New York Times* observed that "the heir
apparent was decidedly fidgety, that he kept changing his position,
and that he did not seem able to keep his hands still,"[23] and the
Daily News agreed and stated that Bertie made an unfavorable
impression.

Examined by Clarke, Bertie stated that he had not seen any cheating, and was ignorant of the accusations until he was told by Lord
Coventry and General Williams; although Gordon-Cumming had
been a good friend for years, Bertie believed he was guilty of cheating.

After twenty minutes of questions from Clarke and Russell,
Bertie was told that he was free to leave the witness box. As Bertie
was turning away, a "sharp clear voice with a cockney accent" rang
out. "Excuse me, your Royal Highness, I have a question or two to
ask you!"[24] This question, not strictly admissible, came from a member of the jury. Bertie wheeled around with a smile, and stood to
attention as the juryman asked him two questions: Had Bertie seen
nothing of the alleged malpractices of the plaintiff? And what had
Your Royal Highness thought at the time of the charges made
against Gordon-Cumming?

To the first question Bertie replied that he had not seen anything
suspicious, although he explained that "it is not usual for a banker to
see anything in dealing cards."[25] To the second, Bertie responded that
"the charges appeared to be so unanimous that it was the proper
course—no other course was open to me—than to believe them."[26]

The queen was horrified by the trial, and Bertie's involvement in
the case:

> *This horrible trial drags along and it is a fearful humiliation to see the
> future king of this country dragged, and for the second time, through the
> dirt just like anyone else in a Court of Justice. I feel it is a terrible hu-
> miliation, so do all the people. It is very painful and must do him and*

his prestige great harm. Oh! If only it is a lesson for the future! It makes me very sad.[27]

The following day: "I hope and think there is no doubt that the verdict will be given against Sir William G Cumming as the evidence is perfectly clear, but even if it is not he will be turned out of the army and society . . . his lawyer, the Solicitor-General most unjustifiably attacked Bertie most unjustly and unfairly. The whole thing must do Bertie harm and I only pray it may be a warning."[28]

The last witness for the prosecution was General Williams. Questioned by Sir Edward Clarke, the general admitted that he had not seen Gordon-Cumming in any way that suggested cheating.

The case for the defense began on the third day of the trial, with Stanley Wilson, the son of the house, in the witness box. Stanley said that he had seen Gordon-Cumming illicitly add counters to his stake twice on the first night and at least twice on the second night, although he could not remember the full details. Stanley was followed into the witness box by Sub-Lieutenant Berkeley Levett, who confirmed that on the first evening he had seen Gordon-Cumming add counters after the hand had finished but before the stake had been paid. He was unsure of other details of the evening's play, and had not witnessed anything on the second night.

Next came Edward Lycett Green, "the emotional force behind the accusations." Lycett Green stated that he had seen Gordon-Cumming twice push counters over the chalk line when he should not have done so; he had considered accusing Gordon-Cumming at the time, but decided against it because he "did not like to make a scene before ladies."[29] At points in the examination Lycett Green contradicted the course of events outlined by Stanley Wilson, and his evidence seemed to be remarkably shaky. Given that Edward Lycett Green had first raised the alarm over Gordon-Cumming's behavior, it "seemed remarkable that he, the prime mover in the affair, seemed unable to say anything without qualifying it with some such remark as, 'I don't exactly remember'. The hedging by the principal accuser certainly weakens the defendants' case. Lycett Green's refusal to remember anything seemed almost like a deliberate policy."[30]

Mrs. Lycett Green followed her husband into the witness box, and confirmed that she had seldom played baccarat before; although she had seen nothing untoward on the first night, she accepted her husband's secondhand version of events as the truth, but did not agree that as a result she had been watching Gordon-Cumming. Mrs. Lycett Green provided a different series of events from those outlined by other witnesses, but stated that she thought she had seen Gordon-Cumming illicitly add to his stake.

After Mrs. Lycett Green had finished giving evidence, her place was taken by her mother, Mrs. Wilson. Examined by Russell, Mrs. Wilson stated that she thought she saw Gordon-Cumming cheat twice by adding additional counters to his stake. When Clarke cross-examined her, he asked if anyone had placed a stake of £15. Mrs. Wilson stated that only her husband had placed such an amount, but Wilson had not played on either night as he disliked both the game and high-stakes gambling. Havers, in his account of the case, regarded it as "rather shocking really, considering that she had sworn to tell the truth . . . to find her coming out with this . . . lie spoken, apparently, with the complete self-assurance that the other members of her family had shown."[31]

The final witness called for the defense was Lord Coventry. He was one of the nonplaying members of the party who had witnessed no cheating, understood little about gambling, and, as a non–soldier, knew nothing of Article 41 of the Queen's Regulations. When cross-examined by Clarke, Coventry confirmed that as far as he was aware, the witnesses had all decided to watch Gordon-Cumming's play on the second night, despite their claims to the contrary.

The Daily Chronicle noted the "obvious doubts which tainted the accusations of the defendants . . . they and the Prince's flunkeys all contradicted each other on material points."[32] Russell's summing up for the defense took the remainder of the day and the court adjourned until the following Monday, when he continued. He referred to a possible thirteen acts of cheating that the defendants were alleged to have seen, and that "we have five persons who believe he cheated, swearing unmistakably they saw him cheat, and telling you how they saw him cheat."[33]

Once Russell had completed his speech for the defendants, Clarke gave his reply, considered by the *Daily Chronicle* to be "a very brilliant, powerful, wily and courageous effort."[34] Clarke pointed to the many inaccuracies in both the written statement prepared by Coventry and Williams, and in the memories of all concerned. He went on to outline that there had been celebrations at the races—the prince's horse had won on the first day, and the St. Leger had been run on the second—combined with the full hospitality of the Wilsons to consider: according to the court reporter for *The Times*, Clarke "alluded to the profuse hospitalities of Tranby Croft, not with any idea of suggesting drunkenness, but as indicating that the guests might not be in a state for accurate observation."[35] He also drew the jury's attention to the gaps in the defendants' memories, where they were so precise about some of their observations but could not remember other key details.[36] Clarke lampooned some of the involved parties, referring to Lycett Green as "a Master of Hounds who hunts four days a week,"[37] while Stanley Wilson was a spoiled wastrel from a rich family who lacked initiative and drive. Above all, Clarke indicated, the defendants, with the exception of Stanley Wilson, saw what they had been told to expect: "the eye saw what it expected or sought to see, there was only one witness who saw Sir William Gordon-Cumming cheat without expecting it—young Mr Stanley Wilson. The others were all told there had been cheating, and expected to see it."[38] At the end of his reply, Clarke's speech was greeted by applause among those in the galleries. The British lawyer Heber Hart later wrote that Clarke's speech was "probably the most conspicuous example of the moral courage and independence of the Bar that has occurred in modern times,"[39] while Clarke considered it to be one of the best speeches he ever made.

When Sir Edward Clarke sat down after completing his speech to the jury, there was a brief clatter of applause from throughout the court. The judge, Lord Coleridge, uttered a fierce and angry cry of "Silence!" This was unusual for him as he had a mild and quiet manner. "This is not a theatre!"[40] According to one newspaper, there was a retort from the back of the court, "You have made it so!"[41] As soon as Clarke made to leave the courtroom, "the overcharged feelings of the spectators again broke out and, unchecked this time, they gave way to their feelings."[42]

On the eighth day of the trial, Bertie did not attend court. He went to Ascot instead, and the waggish *Star* commented that the racing would be a trivial affair compared with the struggle for life and honor now reaching its climax at the Royal Courts of Justice.

On the following day, June 9, Lord Coleridge began his four-hour summing up. His summary was a response to Clarke's, and he went through on a point-by-point basis to discredit the attorney general's speech, although in places his description "was directly contrary to the evidence."[43] The jury retired at 3:25 P.M., and every eye in the courtroom fixed on Gordon-Cumming, "the man whose social life hung in the balance."[44] Gordon-Cumming coped well with this ordeal. "He clasped his gloved hands on his stick, and with composed features waited . . . like a figure of stone."[45]

The jury came back after just thirteen minutes, and Gordon-Cumming turned his cold, gray eyes upon them as the foreman told Lord Coleridge: "We find for the plaintiffs." Hissing and booing broke out from the public and the junior bar. A telegram was dispatched to the prince immediately by Mrs. Wilson, who had brought a form with her for just this purpose. The hissing and booing continued and became louder as the jury filed out of their box. Gordon-Cumming remained seated, "perhaps dazed for the moment with the shock of the stupendous doom which those dreadful words had conveyed; and then, without a word, without a tremor, walked squarely to the well of the court and disappeared into the world that will know him no more."[46]

Scenes outside court following a verdict are often dramatic, and this was no exception. It was not a popular verdict. "The defendants, who had the grace not to smile and who behaved with perfect dignity, were so fiercely mobbed that they had to take refuge under Mr Lewis' sheltering wing in Mr Justice North's court, and then get quietly away."[47]

According to *Reynolds News,* the Wilsons were encircled by a large crowd in the narrow corridors outside the courtroom, and "hissed and hooted and jeered in the most excited fashion."[48] Fearing for their safety, they took refuge in a neighboring courtroom while the people outside crowded around the doors and waited for them to come out.

Bertie escaped the possibility of public humiliation at the Royal Courts of Justice, but at Ascot the crowds were waiting for him. As the royal procession arrived at one o'clock, with the rich scarlet and gold of the liveries of the royal servants glittering in the green landscape, no cheer greeted Lord Coventry, Master of the Buckhounds, as he trotted in front of the royal carriage on a big bay horse. There was no ovation for the royal party, indeed, never had it been received with such coldness. As the Prince and Princess of Wales were driving around the course, there were catcalls and booing and cries of "Oi! Baccarat! Have you bought your counters?" "There's ten pounds more to pay here, sir," and "If you can't back a horse, baccarat!"[49] Princess May of Teck, who was in one of the carriages, described it as "a most unpleasant ordeal."[50] Only Bertie, cutting a fine figure in his dark gray frock coat, seemed to emerge unscathed.[51] On hearing the verdict, he commented that "George Lewis tells me that the Solicitor-General's speech will give the Radicals 100,000 votes at the General Election."[52]

The newspapers had a field day. *The Times* "profoundly regretted that the Prince should have been in any way mixed up, not only in the case, but in the social circumstances which prepared the way for it."[53] The *Review of Reviews* condemned Bertie as "not only a gambler but as a wastrel and whoremonger."[54]

The prime minister, Lord Salisbury, subsequently recommended that Bertie should avoid playing baccarat for six months and then leak a letter to the press stating that the trial had been a lesson to him and he no longer permitted baccarat to be played in his presence.[55] Meanwhile, the queen suggested that Bertie write an open letter to the Archbishop of Canterbury expressing his disapproval of gambling. While Bertie and Lord Salisbury dismissed this suggestion out of hand, Bertie wrote a private letter to the archbishop, expressing his feelings about "the horror of gambling," which he regarded as the equivalent of drunkenness as a social evil, "one of the greatest curses that a country can be afflicted with."[56]

After this, Bertie stopped playing baccarat and took up whist instead, which he also played for money.

A notable feature of the Tranby Croft trial was that, for the first time, the inner workings of the Marlborough House set went on show. The trial revealed that the heir to the throne sat up half the night gambling for massive amounts of money with his cronies; that one of them had been accused of cheating; and that there had been an attempted cover-up. The fact that the Prince of Wales gambled at all was regarded as scandalous by earnest churchgoers, but was seen as endearingly raffish in the opinion of Bertie's working-class subjects; here was further evidence that Bertie, with his smoking, drinking, and womanizing, was indeed "one of us."

The real victim in all of this was Gordon-Cumming. Following the trial, the leader in *The Times* stated that "He is condemned by the verdict of the jury to social extinction. His brilliant record is wiped out and he must, so to speak, begin life again. Such is the inexorable social rule. . . . He has committed a mortal offence. Society can know him no more."[57]

Just like the Churchills and the Beresfords before him, Gordon-Cumming was ostracized. The difference was that Gordon-Cumming would never be allowed back into the royal circle. Anyone who spoke to Gordon-Cumming, or accepted his hospitality, would never be asked to Marlborough House again, and Bertie refused to meet anyone "who henceforth acknowledged the Scottish baronet."[58] On June 10, 1891, the day after the trial, Gordon-Cumming was dismissed from the army and blackballed from his clubs, the Carlton, Guards', Marlborough, and Turf. "So the vengeance was thorough."[59] On the same day, Gordon-Cumming married his fiancée, Florence Garner, by special license at Holy Trinity Church, Chelsea. Gordon-Cumming was faultlessly turned out in a frock coat and pearl-gray gloves, but looked fatigued, while his tiny vivacious bride wore a dove-gray walking dress with a black straw hat. Florence walked up the aisle bubbling with good spirits, a contrast to Gordon-Cumming, but he threw off his gloom as the service proceeded.[60]

When the couple returned to Gordon-Cumming's estate in Scotland, he was greeted by cheering locals who pulled their carriage through the streets by hand. "That the prince and society considered him a social outcast mattered not at all to his people."[61]

It mattered to Gordon-Cumming, though. Despite the beautiful estate of Altyre and the gloomy ancestral castle of Gordonstoun, the presence of a loving wife and local friends, Gordon-Cumming hankered for society. He threw a number of house parties, which Florence hated, especially when one of the guests tried to seduce her and Gordon-Cumming responded, with complete lack of empathy, "My dear child, don't be so silly. You must learn to take care of yourself!"[62] Florence died at fifty-two, exhausted by anxiety and disappointment, and Gordon-Cumming followed her to the grave eight years later, aged eighty-one, having lived "outside society" for forty years.[63] According to his daughter Elma, who later became a successful writer, Gordon-Cumming "never lost that touch of swagger in his walk, the hint of scorn for lesser mortals, the suggestion that he was irresistible. He had worn it for so long that neither trouble nor disgrace nor old age could change his habit."[64]

Opinion is divided as to whether Gordon-Cumming cheated or not. The Duke of Portland, William Cavendish-Bentinck, Bertie's master of the horse, wrote in his memoirs that:

> *I knew Bill Cumming very well, and for a long time liked and admired him, both as a gallant soldier and as a fine sportsman. . . . A friend of mine who went tiger shooting with him was loud in his praise of Bill's sportsmanship, bravery and unselfishness . . . but he had one serious failing: he could not play fair at cards. . . . In the days of duelling, it would have been a brave man who accused Bill of any such thing, as he was a dead shot with a revolver or a pistol. If England had always been at war, or if Bill had always been in pursuit of big-game, everyone would have thought, quite rightly, that no better soldier, or finer fellow in every way, ever existed.*[65]

Gordon-Cumming's problems began when he challenged his accusers. Had he been content to accept a lifetime ban on gambling, he might have maintained his status. The case also points up the disparity between the nouveau riche Wilsons and old money. The Wilsons, hell-bent on convicting Gordon-Cumming, wrecked his career. *The Times* saw the Wilsons as little less than murderers. "With or without their will, [the Wilson family] have been the cause of the social death of a distinguished man. When a man dies physically those who have to do with him remain in seclusion for a time. Those can hardly do less who are indirectly responsible for this far more tragic calamity, the ruin of a fine career."[66]

Daisy Brooke, blamed for Gordon-Cumming's downfall by Mina Beresford, remembered him as "more sinned against than sinning . . . a constant friend, but he cut us all off in his retirement, and I often had sad thoughts of him and always kept a warm corner in my heart for him"[67] Perhaps it is here that we have the real reason for Gordon-Cumming's exclusion from society. In September 1890, three days before the events at Tranby Croft, Bertie had returned early from traveling in Europe. He visited Harriet Street to discover Daisy Brooke "in Gordon-Cumming's arms." What better way, then, to remove Gordon-Cumming for good, than by accusing him of cheating at cards? We have seen Bertie's ruthless streak at work before. Here it was again. Or in the words of one of his circle: "Bertie never forgives."[68] Gordon-Cumming had been taught a painful, and permanent, lesson.

Chapter Eighteen

THE SOCIALITE SOCIALIST

I was as one who had found a new, a real world.
—Daisy, Countess of Warwick

In July 1891, before the dust from the Tranby Croft trial had time to settle, Bertie found himself on the brink of yet another scandal. Charlie Beresford, still furious that he and his wife had been excluded from society, lay stewing on his yacht in the Mediterranean. He was further enraged by the fact that his former mistress, Daisy, was now the lover of the Prince of Wales.

From his state room on the *Undaunted,* Charlie Beresford wrote a threatening letter to Bertie. It was a terrifying ultimatum: Bertie must restore Lady Beresford to her rightful place in society, or he would publish Daisy's letter. Charlie Beresford was using the latest weapon in his war against the Prince of Wales: bad publicity. To ensure that it could not be missed, Charlie Beresford sent his letter to the prime minister, Lord Salisbury. Perhaps Charlie thought that the prime minister would put pressure on the Prince of Wales to resolve the situation, rather than endure disgrace.

Once again, Charlie referred to Bertie as a "blackguard," and not only that but also "a coward!" Dueling may have been outlawed, "but there is a more just way of getting right done than can duelling and that is—*publicity!*"[1] Charlie Beresford sent the letter to his wife, Mina, instructing her to forward it to Lord Salisbury. Mina duly obliged and Lord Salisbury intervened in the matter immediately, and not without good reason. Mina had written to Lord Salisbury making it clear that, not only did her husband have damning evidence to blacken the prince's reputation, but that there was another factor at play. Mina's sister, Lady Lucy Paget, had written a manuscript entitled *Lady River*, a fictionalized account of Daisy's affair with Bertie and others, which, if published, would blacken his name even further.[2] "Several people," Lady Beresford continued, "wanted to make use of the story at the next general election, for purposes of their own." Lady Beresford went on to say that she would accept nothing less than a public apology from the Prince of Wales for excluding her from society.

Shaken by the reference to the next election, as any politician would be, Lord Salisbury drew on all his resources of diplomacy and wrote back to the Beresfords. Salisbury explained to Charlie that, according to "the social laws of our class"[3] it would scarcely be appropriate for Charlie to disgrace his former mistress by making her affair with the Prince of Wales public. This apparently worked, as Charlie agreed to write to Bertie again in a less aggressive manner. However, Mina Beresford was in a less conciliatory mood, and the damage had already been done. Mina's sister Lucy had begun to circulate the manuscript of *Lady River*. This titillating account of Daisy's misdemeanors proved impossible to suppress and provided much scandalized delight when read aloud in society drawing rooms, although Daisy herself remained blissfully unaware of the lurid document.[4] The biggest victim of this vicious attack on Daisy's reputation was not Daisy herself, or even Bertie, though he must have groaned in dismay when he heard about it. It was Bertie's wife, the long-suffering Princess Alexandra, who was humiliated beyond belief by further evidence of her husband's philandering. Discreet affairs were something that every royal wife must tolerate. But now this, so soon after Tranby Croft? Alix had learned about the pamphlet while on holiday with her family in Denmark. Due to return to London to celebrate Bertie's fiftieth birthday, Alix snubbed her husband by traveling out to the Crimea to visit her sister Dagmar, now Tsarina Marie Feodorovna of Russia.

In December, Charlie Beresford arrived back in London and issued an ultimatum to the Prince of Wales. Either Bertie publicly apologize to Lady Beresford and reinstate her in society, and Daisy agree to withdraw from society for a year, or Charlie Beresford would publish an intimate account of Bertie's private life.

The next four days passed in a flurry of damage limitation, with Lord Salisbury negotiating not only with Bertie and Charlie Beresford, but with the queen herself. At the eleventh hour, just as Charlie Beresford was about to call a press conference at which he planned to expose Bertie's affair with Daisy and resign from his position as fourth lord of the admiralty, a settlement was reached. Bertie and Charlie exchanged letters drafted by Lord Salisbury, and Daisy agreed to withdraw from court for a short period of time. This really was not much of a penance for Daisy; everybody loved her—with the exception of Mina—and as acknowledged mistress of the Prince of Wales, she could do as she pleased. At this stage, Bertie's love for Daisy never faltered. The prince continued to write adoring letters to his "darling Daisywife," and Daisy continued to receive his attentions, recalling in later life that "he had manners and he was very considerate."[5] But Daisy was about to experience an unexpected predicament. Although Lord Salisbury's diplomatic intervention had concluded the standoff between Bertie and Charlie, Daisy was in trouble. Daisy's husband, Brookie, had reached the limits of his endurance. There was only so much that he could take. For a decade or more, Brookie had put up with Daisy's dalliances and entertained an endless succession of her lovers at Easton Lodge. Then there was the matter of Daisy selling off the contents of Warwick Castle to finance her expensive lifestyle. The Tranby Croft scandal had been the final straw, with Daisy accused of leaking the details. Now rumors flew that Brookie was preparing to divorce Daisy, naming four-teen correspondents, including Bertie, Charlie Beresford, the Duke of Marlborough, and Lord Randolph Churchill.

Such an action would have been understandable, but there were two mitigating factors. As the Mordaunt and Aylesford cases illus-trated, a high-profile divorce was considered outrageous by Victo-rian society. Brookie had no wish to put Daisy through such a shameful spectacle, and he was also about to succeed to the title of Earl of Warwick. Brookie needed a wife by his side when he became earl, and at least Daisy, for all her faults, was the devil he knew. Daisy was also wildly popular at every level of society, from the Marlborough House set to the landed gentry and the tenants of her estate, Easton Lodge. Daisy, always a generous hostess, had also given way to "recurrent fits of philanthropy, some of it wildly extravagant and mistakenly generous, but indulged in by an impelling desire to help to put things right, and a deep conviction that things as they were were not right."[6] During their final Christmas at Easton, before the Brookes moved to Warwick Castle, Daisy threw a massive party for the children of the estate. The ballroom, with its white walls, Corinthian pillars, and blue ceiling was ablaze with electric light, and dominated by a glittering Christmas tree, so heavily laden with toys and decorations that the foliage could scarcely be seen. Along each side of the ballroom stood tables covered with gifts, including fur-lined coats for the principal household servants, jewelry or trin-kets for others, bags of toys for every child, and fancy articles of dress or warm clothing for the other servants. Every man who worked in the grounds received a new red woolen jersey. A separate table held a collection of silverware and jewelry, which Daisy had provided for each member of her house party. At five o'clock the fifty household servants left their duties in order to arrange themselves on either side of the ballroom, and the village children were ushered in. Behind the children came one hundred outside workmen, gamekeepers, woodmen, gardeners, estate artisans, stablemen, and motormen. Daisy and Brookie had a welcome for everybody, and their eldest daughter, Marjorie, helped Daisy to distribute the presents.[7]

Daisy was resplendent in a beautiful dress designed by Doucet of Paris, made from delicately painted muslin, trimmed with fur and turquoise velvet, and a black picture hat. When the packages had been distributed, Daisy's little son, Leopold, was hoisted onto his brother's shoulders and stripped the presents from the Christmas tree, passing them down to the children. At the end of the party, "cheer after cheer was raised for the earl and countess and their family."[8]

In December 1893, after the old earl died and Brookie became the fifth Earl of Warwick, Daisy and Brookie moved to Warwick Castle. Daisy immediately made a number of improvements, installing bathrooms and electric light. A year later, the period of mourning being at an end, Daisy gave a massive fancy dress ball, "then something of a novelty—on a splendidly lavish scale." Guests from afar were put up by Daisy's neighbors at house parties, and the entire county of Warwickshire buzzed with excitement and the bustle of preparation. The ball was spoken of as "the event of the winter."[9]

Daisy's four hundred guests had been instructed to wear eighteenth-century court dress, with a color scheme of white and gold. Hairdressers had been brought in from London and Paris to ensure that the party guests had appropriately powdered *coiffures*. Warwick Castle had seen nothing like it since the visit of Elizabeth I. Daisy's guests emerged from the frosty night into a reproduction of the court of Louis XVI. Alongside a blazing electric chandelier, five thousand glowing wax candles softened the lighting and flattered the complexions of the ladies. The walls were hung with tapestries and embroidered cloth in silver and yellow, and arum lilies and lilies of the valley had been sent from the South of France. Daisy had spared no expense in re-creating the splendors of the Palace of Versailles just for one night.

Daisy's youngest half sister, Angela, recalled that: "As one stood in the old hall, with its coats of arms and the men in armour, looking out across the river, the countryside decked in its glistening white mantle, the rich colours and fantastic costumes of the guests seemed enhanced by the romantic setting."[10] According to *The World, "every room seemed lovelier than the last one. The gold drawing room was absolutely brilliant, . . ."*[11] while dancing took place in the Cedar Room, which was hung with Van Dykes.

Daisy had dressed up, inevitably, as Queen Marie Antoinette, in a gown of turquoise velvet brocade embroidered with real gold thread in fleur-de-lis and roses. Diamonds glittered at her throat and in her ears; an elaborate headdress with pink, white, and turquoise ostrich plumes and sparkling sapphires bobbed over her hair. Daisy's twelve-year-old daughter, Marjorie, and her friend appeared as Daisy's maids of honor, dressed as shepherdesses in white. As the guests waltzed to the strains of an Austrian band, several individuals could be identified in "cunning combinations of colour and coquetries of costume."[12] Brookie had come as a musketeer, in a ruby-red velvet coat trimmed with red lace and a wig of tumbling curls. His comrades included le Viscomte de Bragalonne (Prince Henry of Pless) and le Comte d'Artagnac (Lord Lovat). Harry Rosslyn, Daisy's half brother, was the Duc de Nemours, and the millionaire coal mine owner Joe Laycock came as an eighteenth-century Indian army officer. Daisy's half sister, Millie Sutherland, dressed up as Louis XV's consort, Marie Leszczyňska, wearing white and silver brocade, with a ruby velvet train and masses of diamonds. Many of the women had dressed as the ladies of Louis XVI's court, including the Duchess de Polignac and the Duchess d'Orléans. Mrs. Alice Keppel, the Scottish beauty, appeared dressed in Rose du Barry antique brocade with silver thread, and powdered hair with three rose-pink feathers and pink satin shoes with diamond buckles.

At midnight, trumpeters in cloth of gold marched through the hall blowing a fanfare to summon the guests to a banquet; forty tables had been laid with hot and cold food in the hall. Dancing continued until dawn, with "minuets, waltzes and champagne"[13] and "it was fairly morning before the echo of the last carriage wheel died away into the bleak countryside."[14]

Daisy's fancy dress ball was hailed as a triumph. "The throng of splendidly gowned and costumed men and women in the setting of the noble rooms of the castle seemed *at the time* to make the gathering worthwhile,"[15] Daisy recalled, arguing that not only had the ball been great fun, but she had provided employment for dozens of servants, dressmakers, musicians, caterers, and florists. "I felt happy in the belief that our ball was giving work to so many people who would otherwise have been idle. The festivities of the Lords and Ladies Bountiful were being translated into terms of meat and bread for the workers."[16] "The ball was a great success," Daisy concluded, a verdict that was echoed by all but one of the newspapers, "an obscure sheet, by name the *Clarion*."[17] The *Clarion* reached Daisy two days later, as she was having her customary breakfast in bed at Warwick Castle. To Daisy's horror, the article in the *Clarion* consisted of a violent personal attack upon Daisy for holding a ball at a time of general misery, a "sham benevolence, a frivolous ignoring of real social conditions."[18] Daisy was so infuriated by this article that she jumped out of bed and took the next train to London. By noon, Daisy was in Fleet Street, the heart of the newspaper industry, searching for the offices of the *Clarion*. Daisy found them in an older building, at the top of a shabby staircase, with the editor's name, Robert Blatchford, on the door.

Daisy walked straight in unannounced, as the editor looked up from his desk. Robert Blatchford showed no surprise as a gracious young woman dressed in the height of fashion appeared in his dingy office. Instead, he stared coldly at Daisy without standing up or giving her a word of welcome. Daisy stared back, thinking to herself that the garment Blatchford wore, something between a dressing gown and a lounge coat, was most undignified.

"Are you the Editor of the *Clarion*?" Daisy demanded.

Blatchford merely nodded.

"I came about this," Daisy went on, thrusting the newspaper under his eyes with the offending page marked in black. Blatchford made no reply, just waited for Daisy to continue.

"How could you be so unfair, so unjust?" Daisy said. "Our ball has given work to half the county, and to dozens of dressmakers in London besides."

"Will you sit down?" Blatchford replied, "while I explain to you how mistaken you are about the real effect of luxury?"[19]

And then Robert Blanchford told Daisy, as a socialist and a democrat, what he thought of charity bazaars and ladies bountiful. Blatchford made plain the difference between productive and unproductive labor, and said that labor used to produce finery was as much wasted as if it were used to dig holes in the ground and fill them up again.

By this new standard, Daisy came to understand that nine-tenths of the money spent on the Warwick ball had been wasted. Such elementary economics as that the only useful labor was labor that produced useful articles, which in turn helped labor to produce again, was all new to her. Although Daisy had had a vague idea that money spent on champagne and delicacies was wasted, she was dismayed to discover that the Blatchford doctrine included cobwebby lace and similar useless and beautiful things in the same category.

Daisy sat and listened, openmouthed. "My old ideas and ideals were all brought to naught, and it was late afternoon before this plain man with the big ideas had ceased speaking. We had both forgotten the lunch hour and the passing of time."[20] Before the end of the talk, Daisy had been convinced that "setting the poor, who themselves needed food and coal and decent housing, to build unnecessary rooms for an evening's employment, to cook dainties for people already overfed, and to make clothes for the rich dancers, was idle work."[21] The great ball, and all its preparations, had not added one iota to the national wealth.

A somewhat dazed Daisy left Fleet Street and returned to the railway station, where she sat waiting for the train back to Warwick. During the journey home, Daisy thought about everything that she had heard, and realized that her outlook on life would never be the same. Daisy reached Warwick Castle just as her guests were going in to dinner, and when she joined the party she made no effort to explain her absence. "I was as one who had found a new, a real world. The crisis I was facing, or had faced, was emotional, and it would have been impossible then to frame such an experience in words."[22]

The following day, Daisy ordered ten pounds' worth of books on socialism, tracked down a retired professor of economics and appointed him as her tutor, and started a period of intense study without delay. "It would be idle to try to follow the circuitous path I trod, but it was Robert Blatchford's honest talk on that memorable day that gave me a vision of how it would be possible to change and modify the unjust conditions of our modern life."[23] "Babbling Brooke" had found a new cause, and it would change her life.

Chapter Nineteen

CAPTAIN LAYCOCK OF THE BLUES

Joe, my Joe—if you could see how my hand shakes
when I write your name. . . .
—DAISY, COUNTESS OF WARWICK

*F*ollowing the critical meeting with Robert Blatchford, editor of the *Clarion* newspaper, Daisy's new career as a philanthropist soon gained momentum. Given Daisy's energy and generosity, this was scarcely surprising. She was no mere do-gooder, posing as Lady Bountiful: she had clearly developed a real sense of social justice, even if this meant plundering the contents of Warwick Castle to finance her ventures. Daisy's achievements were indeed remarkable, and included a school for the local children and needlework instruction for the women of the estate, their output being sold at a shop opened for the purpose in London's West End. This activity, and Daisy's commitments as a society hostess, would have been enough to keep most women busy. But Daisy was not most women, and her private life remained as chaotic as ever.

In 1897, Daisy wrote to Bertie informing him that as she was three months' pregnant, it would be inappropriate for them to be seen together in public. Daisy was, however, concerned that she would lose Bertie as a friend, and her place at court. Bertie responded to Daisy's "beautiful letter" in warm and generous tones:[1]

My own lovely, little Daisy . . . [your letter] gave me a pang after the letters I have received from you for nearly nine years! But I think I could read "between the lines," everything you wished to convey. . . . The end of your beautiful letter touched me more than anything—but how could you, my loved one, imagine that I should withdraw my friendship with you? On the contrary I want to befriend you more than ever. . . . Though our interests, as you have said, lie far apart, still we have the sentimental feeling of affinity which cannot be eradicated by time.[2]

The affair had run its course.

Daisy gave birth to a son, Maynard, on March 21, 1898, and inevitably there was some speculation over the boy's paternity. Brookie was officially the father; Bertie was a putative father, but this is unlikely as he was, by this period, impotent.[3] According to Daisy herself, the father was none other than Joe Laycock, the north country mining heir who had appeared at Daisy's costume ball dressed as an eighteenth-century Indian army officer.

Captain Joe Laycock of the Blues was among the richest men in England, owning huge estates in Durham and Nottinghamshire, where he was "as popular with his miners as he was with the soldiers he commanded."[4] Joe fought in the Boer War with the Sherwood Rangers Yeomanry, an army reserve regiment, and was awarded the DSO in the Second Boer War. Like many men of action, Laycock possessed intense personal magnetism, despite being "the ugliest man I ever saw," according to his daughter-in-law Angela née Dudley-Ward. Laycock was "ugly in that special way with eyes set very far apart, very lithe and yet very powerfully built and with such *vitality!*"[5] Similar to Charlie Beresford in temperament and character, Laycock was very much Daisy's type. "Soldier, horseman, yachtsman, natural leader of men,"[6] Laycock swept Daisy off her feet and she fell passionately in love; a cad in the Flashman mode, Laycock did not entirely reciprocate Daisy's feelings.

Daisy might have developed a social conscience, but when it came to personal relationships she had not matured one whit. "If with the Prince of Wales he had been the captive, she the conquering, he the adoring, she the adored, the reverse was nearer the truth with Laycock. Lady Warwick could still be imperious, was seldom less than demanding, but Laycock was ultimately in the happy position of being the one most desired, the one more loved than loving."[7]

Daisy and Laycock shared a passion for fox hunting, particularly with the Quorn Hunt in Leicestershire, which traditionally offered some of the finest fox hunting in England. The couple loved to ride to hounds, and Daisy had a hunting lodge at Ingarsby Lodge near Houghton on the Hill, Leicestershire. The hunting set chased more than foxes. These were red-blooded folk, for whom field sports merely served as an appetizer for the action to come. Like the Marlborough House set, the foxhunters had their own code, which was very similar: don't ask, don't tell. Everyone knew about the affairs, but nobody said anything.

As a bachelor, Laycock was free to do as he liked, and Daisy had many rivals for his affections. The most notable of these was Kitty, Marchioness of Downshire, a blue-eyed Irish beauty and a superb horsewoman. When Laycock fell from his horse during a hunting accident, it was Kitty who rode cross-country to be by his side, reaching him before Daisy came to the rescue with her pony and trap. Eleven years younger than Daisy, married with three children, Kitty was a serious rival for Laycock's affections,[8] and the source of continual torment for Daisy.

"The mere suspicion [of Laycock's relationship with Lady Downshire] has clouded all these weeks in London," Daisy wrote to him. "Oh say it is not true and that I am a beast to have thought it . . . I am sick with suspense about you know what. . . ."[9] Lady Downshire's husband, Lord Downshire, had similar misgivings about Kitty's relationship with Laycock. "It has nearly broken my heart to hear your name coupled with Joe Laycock as if he was your husband," he wrote Kitty. ". . . It's more than I can stand."[10]

Left to his own devices, Laycock would doubtless have continued to accommodate both women. In the words of the old song, "I could be happy with either 'twere other dear charmer away." However, Daisy had other ideas. While Laycock was in London shopping and packing for a game-hunting expedition in West Bengal, Daisy let herself into his apartment, rifled through his desk, and seized the love letters sent to him by Lady Downshire. Armed with this evidence of Kitty's adultery, Daisy went straight to Lord Downshire. When Laycock found out what Daisy had done, there was a blazing row, and Laycock sailed for India in a towering rage.

Once again, Daisy's possessive and jealous nature meant she had broken the golden rule: *Thou shalt not get found out*. On this occasion, however, Daisy had no George Lewis to protect her and keep the case out of court. Lord Downshire launched divorce proceedings against his wife, Kitty, and the press soon caught the whiff of scandal:

We are likely to be startled next week by one of the prettiest scandals that have amused London society for a good many years. It is the story of a countess, a marchioness and a man. The countess, who is one of our most beautiful women, was in love with him first, but he had the bad taste to weary of her and attach himself to the marchioness, who is rather a commonplace young person . . . they say nothing will stop [the marquess] from bringing divorce proceedings.[11]

During the Downshire divorce trial it emerged that Lord Downshire, already deeply suspicious, had hired a firm of private detectives to spy on Laycock. The detectives confirmed that Laycock had stayed at Kitty Downshire's hunting lodge at Leesthorpe in Leicestershire while Lord Downshire had been away. Evidence gathered from Kitty's servants demonstrated that Laycock had not even made a pretense of sleeping in his own bed. Laycock's bedroom, adjoining Kitty's, had never been used. Further instances of adultery had occurred, and Lord Downshire had discovered his wife to be sending telegrams to Laycock. In addition, he had found a large bundle of letters from Laycock to his wife. Once again, Daisy's interference had made a bad situation even worse. Now that Lord Downshire had launched his divorce petition, there was a real danger that Laycock would feel obliged to marry Kitty, as her divorce would leave her a social outcast. To top it all, Daisy fell from her horse while out hunting and suffered a concussion and a broken arm.

Another unusual element in the case was that Kitty had never been seeking a divorce in the first place. Kitty had been perfectly content to stay married to Lord Downshire, and Laycock had had no plans to marry her prior to the divorce petition being launched. As a counteroffensive, Laycock set private detectives on Lord Downshire to see if he had any dalliances that could prevent a divorce. Sadly for Laycock, this proved to be an expensive and futile gesture. Lord Downshire emerged as a model landlord who butchered his own sheep and drove a cart around his Berkshire estate, selling the mutton to his tenants. Downshire was highly respected for his willingness to work alongside his laborers and join them with his bread and cheese when it was time to rest. And as far as a mistress was concerned, he appeared to have no interest whatsoever in the opposite sex.[12] Lord Downshire remained adamant that he would go through with the divorce, even when his own sister knelt down in front of his horse and cart in tears and begged him to reconsider for the sake of the family name.[13]

Meanwhile, Daisy did everything she could to stop Laycock from marrying Kitty when the divorce became final. Not only did Daisy send dozens of letters, she lobbied Bertie, begging him to agree that it would be a terrible thing if Laycock were to marry Kitty. But Daisy had become an embarrassment, and Bertie was no longer inclined to meddle in her private life and rescue her from the consequences of her own foolishness. Seventy years later many of these letters to Bertie were discovered: unopened. In a last ditch attempt, Daisy even attempted to make Laycock jealous by insinuating that Charlie Beresford wanted her back, "accidentally" enclosing a note from him suggesting they meet while he was in London.[14] This did not make the slightest impact on Laycock, who, for all his faults, was not the jealous type.

The divorce was finalized in April 1902. Lady Downshire was awarded a decree nisi and custody of her daughter, and the sons went to live with their father.

With the pressure of this failing relationship and her increasing commitment to charity work, Daisy fell ill and was diagnosed with "nervous prostration." Her letters to Laycock make sad reading: "Joe, my Joe—if you could see how my hand shakes when I write your name. . . ."[15] In a further letter, Daisy refers to a more troubling development, the fact that she was pregnant: "The big worry we won't talk of [the divorce case], dear one, and about *my* condition—I must do something but think I'll leave it till we have talked it over. . . . Only it makes me shudder!"[16]

It came as no consolation to Daisy that her rival was suffering, too. Lady Kitty had paid the price for her affair with Laycock by becoming a social outcast. But Laycock turned out to be enough of a gentleman to marry Kitty, on November 20, 1902. Laycock wrote to Daisy explaining that he felt compelled to stand by Kitty, but Daisy took the news badly. Daisy's anger rises off the page and so, too, does another emotion, that of the aging beauty who feels she has been humiliated by a younger and more attractive woman.

Daisy wrote back to Laycock in outrage and disbelief: "I cannot believe you to be so utterly callous, heartless and *crooked*. . . . After all the years of love and unchanging loyalty and devotion I have given you, that you can sit down and write to me that offhand note . . . you and that woman have *combined* to make a fool of me. . . . I was to risk and compromise myself, *believing that you wished to get out of this horror,* and have been simply the dupe of you and Lady Down-shire!"[17]

As one biographer remarked, "Fate can be very unkind. Daisy Warwick would meet the great love of her life when she was thirty-eight, beautiful still but over-voluptuous, and he would be five years younger. It was her bad luck. The ages would matter, not very much, but a little, and had they been reversed she would not have lost him."[18] Harsh words perhaps, by modern standards: no woman would con-sider herself "too old" for a love affair at the age of thirty-eight, but Anita Leslie summed up the situation effectively.

While Laycock and Lady Kitty were on honeymoon at the Paris Ritz, a message arrived that Daisy had taken an overdose. Laycock rushed back to London, to be greeted by a perfectly healthy Daisy, who said: "I thought you'd had enough of that!"[19]

Daisy was, however, facing a serious medical issue. It appears that she had finally decided to "do something" about her condition. In 1900, when termination was illegal in the United Kingdom, this was a daunting task. Failing to find any doctor in London willing to per-form the procedure, Daisy went to Paris and visited an abortionist. On the way back to the hotel, Daisy's train was involved in a minor accident and Daisy and her fellow passengers were forced to walk a mile down the track. This, and Daisy's fatigue, upset "the arrange-ments" put in place by the abortionist, but by Sunday Daisy was back at Warwick Castle, with a sympathetic girlfriend, Blanchie Gordon-Lennox, to look after her and deflect inquiries from a concerned Brookie while she waited for the planned miscarriage. Laycock came to visit the following day, and then, despite being in excruciating pain, Daisy was up and about again. But, while carrying out an en-gagement, Daisy contracted a chill. That night, there was a recep-tion at Warwick Castle, but Daisy was too ill to come downstairs.[20] Despite this, Daisy left the castle at Laycock's behest and traveled to London, where her condition deteriorated. After seeing a sympathetic doctor, Daisy managed to return to Warwick Castle in a state of "un-speakable pain and suffering."[21]

"I tried to crawl about Sunday but had to go to bed and Monday night the 'thing' happened. On Tuesday 1 I was very ill, blood poisoning, followed by inflammation of the kidneys and only my strength of *will* has brought me through the most awful time of pain I have ever known. . . . Please burn this at once. It is awful to have to write but your denial made it necessary."[22] Laycock's refusal to burn after reading does at least provide an insight into their relation-ship and the shocking truth about abortion in the 1900s.

The following night Daisy developed septicemia and was criti-cally ill for several days, saved only by the eminent surgeon Sir John Halliday Croom and her own formidably strong constitution. Despite being weakened by hemorrhage and morphine, Daisy man-aged to write to Laycock: "I find it difficult even today to put words together so as to reach your heart my darling. . . . Don't let's ever mention 'love' again. It has bought hell to us both."[23]

This was not entirely the end of the affair. Although Kitty had become chatelaine of Wiseton Hall, Laycock's country house in Not-tinghamshire, and her horses were in the stables, and her curtains at the windows, Laycock continued to visit Daisy. While Kitty was pregnant with their first child, Laycock took Daisy to Paris. Some months later at the age of forty-two, Daisy discovered that she was, once again, pregnant. This time, she chose to keep the baby, despite the discomfort of being heavily pregnant at her daughter Marjorie's wedding to Viscount Helmsley. The baby was born on April 3, 1904, and christened Mercy because that was Daisy's response upon hear-ing that she was pregnant again.[24]

Although Laycock did not rush to see his new daughter, over time he maintained his relationship with Daisy. On one level this is un-derstandable, as they had not one but two children together, May-nard as well as Mercy. Daisy and Laycock continued to meet and correspond, and Laycock genuinely seems to have been the love of her life.

Meanwhile, Bertie increasingly sought comfort from an unusual source: a prim, unmarried woman named Agnes Keyser who ran a nursing home for army officers in Grosvenor Crescent. Agnes Keyser was the most unusual of Bertie's close female friends in two respects: Agnes was unmarried, or in the words of Anita Leslie, "Miss Keyser was the only 'bachelor girl' in the King's life and she really loved him."[25] Also, Agnes did not conform to Bertie's physical type. Rather, she appears to have fulfilled the role of nanny and nurse toward the aging Bertie: the couple became acquainted when Agnes was forty-six and Bertie fifty-eight. Leslie's theory is that by this stage of his life, although Bertie desired female company, he also longed for peace and quiet.[26] Agnes Keyser could provide this—making her role in Bertie's life unique. A "well-born girl who devoted her life and personal fortune to nursing,"[27] Agnes Keyser was born in Great Stanmore, Middlesex, in July 1852, the daughter of Charles and Margaret Keyser, a wealthy Anglo-Jewish couple comfortably assimilated into the British upper classes. Charles Keyser, a member of the Stock Exchange, had read for the bar but never practiced as a barrister, and devoted himself to scholarship and philanthropy. Agnes had a comfortable and conventional childhood and was presented at court, but it soon became obvious that Agnes was not going to marry simply because it was expected of her. Indeed, the independent-minded Agnes had no desire to get married at all, despite the fact that she loved men and had very poor relationships with women.[28] Agnes also possessed the distinction of independent wealth, giving her considerable freedom. To the bewilderment of her rich, respectable family, she decided to take up a career in nursing, when nursing was considered a less than respectable occupation and there were no professional careers open to women.

Agnes was introduced to Bertie in 1898, and he dined regularly at the family home, 17 Grosvenor Crescent. When the Boer War broke out in 1899, Agnes and her younger sister, Fanny, tried to set up a nursing home for officers at Grosvenor Crescent, but when this proved too costly, Bertie set up a trust and asked his rich friends for donations. Among those who subscribed were Sir Ernest Cassel, Arthur Sassoon, Nathaniel Rothschild, Lord Burnham, Lord Sandwich, Lord Iveagh, and the Hambro banking family. As a result, 17 Grosvenor Crescent became the King Edward's Hospital for Officers, which would nurse 275 officers during the Boer War. Gentlemen from the Household Cavalry and the Guards Brigade were especially welcome, but Agnes, who was something of a snob, could not tolerate the prospect of entertaining other ranks. Agnes and Fanny's nursing home offered congenial conditions for the wounded officers: medical and surgical care was given for free by eminent physicians and surgeons, and the butler poured drinks before dinner every evening.[29] Subsequently, officers were charged a nominal sum for their care—around twenty-five shillings a day. Following the end of the Boer War in May 1902, Bertie suggested that there was a need for such a hospital during peacetime. He gave it his name and Agnes's hospital became the King Edward VII's Hospital for Officers: Sister Agnes Founder.[30] Agnes lacked formal medical training, but was an excellent administrator. In another period of time, Agnes would have made a formidable matron.

There was something of the dominatrix about Agnes. It was said that "she liked men, sick men, wounded men, impecunious men, men she could dominate and scold and pamper. She liked men stretched out in bed or in wheelchairs; best of all she liked to hold their hands as they went under their anaesthetic. The nursing staff feared her, and so did ladies who visited her patients."[31]

Bertie was a natural patron for Agnes's hospital. Genuinely interested in scientific progress, and in medicine in particular, Bertie once told his doctors that he wished a cure for cancer might be found before he died. The hospital at 17 Grosvenor Crescent also provided respite for Bertie, located as it was so close to Buckingham Palace.

Bertie seemed to find "absolute content with this handsome, formidable, middle-aged woman, especially in moments of stress when he could dine alone with her without arousing gossip or envy."[32] Unlike Bertie's other mistresses, Agnes was not interested in society and had no interest in competing with ambitious hostesses. Instead, she made sure she was always available whenever Bertie dropped in, as a good listener with medical knowledge who could take his pulse while he unburdened himself. Perhaps that unflappable, patient, no-nonsense Agnes provided Bertie with the "cosy comfort of an English nanny—that cosy fireside glow which most of his subjects had enjoyed in childhood."[33] The royal family respected the fact that Agnes studiously avoided all publicity and asked for nothing more than funds to keep her "home" running. Bertie dropped in frequently when in London, and Agnes did a formidable holding operation keeping the press at bay. The staff, and the military patients, must have known that Bertie was a regular visitor, but they wisely kept their mouths shut.

Agnes also took an active, professional interest in Bertie's health. Instead of offering him elaborate rich meals, Agnes offered simple nursery food: wholesome Irish stews and rice puddings, and discouraged him from smoking "those wretched cigars which aggravated his bronchitis."[34] A wonderful picture emerges of the greatest libertine of his age sitting with a nurse and spooning up his rice pudding, to be reprimanded by Agnes, in her starchy nurse's uniform, if he asked for second helpings.[35] "And if the worthy matron of this charitable establishment occasionally thinks it is time for a lie-down—well, *honi soit qui mal y pense* (shame on him who thinks evil of it)."[36]

Chapter Twenty

THE LAST MISTRESS: ALICE KEPPEL

*That terrible moment when the King would "drum with irritable
fingers upon the arm of his chair or upon the dinner table."*
—VITA SACKVILLE-WEST, *THE EDWARDIANS*

lice Keppel was the ultimate mistress; she was also
Bertie's last mistress. During her reign as the *mâi-
tresse en titre,* or mistress in chief, Alice Keppel carved a special place
in history. The fame of her liaison with the Prince of Wales "re-
sounded throughout Europe and gave her terrific *réclame* in France,
where the power of a wise mistress has always been regarded with
respect . . . a mistress is the one who rules and gives favours, not merely
a woman who sleeps with a man out of wedlock."[1] Alice was born to
the role: a product of the Scots upper classes, she was sensible, practical,
and diplomatic; indeed, in Alice's case the post of royal mistress could
be classified as a profession, like being a lady-in-waiting or an ambassador. A tomboy at heart, Alice possessed that combination of high
spirits and independence that Bertie always found so attractive.

Alice Frederica Edmonstone, or "Freddie" to her family, was born
on April 29, 1868, in Strathblane, Scotland. Alice's father was the
4th Baronet Edmonstone and a retired admiral in the Royal Navy,
and her maternal grandfather had been a governor of the Ionian Islands. Alice grew up at Duntreath Castle, the Edmonstones' home

since the fourteenth century. It was a wedding gift from King Robert III of Scotland to his daughter Mary Stewart, Princess of Scotland, when she married her fourth husband, Sir William Edmonstone of Culloden in 1425. They had a son whom they named Sir William Edmonstone of Duntreath.[2]

At first glimpse, Duntreath is an austere castle, set among rugged moorland. But once inside, far from being "a dour Scottish fastness, reeking of Balmorality," Duntreath was "romantic . . . gay with a touch of Frenchness in its salons *en enfilade* and premeditated perspectives. One fled from terror to enchantment. The atmosphere of the place was complex: half mediaeval, half-exotic. The Greek goddess wedded to the Scottish ogre."[3] "The masculinity of the castle, as characterised by the gun-room, the billiard room, the armoury, the dungeons and even the haunted Oak Room, was compensated for by the overpowering scent of the tuberoses, grown in the greenhouse, with which Alice's mother kept the rooms filled throughout the year. . . ."[4]

Alice's mother had refurbished the castle fifteen years earlier, making it comfortable and luxurious despite the forbidding exterior. Alice was the youngest of seven sisters, and had one little brother, Archie. Growing up, it was the shy delicate Archie to whom Alice felt closest; but, like Lillie Langtry and Daisy Warwick, Alice was happiest out of doors, playing boys' games with the gillies' sons. The little education Alice received was at the hands of her governess, and designed to prepare her for the marriage market: while Archie expected to go to Oxford, Alice needed to find a husband. The Edmonstones were not a wealthy family, and when their father died in 1888 it was essential that Alice, the only daughter still unmarried, make a good match.

To all intents and purposes, Alice did: she married the Honorable George Keppel, son of the 7th Earl of Albemarle. The Keppel family had a history of service to the British royal family, being descendants of Arnold Joost van Keppel, who had accompanied King

William III of England to Britain in 1688 and been given the title of
Earl of Albemarle in 1696. The Hon. George was a handsome, well-
set-up man four years Alice's senior, a lieutenant in the Gordon High-
landers who stood nearly six foot eight in his bearskin and curled his
moustache every morning with hot tongs. Harold Acton once observed that "one could picture him waltzing superbly to the strains
of 'The Merry Widow.' "[5]

Alice, at twenty-three, was a handsome Scotswoman, small but
beautifully proportioned, with magnificent auburn hair, alabaster
skin, and turquoise eyes. If Alice's admirers found something Mediterranean about her curvy figure and superabundant vitality, they
were correct. Alice's maternal grandmother had come from the Greek
island of Zakynthos.[6] Alice and George were married on June 1,
1891. Their first house was 7 West Halkin Street, Belgravia; then
they moved to 2 Wilton Crescent, part of the Grosvenor estate, built
by Seth Smith and Thomas Cubitt in the 1820s, a suitable base for
their role in London. In many respects, Alice and the Hon. George
had a good marriage; there was enormous affection on both sides.
Sadly, there were financial problems from the start: neither of them
possessed much in the way of money, making it difficult for Alice to
launch herself into London society. Like Alice, the Hon. George
came from one of those aristocratic families that had seen better days.
A "younger son," with no inheritance to look forward to, George had
income apart from his army pay and a small allowance from his father.
There was a certain symmetry in their financial plight, which perhaps
explains their compatibility. Keeping up with society, attending dinner parties and giving them in return, staying in country houses and
possessing the clothes to wear while doing this presented a real difficulty. It was Alice who resolved the issue in her characteristically
pragmatic fashion with a discreet series of affairs, selecting men from
the fringes of the Marlborough House set who contributed to her
upkeep. Alice's first affair was with Ernest Beckett, 2nd Baron
Grimthorpe, later assumed to have been the father of Alice's first

daughter, Violet. Alice also had an affair with Humphrey Sturt, 2nd Baron Alington. The Hon. George accepted this behavior with admirable restraint, the model of the *mari complaisant*.[7] Alice Keppel also possessed another characteristic, a vital asset for a woman chronically short of money. According to her daughter Sonia, throughout her life Alice "was irresistibly attractive to bank managers."[8]

"There was one in particular, a most useful Mr Montagu of the Westminster Bank at Victoria Gate," recalled Sonia.[9] Alice would walk across the park "with the tirelessness of a Scots gillie"[10] to visit Mr. Montagu in his private office. "Once inside it, he would place Mamma opposite him, with myself between them, and make his opening remarks in a reverently low tone as though he was praying in church. Usually, whatever the season, Mamma was veiled. Placing her umbrella or parasol on the table, then she would lift her veil, and Mr Montagu seemed to catch his breath a little as he beheld her beautiful face."[11]

Thus, the usually prosaic discussion about overdrafts would become "utterly delicious," Alice's request for further funds would be granted, and then she would sweep out, with her little girl by her side, leaving Mr. Montagu unable to return to his dusty ledgers while the faint smell of "fresh green sap" that was Alice Keppel's personal fragrance lingered on in the dark office.[12]

Beautiful, vivacious Alice and the man they liked to call "Edward the Caresser" were made for each other: their relationship was inevitable. But exactly when they first met is the subject of much conjecture. Biographer Anita Leslie maintains that Alice was introduced to Bertie at Sandown Races, where Bertie was of course immediately impressed by "the delectable Alice's" lovely face and fashionably curved figure.[13] Alice, at twenty-nine, and at the height of her beauty, bowled over the fifty-six-year-old Bertie with her "turquoise eyes, extraordinary attraction of *manner*," and her husky voice.[14]

Another theory is that the couple were introduced by Baroness de Stoeckl on the French Riviera in 1898, as the Baroness thought Bertie might be "amused" by Mrs. Keppel.[15] Raymond Lamont-Brown suggests that Bertie first encountered Alice Keppel at a ball given by Harty-Tarty, now the 8th Duke of Devonshire, to celebrate Queen Victoria's Golden Jubilee. The ball, at Devonshire House, Piccadilly, on July 2, 1897, was attended by Bertie and Alix, the Duke and Duchess of York, and everyone who was anyone in society. Alice Keppel was among the guests, dressed as the Duchess de Polignac, one of Marie Antoinette's courtiers.[16] Meanwhile, Sir Philip Magnus claimed that the Keppels first entertained Bertie to dinner on February 27, 1898,[17] where the other guests remarked on their astonishing display of sexual chemistry. An "understanding" between the prince and Mrs. Keppel "arose almost overnight" according to one eyewitness.[18] So strong was this "understanding" that a full-blown affair developed immediately, and Mrs. Keppel became established as "official mistress" within weeks.

Bertie needed a different type of mistress by this stage. Daisy Warwick had become a liability and bored him with her campaigning and progressive views. Less athletic now, but still demanding, Bertie required a younger woman to keep him interested, but no longer the sort of girl like Lillie, who would slide downstairs on a silver tray or pop ice cream down his neck.[19] With his best years behind him, Bertie had finally become aware of the whims of his subjects; decorum, not scandal, was now the order of the day. Alice Keppel filled the role perfectly, "a lady so different from Lady Warwick, so discreet, so restful, so undemanding—the perfect mistress for an ageing man."[20]

There is no reason to suppose that Bertie departed from his usual seduction technique when he encountered Alice Keppel: the expression of charmed and obvious interest, the affectionate glance, and, in due course, the arrival of a letter from Sir Francis Knollys suggesting that Alice might like to ask Bertie for afternoon tea when the Hon. George would not be at home. As the Hon. George had just been accepted for membership at the exclusive St. James's Club in Piccadilly, this would not present a problem. Alice would have known exactly what to expect, from her previous experiences with society lovers. The maid would enter with a tray of tea and cakes, and retire discreetly. In the drawing room, flirtation would ensue, a passionate embrace, perhaps—many of Bertie's ex-lovers complained about his excessive sentimentality—and possibly even full sexual intercourse, though a combination of Bertie's weight and ill health would have made this awkward. Alice's comparative youth and fitness was in her favor. She could perform her duties, jockey-style, while Bertie lay beneath her. It is said that in his own quarters, Bertie had a "hanging harness, complete with footholds" to make intercourse more feasible.[21]

Alice swiftly became Bertie's beloved little "Mrs. George" and their relationship was established. Although the affair started so quickly, it did not burn out; Mrs. George and Bertie were made for each other. Promotion to the rank of royal mistress brought its rewards: Alice and her family moved from their old, narrow house in Wilton Crescent to an impressive new residence at Portman Square, where Alice could entertain her royal lover in style. Over the years, Alice's daughters came to accept Bertie's visits as part of the routine of family life. Vita Sackville-West, lover of Alice's daughter, Violet, recalled visits to Portman Square during childhood: "Often when I went to their house I used to see a discreet little one-horse brougham waiting outside and the butler would slip me into a dark corner of the hall with a murmured 'One minute, miss, a gentleman is coming downstairs' so that I may take my choice whether it was the King or the doctor."[22] Violet herself remembered "a fat bald gentleman who smelt of cigars and eau-de-Portugal, whose fingers were covered in rings and to whom one curtsied endlessly"[23]

Sonia, Alice's younger daughter, born in 1900, had memories of being dressed up and given firm instructions by her nanny before being sent downstairs to the drawing room. " 'Be sure to curtesy to the king,' nanny would say,"[24] but Sonia was too nervous to raise her eyes above the gentleman's midriff, so sometimes ended up curt-sying to Sir Ernest Cassel by mistake.

Violet and Sonia were taught to call Bertie "Kingy." Fortunately, "Kingy" loved children and was very indulgent, allowing Sonia to play a fascinating game. "On his outstretched and immaculately trou-sered legs, she would place two pieces of bread, buttered side down. Bets of a penny each would be laid on which piece of bread would slide down more quickly; the winning piece always being more but-tery. "The excitement was intense while the contest was on."[25] Ber-tie must have been particularly indulgent toward Sonia to allow this contest to take place. He was noted for being obsessively well turned out, and could not bear to wear anything with a spill or a stain. On one occasion, when he suffered a splash of spinach to his starched white shirt, he was so angry that he plunged both hands into the serving dish and smeared the rest across his shirt, leaving the table with a laugh and going upstairs to change.[26]

At the height of her affair with Bertie, Alice was extraordinarily beautiful. "I can picture her as she lay back among her lace pillows, her beautiful chestnut hair unbound around her shoulders," recalled Sonia. "And I can see the flowers sent as oblations to this goddess, the orchids, the malmaisons, the lilies. Great beribboned baskets of them, delivered in horse-drawn vans by a coachman and atten-dant in livery. They would have been banked in tall, cut-glass vases about her bed."[27] Alice's bedroom was always full of the scent of flowers, and "a certain elusive smell, like fresh green sap, that came from herself."[28]

Violet remembered that "my mother began as an atmosphere . . . luminous, resplendent . . . she not only had a gift of happiness, but she excelled in making others happy. She resembled a Christmas tree laden with presents for everyone."[29]

Alice soon proved her worth as the royal mistress, taking a vital role in alleviating Bertie's boredom. Alice knew how to entertain

Bertie as few others did. So many of Bertie's hosts and hostesses dreaded "that terrible moment when the king would 'drum with irritable fingers upon the arm of his chair or upon the dinner table' . . . for the King, genial as he could be, was known to lose interest easily." But everything seemed easier when Alice was present, "therefore he wanted her constantly at hand, at every house party and every dinner, and to be alone with at the end of a tiring evening."[30]

As a mistress, Alice Keppel "took her post seriously and her wellbred, handsome husband raised no objections. Discreet, intelligent, and well informed, she became even more so as the king's intimate companion."[31] Raised in a family devoted to service, Alice was almost fulfilling a ceremonial function in her role as the king's mistress. Alix seemed to respect this, and treated Alice as a friend. Unlike Daisy Warwick, Alice was often invited to stay at Sandringham. Once she had become his mistress, Alice was entirely faithful to the king, despite the fact that "he was gross, he was still sensual, he was indeed still unfaithful all round."[32] Somehow, despite these characteristics, Bertie "remained extraordinarily endearing—a man of sensitivity, a man who could laugh at small joys and weep at his friends' sorrows, a man whom it was hard to know and not love."[33]

Chapter Twenty-one

GOLDEN YEARS

God save the king, and preserve Mrs Keppel from his rage!
—ALICE KEPPEL

Despite her beauty, charm, and diplomacy, Alice Keppel was not popular with everyone. The Duke of Norfolk, head of the country's leading Roman Catholic family, would not invite Alice to Arundel Castle, his stately home in Sussex, and she was banned from Welbeck Abbey, Nottinghamshire, home of the Duke of Portland.

The French took a different view. When Alice traveled to France with Bertie, she was treated like a queen. At Biarritz, on the Atlantic coast, Bertie holidayed at leisure with Alice as though they were an old married couple. Bertie and Alice repaired to Biarritz every Easter, while Alix traveled and the Hon. George went off to that job at Lipton's tea company so helpfully provided by Bertie.[1] The French, it is always said, "understand these things," and it was in Biarritz that the couple could truly be themselves, away from other royalty and politicians.

Alice and Bertie always made the journey to France separately. Alice traveled with her daughters, Violet and Sonia, their governess, Miss Draper, their nanny, and a succession of "studded wardrobe-trunks, standing up on end and high enough to stand in; hat-boxes, shoe boxes; rugs; travelling cushions and [Alice's] travelling jewel-case."[2]

It was here that Sonia witnessed an extraordinary transformation. From a small case, Alice unpacked a small pillow, a shapeless nightgown, and a mobcap. The nightgown went over Alice's beautiful body, and her luxuriant red hair was piled underneath the mobcap, before she covered her face in a thick layer of grease. After Sonia had been put to bed in the upper berth, Alice put on a black eye mask, took a sleeping pill, and "lay for dead till morning." Unable to sleep, Sonia would look down from her bunk at this strange apparition, "at Mama and in the weird blue ceiling light her white face its black-bandaged eyes looked ghastly."[3] The following morning, the attendant from the restaurant car would appear with steaming hot coffee and suppress a gasp of astonishment as the eye mask was removed and he would gaze into those sleepy turquoise eyes at close range.[4]

Bertie traveled to Biarritz under his nom de guerre as the "Earl of Chester," although his entourage, consisting of thirty servants and his white fox terrier Caesar were as clearly identifiable as his portly figure and imperial beard. Bertie requisitioned three private railway carriages, and three cars and chauffeurs were sent on ahead.[5] At Biarritz, Bertie checked into the Hôtel du Palais, while Alice and her daughters stayed at Sir Ernest Cassel's magnificent residence, the Villa Eugénie, built by Napoleon III.

The Biarritz vacation was a family holiday, but not one that made any concessions to Alice's family. Violet and Sonia found the trips stultifyingly dull, as did Sir Ernest Cassel's daughter, Maudie: "We are his servants quite as much as the housemaid or the butler."[6] The girls' nanny didn't care much for Biarritz, either. "Our clothes were hard put to it to compete with those of Sir Ernest's grandchildren, Edwina and Mary. And I suspect that Nannie put in several clandestine hours overtime washing and ironing, sensitively conscious of the inferior quality of the lace on our knickers."[7] The condition of her underwear had always been something of an issue for young Violet, who envied her young neighbors, the Alingtons, who always had "real" lace on their underclothes.[8]

After Bertie had spent a morning with his diplomatic bags, a necessity for the head of state even when he was *en vacances,* Alice would meet him at 1:15 every afternoon and they would walk along the promenade arm in arm before luncheon at the Hôtel du Palais. Luncheon was, like all Bertie's meals, an elaborate affair, and Alice, once curvaceous, slowly gained weight as she settled into their relationship. Indeed, so comical did the pair look together that Princess Alexandra once summoned one of her ladies-in-waiting over to the window and pointed, laughing helplessly, at Bertie and Alice sitting fatly side by side as they drove around the grounds of Sandringham in a little carriage.[9]

Afternoons were reserved for sightseeing, walking among the sand dunes, or going to the races at La Barre in the three claret-colored cars. They dined at 8:15 and visited the casino and spent the evening playing interminable games of bridge, which Bertie must never be allowed to lose,[10] until midnight. Bertie was not a good bridge player and Alice was often required to placate him.

Alice and Bertie were avid bridge players. The game was de rigueur at all events Bertie attended and he liked to play for high stakes. Several stories did the rounds about Mrs. Keppel's technique. On one occasion, when, as king, Bertie admonished Alice for fluffing her cards, Alice excused herself by replying that she could never tell a king from a knave. On another, when Alice was given a difficult hand to play, she commented, "God save the king, and preserve Mrs Keppel from his rage!"[11]

Easter Day brought a concession to the children in the form of elaborate eggs. Sonia recalled "lovely little jewelled Easter eggs given by Kingy and Sir Ernest, particularly an exquisitely midget one in royal blue enamel, embossed with a diamond 'E' and topped by a tiny crown in gold and rubies."[12]

Then came the picnic. Bertie had an inexplicable preference for picnicking at the side of the road, despite the fact that he had one of the most recognizable faces in Europe. The roads in and out of Biarritz were always busy, and nothing could have seemed more incongruous than the sight of the Prince of Wales tucking in, complete with tables, chairs, silver, and service by footmen, as the cars slowed down to watch.

This was an elaborate Edwardian picnic, with a table covered by a linen cloth, laid with the finest silver cutlery and porcelain plates, and every variety of food.[13] Caesar the fox terrier sat on Violet's knees, despite the fact that the little girl loathed the dog and complained that he smelled. "Always he was accompanied by his dog Caesar, who had a fine disregard for the villa's curtains and chair-legs, but a close regard for me."[14] After Biarritz, the couple traveled up to Paris. Bertie would stay in his usual suite at the Hotel Bristol, and Alice and her family at Sir Ernest Cassel's apartment in the Rue de Cirque. In Paris, Alice shopped at Worth.

Wrote Violet:

I have vivid memories of the first time I accompanied my mother to the dressmaker, where she was received like a goddess. Monsieur Jean [Worth] supervising her fitting in person, the vendeuses quite shamelessly forsaking their other clients to vie with each other in flattering epithets. Il y avait de quoi. My mother had everything that could most appeal to them, lovely, vivacious, feted, fashionable, with a kind word for each of the anonymous old crones who had been for years in the establishment. . . .[15]

Alice also accompanied Bertie to his favorite restaurants, under constant surveillance from his detectives. This was before the days of the Royal Protection Squad, a crack group of police officers specifically detailed to take care of the royals. Instead, Bertie was always accompanied by his royal equerry and a detective, to keep him under surveillance at all times. Alice was always concerned about

Bertie's security. It made her nervous that, as they strolled arm in arm along the boulevards of Paris, Bertie would not hesitate to stop and take the time of day with anyone who approached him. Nervously, Alice hovered close by, and could not wait to get him back to the safety of his suite at the Hotel Bristol. Alice's fears were not without foundation. On April 4, 1900, Bertie and Princess Alix arrived in Brussels en route to Copenhagen. Their train was just beginning to pull out of the Gard du Nord station when a man fired a pistol at Bertie through their open carriage window. Bertie remained unruffled, commenting merely that his would-be assassin was a poor fool. The gunman, a Belgian youth named Jean-Baptiste Sipido, was protesting against the Boer War.[16] Bertie telegrammed Alice to say, "I don't think there was a bullet in it. He was at once seized."[17]

Bertie's security remained Alice's primary concern. On one occasion, they were lunching in a restaurant at Saint-Cloud. Tables had been spread outside in the garden, under the trees. Bertie, Alice, a secretary from the British Embassy, and a handful of French aristocrats were seated at a table in a prominent position. As the lunch progressed, Alice became increasingly worried about a man at a table nearby who had, she claimed, a "criminal face."[18] As she glanced around, Alice noted that the garden was a real security risk: there were gaps in the wall through which an assailant, or even a group of assailants, might launch themselves. Sir Frederick Ponsonby, Bertie's private secretary, reassured Alice, telling her that Bertie had plenty of police protection nearby. But Alice continued to worry, and insisted on speaking to the chief of police, Monsieur Lepine, asking him to check the police presence. With a broad smile, Monsieur Lepine confirmed that all the diners at the nearby tables were in fact police officers and their wives—including the individual with the "criminal face!"[19]

Alice's role of chief mistress also included a diplomatic function, with Alice acting as informal liaison officer. Rather than have elaborate meetings to discuss policy and diplomatic issues where he received his ministers in a royal audience, Bertie preferred to turn these encounters into social occasions. Here he could rely on his close friends and advisers such as Admiral Lord Fisher, Sir Charles Harding, Sir Ernest Cassel, Sir Francis Knollys, and Ponsonby—alongside Alice Keppel. "Alice evolved as the perfect amateur diplomat for the king; her circumspection and discretion came naturally to her and she was completely loyal to the king . . . she was a consummate liaison officer."[20]

Skilled at keeping the conversation flowing while Bertie took in information by listening rather than reading reports, Alice kept the talk flowing so that Bertie could pick up the intelligence he needed. Royal biographer Raymond Lamont-Brown gives us one particular example. In 1907, Kaiser William II visited Highcliffe Castle, home of Major-General Edward Stuart-Wortley. Bertie did not attend this dinner, but Alice came over for dinner from Crichel Down with a party after the kaiser had enjoyed a day's shooting. Alice was placed next to the kaiser at dinner, despite the fact that he had publicly denounced Bertie's relationship with Alice, or "Favorita" as he referred to her. Alice was, of course, more than capable of rising to the challenge and attempted to defuse the situation rather than creating the tense atmosphere that might have been expected. The Austro-Hungarian diplomat Count Albert von Mensdorff Pouilly-Dietrichstein later wrote in his journal: "It was amusing to see how, at table, in disregard of all rules of precedence, the *Favorita* was seated next to the Kaiser, so she might have the opportunity of talking to him. I would like to know what sort of report she sent back to Sandringham."[21]

Lord Hardinge of Penshurst, permanent undersecretary at the Foreign Office, had a high opinion of Alice's tact, loyalty, and discretion:[22]

I would like here to pay a tribute to her wonderful discretion, and to the excellent influence which she always exercised upon the King. She never utilised her knowledge to her own advantage, or that of her friends; and I never heard her repeat an unkind word of anybody. There were

one or two occasions when the King was in disagreement with the For-
eign Office and I was able, through her, to advise the King with a view
to the policy of the Government being accepted. She was very loyal to the
King and patriotic at the same time. It would have been difficult to find
any other lady who would have filled the part of friend to King Edward
with the same loyalty and discretion.[23]

If Bertie had adopted a "sofa-style" form of government, Alice's advice and support were indispensable for its smooth running. The supreme example of Alice's ability to drop a word or two in Bertie's ear when it mattered was the potential crisis of 1908 when Henry Campbell-Bannerman resigned as prime minister on health grounds and Herbert Asquith was elected as his replacement. Bertie and Alice were on their annual jaunt in Biarritz when the news was announced. Constitutionally, Bertie was required in London to swear in the new premier and attend a Privy Council meeting. But Bertie, who had no intention of breaking off his vacation with Alice, point-blank refused to return. This resulted in a predictable outcry in the press before Alice defused the situation with the skill of a born spin doctor by suggesting that Asquith travel out to Biarritz instead. Asquith arrived in Biarritz on May 7, 1908, and went straight to the Hôtel du Palais, where Alice was waiting for him. She must have briefed Asquith well, for his appointment was confirmed with the minimum of fuss: "I presented [the King] with a written resignation of the office of Chancellor of the Exchequer; and then he said, 'I appoint you Prime Minister and First Lord of the Treasury,' whereupon I knelt down and kissed his hand. *Voila tout!*"[24] Then Bertie invited Asquith to breakfast and they spent the next hour running through the details of the new cabinet.

The following day, Asquith thanked Alice for her support. "I must send you a line of most sincere thanks for your kind words and wise counsels, which I shall treasure and (I hope) profit by."[25]

As well as being constantly anxious over Bertie's security, and keeping a weather eye out for assassins, Alice worried about Bertie's health. This was not without foundation. By the age of sixty, Bertie was morbidly obese. At five feet six inches in height, he was not tall, but weighed over 225 pounds with a waist measurement of forty-six inches. Always a keen trencherman, Bertie had become a compulsive eater, and Princess Alix was horrified by his voracious appetite. Even Alice Keppel was powerless when it came to suggesting that Bertie limit his food intake. And, although never a drunk, Bertie had started to drink heavily during the day, tippling champagne, Chablis, claret, and brandy alongside a succession of heavy meals.[26]

A heavy smoker, Bertie suffered from bronchitis and emphysema, the result of a lifetime's chain-smoking Royal Derbies, Laurens, and Dembergi's Egyptian cigarettes and Henry Clay Tsars and Corona y Coronas cigars.[27] Recurrent coughing fits were treated with a throat spray to soothe symptoms that Bertie, and his family, secretly suspected were those of cancer. In keeping with the fashion of the time, Bertie traveled to Marienbad every year for the "cure." This was the nineteenth-century equivalent of a spa break, an austere regime of diet, exercise, and drinking and bathing in the waters that were believed to have curative powers. For the more stubborn cases, there were enemas and a mild form of electric shock treatment, which was recommended for impotence. Alice never accompanied Bertie to Marienbad. While Biarritz was "safe," a town where the couple were unlikely to run into major royalty, Marienbad was popular with the key players of the European royal families and Alice's presence would be an embarrassment.

But even trips to Marienbad were not sufficient to tackle Bertie's dreadful combination of obesity, chronic ill health, and lack of exercise, exacerbated by a knee injury sustained when Bertie fell downstairs at Baron Rothschild's house, Waddesdon Manor in Buckinghamshire. According to Brookie, Daisy Warwick's husband, it appeared that Bertie had slipped on the spiral staircase. Brookie hurried inside, and "found the Prince where the butler had left him, sitting on a step of the main circular staircase. He smiled reassuringly at me, although I could see at a glance that he must be in great pain, and said: 'I fear I have broken something in my leg; my foot slipped, and as I fell I heard a bone crack.' Two servants came up at that moment bearing a long invalid chair, and fearing from what the Prince had said that he had split or broken his knee-cap, I tied his leg straight out onto one of the parallel carrying poles. Then the local doctor arrived, and the Prince was allowed to sit on a sofa with his leg down, to have his breakfast before leaving. I have always thought that but for the severe strain involved by his straightened leg the subsequent illness would not have been so long or so difficult—but I will not blame the doctor. The Prince was ever the kindliest of men, and his great anxiety was to reassure Baron Ferdinand, who was too grieved to think he should have met with a serious accident under his roof."[28]

To make matters worse, the chair broke as Bertie was being carried to his train, and he was unceremoniously dropped on the passenger bridge. Bertie's knee never recovered from this incident. Alice Keppel was particularly concerned about the knee, and wrote to Bertie's close friend, Portuguese diplomat the Marques de Soveral, urging him to get medical attention. Bertie "writes that it is very painful and stiff and that massage does it no good or rather harm as there is a slight 'effusion' on it. This I know ought to be seen at once, for if he gets water on the knee this might mean a stiff knee for life . . . do try what you can with your famous tact and, of course, don't tell anyone *I* wrote to you. . . ."[29]

In 1901, as Queen Victoria lay on her deathbed, Bertie was preparing to leave for Osborne to be with the dying queen. Alix was away in Sandringham, and Alice at home with the Hon. George. On Queen Victoria's last night on earth, it seems that the only person Bertie wanted to see was Agnes Keyser. Bertie dined alone with

Agnes at 17 Grosvenor Crescent, and sat by the fire telling her that he felt unworthy to succeed the queen; then he left at dawn, taking a special train to the Isle of Wight.[30]

Queen Victoria finally passed away at 6:30 P.M. on January 22, 1901, "surrounded by her children and grandchildren,"[31] and Bertie, at long last, became king. Court rumors circulated that, as soon as the queen was dead, Alix knelt and kissed her husband's hand and addressed him as "Sire!"[32] But Bertie, overwhelmed with loss, could only say: "It has come too late."[33] Alice Keppel was at home with her husband when she heard the news. They were not invited to the funeral.

Following Bertie's accession to the throne, there was consternation among his lady friends that they might be dropped, just as Prince Hal had dropped Falstaff when he became Henry V. "When he succeeded to the throne he wrote to diverse of these ladies to say that though called to the other serious duties he hoped still to see them from time to time."[34] One apparent victim of Bertie's accession was the actress Réjane, who had been Bertie's mistress briefly in the early '90s. In Denmark, some weeks after his succession, Bertie had walked right past her without acknowledging her. But the following day, Réjane received a diamond clip with a note that read: "With apologies from the King of England who is no longer the Prince of Wales."[35]

Alice Keppel, as Bertie's mistress in chief, had most to fear at this time, and became the object of snide comments from the young Winston Churchill. Writing to his mother, Jennie, and speculating as to her role in the new administration, Churchill made some disparaging comments about Bertie's future court and sneeringly inquired whether "the Keppel" would be appointed 1st Lady of the Bedchamber.[36] The Keppel retained her position and would be one of the most conspicuous guests at the coronation.

The coronation of King Edward VII had been scheduled for June 26, 1902. Bertie, although happy, was unwell. He had attended the spring race meetings, particularly enjoying the Coronation Derby at Epsom, but the weather was cold and wet, and Bertie caught a chill. Despite this, Bertie refused any requests to rest and attended a huge luncheon party for the diplomats visiting London for the coronation, and then went on to the coronation rehearsal at Westminster Abbey. At this point, Bertie was suddenly struck down with intense abdominal pain and an alarmingly distended belly. Bertie's physicians, suspecting appendicitis, knew that Bertie required an operation immediately. Sir Frederick Treves, his surgeon, examined the king and found a hard swelling in his abdomen. Treves informed the royal physicians, Francis Laking and Sir Thomas Barlow, that the king was in grave danger. When Bertie asked what would happen if he refused the operation, he was told in no uncertain terms that he would die. Bertie refused to cancel the coronation, saying: "I will go to the Abbey, even if it kills me."[37] Laking sternly replied that if the king insisted on going to the Abbey, it *would* kill him. Eventually, he was persuaded that to refuse the operation really would be letting his subjects down. The coronation was canceled and the gala dinner for five hundred, prepared by the celebrity chef César Ritz, had to be distributed among the London poor, who feasted on jellied strawberries and snipe stuffed with pâté de foie gras. Monsieur Ritz, when he learned of this, collapsed with a seizure.[38]

As wild rumors and speculation circulated that the king was dying of cancer and would not live to see his own coronation, a bulletin, signed by Bertie's doctors, was duly posted on the railings of Buckingham Palace: "The King is undergoing a surgical operation. The King is suffering from perityphilitis. His condition on Saturday was so satisfactory that it was hoped that with care His Majesty would be able to go through the Coronation ceremony. On Monday evening a recrudescence became manifest, rendering a surgical operation today."[39]

Rather to the dismay of Treves, Alix insisted on remaining at her husband's side for the operation. Given her interest in nursing, this was perhaps understandable, but as a laywoman she was clearly unprepared for the grisly reality of surgery. "Indeed, she helped to hold [Bertie] struggling during the administration of chloroform."[40] Treves later wrote: "I was anxious to prepare for the operation but did not like to take off my coat, tuck up my sleeves, and put on an apron whilst the Queen was present."[41] When Treves asked Alix to leave, she released her hold on the unconscious Bertie and quietly walked out.

Treves operated on the king and found a large abscess on his appendix, which when drained, contained over a pint of pus. Bertie would have died of blood poisoning had it not been removed. It was not necessary to remove his appendix. Before the operation, Bertie wrote a letter to Alice Keppel in which he said that "if he were dying, he felt sure that those about him would allow her to come to him."[42]

Bertie's first words on coming around from the operation were: "Where's George?" This is commonly supposed to be a reference to his son, but the inquiry could just as easily have been Bertie calling for his faithful companion, his "dear Mrs George."

The coronation finally took place six weeks later on August 9, 1902. Daisy, Countess of Warwick, attended the coronation in her own right, as a peeress, rolling up to Westminster Abbey in the old family coach.[43] According to Lord Rosebery, Daisy was second only to Queen Alexandra for "stately grace and absolute beauty."[44] In a break from tradition, Bertie invited many of his former mistresses to the coronation.

Alix, now queen at last, outshone them all in a "dress of golden Indian gauze, glittering in state jewels, with a sceptre in either hand, walking slowly up Westminster Abbey, her fantastically long violet-velvet train behind her, a canopy held over her head by four tall duchesses."[45]

Alix accepted the coronation ceremonies reverently and prayed throughout the ceremony; and she "prayed devoutly as the oil was placed on her brow."[46] Four tall peeresses, Daisy's sister Millie Sutherland among them, placed the crown on Alix's head. As soon as Alix had been crowned, there was a remarkable scene: all the peeresses, in one graceful movement, placed their coronets on their own heads. "Their white arms arching over their heads," Bertie later declared, had resembled "a scene from a beautiful ballet."[47] As she took her place alongside the newly crowned King Edward VII, did Alix cast a swift glance at her rivals in the king's loose box? There was no need to: Alix must have known that she had won all around.

Chapter Twenty-two

FAMOUS LAST WORDS

Because Kingy was such a wonderful man.
—THE HON. GEORGE KEPPEL, HUSBAND OF ALICE

A few days before setting off on his annual jaunt to Biarritz with Alice Keppel on March 6, 1910, Bertie quarreled with Alix, who regarded him as too ill to travel. Once at Biarritz, Bertie caught a chill and was confined to his suite at the Hôtel du Palais. Alice, increasingly concerned about Bertie's health, wrote to the Marques de Soveral, saying, "the King's cold is so bad that he can't dine out, but he wants us all to dine with him at 8.15 at the Palais, SO BE THERE. I am quite worried *entre nous* and have sent for the nurse."[1] Alice's use of capitals, unusual for her, indicates just how worried she must have been.

After a week or so, Bertie's condition improved and he was able to get out and about, but Alix was adamant that Bertie must leave "that horrid Biarritz" as soon as possible and join her on the new royal yacht, the *Alexandra*.[2] Bertie refused, and Alix went without him to stay with her brother, King George of the Hellenes, in Corfu.

Bertie's refusal to return to England resulted in his longest stay in Biarritz, for seven weeks, and the longest period of continuous time that he had spent with Alice by his side. Perhaps he knew that the end was in sight. On his last day in the resort, Bertie went out onto his balcony and stood gazing across the promenade to the sea, and said: "I shall be sorry to leave Biarritz. Perhaps for good."[3]

On the way back to England, Bertie caught another chill and developed bronchitis. Despite this, Bertie worked like a horse on his royal duties and social obligations, so much so that by the end of April Alice was sending him home early from a dinner, because he looked so unwell, breathless, coughing, and gray.[4] The queen was sent for, and returned from Corfu to be horrified by Bertie's appearance. By the following morning, May 6, Bertie was worse, but he insisted on getting up, getting dressed, and conducting business as usual. Sir Ernest Cassel arrived at lunchtime, bringing an envelope containing £10,000 (over £1.6m) in banknotes, a financial settlement for Alice, perhaps.[5] Bertie must, by now, have understood that he was dying, and he needed to provide for Alice's future. Despite a series of heart attacks in the afternoon, Bertie refused to go to bed and told the queen and his doctors that he intended to keep on working until the end. Bertie's mood improved slightly later in the afternoon, when he was told that his horse, Witch of the Air, had won the 4:15 at Kempton Park.[6] Bertie's official famous last words were: "I am so glad."[7]

There is some dispute as to how Bertie passed his last night on earth. Some biographers have suggested that Alix sent for Alice Keppel when she knew that Bertie was dying. While it is tempting to think that the long-suffering, generous Alix was determined to do the right thing and offer Alice her chance to say farewell, other accounts, from Viscount Esher and Wilfrid Scawen Blunt, present a different version of events. According to Bertie's doctor, Sir Francis Laking, an increasingly frantic Alice Keppel had been calling at Buckingham Palace throughout the day, and had sent Alix the letter Bertie had written to her at the time of his appendix operation, which said that "if he were dying, he felt sure that those about him would allow her to come to him."[8] Alix had no option but to instruct Sir Francis Knollys to send for Alice.

According to Alice, she was received by the queen in tears, who proceeded to sob on her shoulder and tell Alice not to worry, that the royal family would take care of her.[9] Sir Francis Laking's memory of the scene was somewhat different.

Alice arrived, distraught with grief, and was ushered into the royal presence, where she curtsied to Queen Alexandra and Princess Victoria and was led to sit down beside Bertie. Bertie was drifting in and out of consciousness by this time, and kept toppling forward in his chair. Indeed, it is unlikely that he realized who Alice was. The envelope of cash still sat beside him, untouched. According to Sir Francis Laking, Bertie took her hand, and told Alice not to cry, before calling out to Alix and asking her to join them. "You must kiss her," he insisted to his wife. "You must kiss Alice."[10] This must have been a horrific request for Alix, but she complied and offered her cheek to Alice. Again, this peculiar request may have been the result of Bertie's incoherence; perhaps he mistook Alice for a family member, and that is why he did not hand over the money.

By this time, according to Sir Francis Laking, Bertie's mind had begun to wander. Forgetting that he was in the presence of the queen, Bertie stuttered: "I want to pee."[11]

Mercifully, Alix was so deaf that she didn't catch the meaning of his request. "What was that?" she asked Sir Francis. "He is asking for a pencil, Ma'am," replied Laking, with presence of mind.[12] As Bertie passed into unconsciousness again, and Alice had become hysterical, Alix whispered to Laking: "Get that woman away."[13]

This was not an easy task. Alice refused to leave Bertie's side, until Laking told her sternly that the king had asked to be left alone with Alix. Led out of the room by Princess Victoria, Alice gave herself up to grief and shrieked, at the top of her voice, so that all the pages and footmen in the passage outside could hear, "I never did any harm, there was nothing wrong between us. What is to become of me?"[14] Despite Princess Victoria's valiant efforts to calm her down, Alice was carried into Sir Edward Ponsonby's room in "a wild fit of hysterics," where she remained for several hours.[15]

It was, according to Lord Esher, a close friend of Bertie's,[16] "a painful and rather theatrical exhibition, and ought never to have happened."[17]

Sir Francis Knollys, when he discovered the envelope of money, returned it to Sir Ernest Cassel, who duly sent it back, saying that the cash represented "interest I gave to the King in financial matters I am undertaking."[18]

Bertie died just before midnight. Afterward, "in a terrible state of despair," Alix told Francis Laking:

> *I would not have kissed her, if he had not bade me. But I would have done anything he asked of me. Twelve years ago, when I was so angry about Lady Warwick, and the King expostulated with me and said I should get him into the divorce court, I told him once for all that he might have all the women he wished, and I would not say a word; and I have done everything since that he desired me to do about them. He was the whole of my life and, now he is dead, nothing matters.*[19]

Had the women been able to weep together and share their grief, Alice would have agreed with Alix that now that Bertie was dead, "nothing matters." However, Alice had to ensure her own survival. For the first time, the knowledge that she was merely a mistress, and not a queen, hit home and the message was hard to take.

After she left Buckingham Palace for the last time, Alice did not go back to 16 Portman Square. Indeed, she never went home again. Crowds had already gathered outside the house and she knew that once the king was dead, she and her family would be subjected to intense scrutiny. Instead, Alice went to stay with her friends Arthur and Venetia James in their house in Grafton Street. The sudden exit from Portman Square occasioned some comment among gossips and royal watchers. Was Alice bankrupt? they asked. Had she fled from her creditors? This rumor at least was unfounded. Alice was still wealthy.

The following morning, Violet and Sonia woke to the news that Kingy had died. They were dressed in mourning, including underwear threaded with black ribbon, and escorted to Venetia James's house, but they were not allowed to go straight to their mother. The next day, when Sonia and Violet were eventually ushered into Alice's bedroom, she seemed almost like a stranger to them: "We went up to her bed and she turned and looked at us blankly, and without recognition, and rather resentfully, as though we were unwelcome intruders."[20]

Alice came to her senses in a day or so, and with her old resilience set off to Marlborough House to sign the book of condolence opened in Bertie's memory. To Alice's horror, she discovered that the new King George, and his wife, Queen Mary, had banned her from signing the book and she was refused admission. But instead of admitting defeat, even as she reeled away from Marlborough House, the scene of her past triumphs, Alice was already at work on her side of the story. Over the coming days, she circulated her version of events, in which Queen Alexandra sobbed on her shoulder and vowed to look after her. She even set about inviting small groups of former "friends" to dine with her, denying of course that there was anything so inappropriate as a dinner party during this period of heavy mourning, but was instead merely the opportunity for friends to talk about the past.[21] Alice even asked if she could take on Caesar, Bertie's dog. But this request, too, was denied, even though Alix had hated the fox terrier.[22] Another snub came from the kaiser; when Alice wrote asking to meet him when he arrived in London for Bertie's funeral, he refused to see her. That diplomatic breakthrough when Alice had sat next to him at dinner might just as well have never happened.[23]

As a member of the Norfolk Yeomanry, the Hon. George Keppel should have played an important part in the funeral parade, but he was not invited. It had obviously been decided that having the late king's mistress's husband in the funeral cortege would be too embarrassing.

There was to be no repeat of the notorious "loose box" at Bertie's funeral. Alice was now outside the royal circle. But she did at least receive an invitation, and arrived, dressed in full mourning, as one observer snidely remarked (as though Alice would have worn anything else),[24] slipping in discreetly by a side door.

At Bertie's funeral service, Caesar the fox terrier was among the mourners. Young Vita Sackville-West attended, with her father, and her diary entry captured the pathos of the scene: "Everyone cried when they saw the King's little dog following the coffin."[25]

Little Sonia Keppel, distressed by her mother's strange behavior, the death of Kingy, and moving house at short notice, burst into tears and wept in her father's arms. "Why," she asked George Keppel, "why does it matter so much, Kingy dying?"[26]

"Because Kingy was such a wonderful man," replied the Hon. George. "Poor little girl. It must have been very frightening for you. And for all of us, for that matter. Nothing will ever be quite the same again."[27]

AFTERTHOUGHTS

In the second volume of Daisy's memoirs, *Afterthoughts,* she recalled Lillie Langtry in later life, during World War I:

> Lady de Bathe was certainly one of the loveliest creatures I have ever seen. I have often remembered a conversation that we had as we strolled through the gardens at Easton one summer evening during the War.
>
> "Whatever happens, I do not intend to grow old!" exclaimed Lily [sic] Langtry suddenly, and with these words I saw a flash of her beautiful eyes. "Why shouldn't beauty vanquish time?"
>
> I forget what I answered, for I was busy analyzing what she had said. I stole a glance at her, and certainly Time's ravages, although perceptible to the discerning eye of one who had known her at the zenith of her beauty, were disguised with consummate artistry, while her figure was still lovely.
>
> But it came to me then that there was tragedy in the life of this woman, whose beauty had once been world-famous, for she had found no time in the intervals of pursuing pleasure to secure contentment for the evening of her day. Now that she saw the evening approach, Lily

[sic] Langtry could only protest that it was not evening at all, but just the prolongation of a day that was, in truth, already dead. . . . The Jersey Lily clung to her beauty even when it was passing . . . the world of easy triumphs was slipping from her grasp.[1]

Daisy went on to conclude that she felt Lillie was living in the past, while she, Daisy, preferred to live in the future. "I have found that life becomes increasingly interesting the more I identify myself with worth-while causes, and the less I think about personal matters and my own age."[2]

Daisy's worthwhile causes included standing for the parliamentary seat of Warwick and Leamington Spa as the Labour party candidate in 1929, against the charming and debonair young Anthony Eden, rescuing circus ponies, and adopting a pet monkey, which set fire to Easton Lodge, burning a substantial part of the mansion to the ground. Faced with bankruptcy, Daisy even attempted to blackmail King George V with a cache of letters from Bertie. When this failed, Daisy brought out two volumes of memoirs instead, *Life's Ebb and Flow* and *Afterthoughts*. Touted as deeply shocking, these books instead provide a wealth of insight into the privileged life of the Marlborough House set and the British upper classes before World War I. Eccentric and life-affirming to the end, Daisy had a huge circle of friends, including H. G. Wells and Charlie Chaplin. Daisy died in 1936, aged seventy-eight.

In *Afterthoughts*, Daisy wrote: "As I strolled along the garden paths with the Jersey Lily I was deeply sorry for her, realising as I did that she had no resources within herself and was living on memories— for memories do not carry one forward, and inevitably one reaches a period when one has exhausted them."[3]

In fairness to Lillie, she had a lot to remember. Lillie achieved great fame as a celebrity, rather than an actress, became a successful racehorse owner, and in 1907 attained the respectability she craved when her young husband, Hugo de Bathe, succeeded to the title of baronet, but their marriage was a troubled one and the couple lived apart, Lillie in Monaco and Hugo in Venice.

There exists an extraordinary photograph of Lillie in her final years, taking a stroll after lunch in Monte Carlo; elegant Mediterranean palms are visible in the background. Imperious in a cloche hat and fur coat, Lillie is flanked by Sir Walter de Frece and his wife, "Lady de Frece." In a previous incarnation, Lady de Frece was music hall star Vesta Tilley. In this early example of a "pap" shot, Sir Walter, in tweeds and homberg, is staring warily down the camera and grasping his walking stick as though about to lash out at the photographer. It is a snapshot of Britain's vanished stage aristocracy: Lillie, the mistress of the Prince of Wales, now married into the peerage; Vesta, the male impersonator who once twirled a top hat and cane in white tie and tails while claiming to be "Burlington Bertie,"[4] the epitome of the idle aristocrat, now immaculate in a fur-trimmed coat, eyes demurely downcast. None of these people want to be in the photograph. A curious state of affairs for two women who once courted fame.

Daisy was right about the tragedy. Before Lillie married Hugo in 1899, she had a violent and unhappy relationship with George Alexander Baird, an amateur jockey and boxer known as "the Squire."[5] A violent alcoholic, the Squire would beat Lillie up one day and shower her with diamonds the next. The Squire would doubtless have killed Lillie, but in 1893 he was found dead in his New Orleans hotel room following a massive binge. Lillie became estranged from her daughter, Jeanne-Marie, over the vexed issues of Jeanne-Marie's paternity, although Lillie had the comfort of seeing Jeanne-Marie marry into the peerage.

Lillie retired to Monte Carlo, a sad and bitter woman who lived alone apart from her devoted maid, Mathilde Peat. "I have lost my daughter, the only thing that is dear to me, my life is sad indeed,"[6] Lillie told one old friend; an employee from Lillie's Monte Carlo villa recalled that Lillie cried herself to sleep every night. Lillie died of complications following bronchitis in 1929.

As for Ned Langtry, his story was never going to end happily. While Lillie's star ascended and she became a household name, Ned succumbed to alcoholism. He was occasionally to be found outside theaters where Lillie was playing, desperate to see her. One night, Ned was picked up in Liverpool, after stumbling deliriously off the Belfast ferry. Drunk and confused, possibly after a head injury, he was taken to Chester Asylum, where he died. Nobody believed his claims to be the husband of Lillie Langtry.[7]

After the death of Bertie, Alice Keppel exploited her fame as the late king's mistress, although the family of King George V regarded her as an embarrassment. In later years, Alice became something of a parody of herself, and inspired a memorable portrait in Virginia Woolf's diary for March 10, 1932: "I had lunched with Raymond [Mortimer, the critic] to meet Mrs Keppel; a swarthy thick set raddled direct—'My dear', she calls one—old grasper: whose fists had been in the moneybags these 50 years: And she has a flat in the Ritz."[8] Alice also had a Rolls-Royce waiting. But under the magnificent furs and great pearls, Alice's dress was shabby. On one level, Woolf rather admired Alice's directness and humor, but she was dismayed to learn that Alice was off to Berlin to hear Hitler speak.

Alice Keppel's older daughter, Violet, who grew up to be self-centered and attention-seeking, claimed that she was Bertie's daughter until the day she died. There was no evidence for this. Violet Keppel was born in 1894, four years before Alice was introduced to Bertie, and there was no suggestion they had met before that time. It is possible, however, that Sonia was the daughter of Alice and Bertie. Born in 1900, Sonia did have a likeness to Bertie, and later wrote *Edwardian Daughter,* in which she did nothing to dispel this rumor, as both sisters lived on in the shadow of their increasingly eccentric and difficult mother. Sonia married Henry Cubitt and their granddaughter, Camilla, was for many years the mistress of Charles, the current Prince of Wales. Charles and Camilla were married in 2005.

The image of Daisy and Lillie, all rivalry behind them, walking arm in arm in the gardens of Easton Lodge is a compelling one. Those gardens are a ruin now, despite the best efforts of volunteers, but on a warm, quiet day in the summer, it is possible to roam alone through what remains of Easton Lodge and catch a glimpse of times past: the Edwardian long golden afternoon, an echo of laughter, a splash of sunlight through flickering leaves, the scent of Eau de Portugal cologne, the faint whiff of cigar smoke, a stifled giggle. If one is to catch something of Bertie's spirit, it is here, in the ruins of Daisy's beautiful gardens.

NOTES

INTRODUCTION

1. Theo Aronson, *The King in Love: Lillie Langtry, Daisy Warwick, Alice Keppel and Others* (New York: Harper and Row, 1988), p. 219.
2. Ibid.
3. Virginia Cowles, *Gay Monarch: The Life and Pleasures of Edward VII* (London: Harper, 1956), p 214.
4. Christopher Hibbert, *Edward VII: A Portrait* (London: Allen Lane, 1976), p. 41.
5. Anita Leslie, *Edwardians in Love* (London: Hutchinson, 1972), p. 296.
6. Anita Leslie, *The Marlborough House Set* (New York: Doubleday, 1973), p. 252.
7. Ibid.
8. John Pearson, *Edward the Rake: An Unwholesome Biography of Edward VII* (New York: Harcourt Brace Jovanovich, 1975), p. 131.
9. Leslie, *Edwardians in Love,* p. 294.
10. Anne Sebba, *Jennie Churchill: Winston's American Mother* (London: John Murray, 2007), p. 96.
11. https://maggiemcneill.wordpress.com/2014/05/08/lillie-langtry/.
12. Leslie, *Edwardians in Love,* p. 123.
13. Aronson, *The King in Love,* p. 58.
14. Lillie Langtry, *The Days I Knew* (North Hollywood, Calif.: Panoply Publications, 2005), p. 99.
15. Aronson, *The King in Love,* p. 60.
16. Leslie, *Edwardians in Love,* p. 153.

1. A YOUTHFUL INDISCRETION

1. Christopher Hibbert, *Edward VII: A Portrait* (London: Allen Lane, 1976), p. 40.
2. Ibid.
3. Ibid.
4. The late Lord Litchfield's comment on the impact of military school, circa 1982.
5. Ibid.
6. Ibid.
7. Ibid., p. 41.
8. Jane Ridley, *Bertie: A Life of Edward VII* (London: Vintage, 2003), p. 54.
9. Allen Andrews, *The Follies of King Edward VII* (London: Lexington, 1975), p. 75.
10. Giles St. Aubyn, *Edward VII: Prince and King* (London: Collins, 1979), p. 63.
11. Ibid.
12. Ibid.
13. Ibid.
14. Ibid., p. 64.
15. Ibid.
16. Ibid.
17. Ibid.
18. Ibid.
19. Ibid.
20. Ibid., p. 65.
21. Ibid., p. 66.
22. Ibid.
23. Ibid.
24. Ibid.
25. Ibid.
26. Hibbert, *op. cit.*, p. 46.
27. St. Aubyn, *op. cit.*, p. 67.
28. Andrews, *op. cit.*, p. 76.
29. Ibid.
30. Ibid.
31. Ridley, *op. cit.*, p. 57.
32. Hibbert, *op. cit.*, p. 47.
33. Ibid.
34. Ibid., p. 48.
35. Ibid.
36. Ibid., p. 47.
37. Ibid., p. 49.
38. Ibid.
39. Ibid.
40. Ibid.

41. Ibid., p. 50.
42. Ibid.

2. A ROYAL WEDDING

1. Jane Ridley, *Bertie: A Life of Edward VII* (London: Vintage, 2003), p. 73.
2. Denis Judd, *Edward VII: A Pictorial Biography* (London: Macdonald and Jane's, 1975), p. 29.
3. http://www.express.co.uk/news/royal/382032/The-first-Queen-of-Hearts.
4. Ibid.
5. http://www.guildhallhistoricalassociation.org.uk/docs/TheWeddingofthePrince ofWales.pdf.
6. Ibid.
7. Christopher Hibbert, *Edward VII: A Portrait* (London: Allen Lane, 1976), p. 60.
8. Ibid., pp. 60–61.
9. Ibid., p. 60.
10. http://www.guildhallhistoricalassociation.org.uk/docs/TheWeddingofthePrince ofWales.pdf.
11. Hibbert, *op. cit.,* p. 61.
12. Ibid.
13. Ibid.
14. Allen Andrews, *The Follies of King Edward VII* (London: Lexington, 1975), p. 83.
15. Hibbert, *op. cit.,* pp. 61–62.
16. Ibid., p. 62.
17. Ibid.
18. Ibid.
19. Ibid.
20. Ibid., p. 63.
21. Ibid.
22. Ibid.
23. Ibid.
24. Ibid., p. 64.
25. Ibid.
26. Ibid.
27. Ibid.

3. "GAY PAREE AND LONDON LOWLIFE"

1. Giles St. Aubyn, *Edward VII: Prince and King* (London: Collins, 1979), p. 83.
2. Anita Leslie, *Edwardians in Love* (London: Hutchison, 1972), p. 281.
3. Denis Judd, *Edward VII: A Pictorial Biography* (London: Macdonald and Jane's, 1975), p. 30.
4. Ibid.
5. Leslie, *op. cit.,* p. 282.

6. Judd, *op. cit.,* p. 30.

7. Leslie, *op. cit.,* p. 282.

8. Ernest Dudley, *The Gilded Lily* (London: Odhams Press, 1958), p. 43.

9. Cowles, Virginia, *Gay Monarch: The Life and Pleasures of Edward VII* (London: Harper, 1956), p. 214.

10. Dudley, *op. cit.,* p. 43.

11. Ibid.

12. John Pearson, *Edward the Rake: An Unwholesome Biography of Edward VII* (New York: Harcourt Brace Jovanovich 1975), p. 50.

13. Christopher Hibbert, *Edward VII: A Portrait* (London: Allen Lane, 1976), p. 99.

14. Pearson, *op. cit.,* p. 52.

15. Ibid.

16. Ibid.

17. Ibid.

18. Ibid., pp. 59–60.

19. Diana Souhami, *Mrs Keppel and Her Daughter* (New York: St. Martin's Press, 1996), p. 34.

20. Jane Ridley, *Bertie: A Life of Edward VII* (London: Vintage, 2003), p. 31.

21. Pearson, *op. cit.,* p. 44.

22. Ibid.

23. Allen Andrews, *The Follies of King Edward VII* (London: Lexington, 1975), p. 98.

24. Ibid., p. 92.

25. Ibid., p. 98.

26. Ibid., p. 101.

27. Joanna Richardson, *The Courtesans* (New Jersey: Castle Books, 2004), p. 3.

28. Katie Hickman, *Courtesans* (London: Harper Perennial, 2003), p. 234.

29. Ibid., p. 278.

30. James Brough, *The Prince and the Lily* (London: Coronet, 1975), p. 146.

31. Hickman, *op. cit.,* p. 281.

32. Ibid., p. 303.

33. Ridley, *op. cit.,* p. 166.

34. Richardson, *op. cit.,* pp. 20–21.

35. Ibid., p. 23.

36. Leslie, *op. cit.,* p. 70.

37. https://en.wikipedia.org/wiki/Boson_de_Talleyrand-Périgord.

38. Leslie, *op. cit.,* p. 71.

39. Ibid., p. 72.

40. Ibid.

41. Pearson, *op. cit.,* p. 49.

42. Ibid.

43. Giles St. Aubyn, *Edward VII: Prince and King,* p. 156.

44. Ibid.

45. Ibid.

46. Ibid.

47. Ibid., p. 157.

48. Ibid.

49. Ibid.

50. Ibid., p. 158.

51. Ibid., p. 159.

4. *MORDAUNT VS. MORDAUNT*

1. John Pearson, *Edward the Rake: An Unwholesome Biography of Edward VII* (New York: Harcourt Brace Jovanovich 1975), p. 66.

2. Ibid.

3. Ibid.

4. Christopher Hibbert, *Edward VII: A Portrait* (London: Allen Lane, 1976), p. 106.

5. Roger Wilkes, "Sex Mad—and Off to the Asylum to Prove It," *Daily Telegraph,* January 16, 2002.

6. Jane Ridley, *Bertie: A Life of Edward VII* (London: Vintage, 2003), p. 125.

7. Michael Havers, Edward Grayson, and Peter Shankland *The Royal Baccarat Scandal* (London: Souvenir Press, 1988), p. 20.

8. Hibbert, *op. cit.,* p. 107.

9. Ibid.

10. Pearson, *op. cit.,* p. 67.

11. Havers, *op. cit.,* p. 20.

12. Theo Lang, *My Darling Daisy* (London: Michael Joseph, 1966), p. 39.

13. Ibid.

14. Havers, *op. cit.,* p. 20.

15. Hibbert, *op. cit.,* p. 107.

16. Ibid., pp. 107–8.

17. Ibid., p. 108.

18. Ibid.

19. Ridley, *op. cit.,* p. 133.

20. Ibid.

5. JENNIE CHURCHILL, THE DOLLAR PRINCESS

1. Anne Sebba, *Jennie Churchill: Winston's American Mother* (London: John Murray, 2008), pp. 16–17.

2. Anita Leslie, *Jennie: The Mother of Winston Churchill* (Maidstone, UK: George Mann, 1969), p. 8.

3. Ibid., p. 9.

4. Ibid., p. 11.

5. Ibid.

6. Ibid., p. 15.

7. Sebba, *op. cit.,* p. 28.
8. Ibid., p. 23.
9. Leslie, *op. cit.,* p. 11.
10. Ibid., p. 16.
11. Ibid., p. 17.
12. Ibid.
13. Ibid., p. 18.
14. Ibid., p. 19.
15. Ibid.
16. Leslie, *op. cit.,* p. 22.
17. Sebba, *op. cit.,* p. 35.
18. Leslie, *op. cit.,* p. 24.
19. Ibid.
20. Ibid.
21. Ibid.
22. Ibid., p. 26.
23. Ibid.
24. Ibid.
25. Ibid., p. 39.
26. Sebba, *op. cit.,* p. 40.
27. Leslie, *op. cit.,* pp. 27–28.
28. Ibid., p. 28.
29. Sebba, *op. cit.,* p. 49.
30. Ibid., p. 29.
31. Ibid., p. 51.
32. Ibid., p. 52.
33. Leslie, *op. cit.,* p. 32.
34. Sebba, *op. cit.,* p. 55.
35. Ibid., p. 53.
36. Leslie, *op. cit.,* p. 37.
37. Sebba, *op. cit.,* p. 58.
38. Ibid., p. 59.
39. Ibid., p. 61.
40. Ibid., p. 62.
41. Leslie, *op. cit.,* p. 59.
42. Ibid., p. 39.
43. Ibid.
44. Ibid., p. 40.
45. Ibid., p. 42.
46. Ibid.
47. Sebba, *op. cit.,* p. 68.
48. Leslie, *op. cit.,* p. 117.

6. THE AYLESFORD SCANDAL

1. Anita Leslie, *Edwardians in Love* (London: Hutchinson, 1972), p. 68.

2. Ibid., pp. 84–85.

3. Ibid., p. 85.

4. Allen Andrews, *The Follies of King Edward VII* (London: Lexington, 1975), p. 125.

5. Leslie, *op. cit.,* p. 85.

6. Ibid.

7. Ibid.

8. Ibid., p. 86.

9. Ibid., p. 87.

10. Ibid., p. 86.

11. Ibid.

12. Ibid.

13. Ibid., p. 87.

14. Ibid., p. 86.

15. Ibid., p. 87.

16. Ibid.

17. Ibid., p. 92.

18. Leslie, *op. cit.,* p. 87.

19. Ibid., p. 91.

20. Jane Ridley, *Bertie: A Life of Edward VII* (London: Vintage, 2003), p. 187.

21. Ibid.

22. Leslie, *op. cit.,* p. 87.

23. Ibid., p. 88.

24. Ridley, *op. cit.,* p. 190.

25. Leslie, *op. cit.,* p. 88.

26. Ridley, *op. cit.,* p. 188.

27. Leslie, *op. cit.,* p. 88.

28. Ibid.

29. Ibid.

30. Ibid., p. 91.

31. Ridley, *op. cit.,* p. 186.

32. Leslie, *op. cit.,* p. 89.

33. Ibid.

34. Ibid., p. 88.

35. Ibid., p. 89.

36. Ibid., p. 90.

37. Ibid.

38. Ibid., p. 91.

39. Ibid., p. 90.

40. Ibid.

41. Ridley, *op. cit.,* p. 198.

42. Anita Leslie, *The Marlborough House Set* (New York: Doubleday, 1973), p. 63.

43. Leslie, *Edwardians in Love*, p. 92.

44. Ibid., p. 93.

45. Ibid.

46. Ibid.

47. Ibid., p. 92.

48. Ibid.

7. THE JERSEY TOMBOY

1. Lillie Langtry, *The Days I Knew* (North Hollywood, Calif.: Panoply Publications, 2005), p. 15.

2. Ibid., p. 17.

3. Ibid.

4. Ibid., p. 20.

5. Ibid., p. 22.

6. Ibid., p. 23.

7. Ibid., p. 25.

8. Ibid., p. 26.

9. Ibid.

10. Ibid.

11. Ibid., p. 27.

12. Ibid., p. 28.

13. Laura Beatty, *Lillie Langtry: Manners, Masks and Morals* (London: Vintage, 2000), p. 25.

14. Ibid., p. 25.

15. Langtry, *op. cit.*, p. 29.

16. Ibid.

17. Beatty, *op. cit.*, p. 17.

18. Ibid.

19. Langtry, *op. cit.*, p. 24.

20. Beatty, *op. cit.*, p. 23.

21. Ernest Dudley, *The Gilded Lily* (London: Odhams Press, 1958), p. 32.

22. Theo Aronson, *The King in Love* (New York: Harper & Row, 1988), p. 26.

23. Dudley, *op. cit.*, p. 34.

24. Aronson, *op. cit.*, p. 26.

25. Ibid.

26. Beatty, *op. cit.*, p. 25.

27. Dudley, *op. cit.*, p. 34.

28. Langtry, *op. cit.*, p. 30.

29. Ibid.

30. Ibid.

31. Ibid.

32. Ibid.

8. TAKING LONDON BY STORM

1. Lillie Langtry, *The Days I Knew* (North Hollywood, Calif.: Panoply Publications, 2005), p. 31.
2. Ibid.
3. Ibid.
4. Laura Beatty, *Lillie Langtry: Manners, Masks and Morals* (London: Vintage, 2000), p. 32.
5. Langtry, *op. cit.,* p. 33.
6. https://en.wikipedia.org/wiki/Thomas_Jones,_7th_Viscount_Ranelagh.
7. Theo Lang, *My Darling Daisy* (London: Michael Joseph, 1966), p. 34.
8. Frances, Countess of Warwick, *Life's Ebb and Flow* (New York: William Morrow, 1929), p. 47.
9. Ibid.
10. Langtry, *op. cit.,* 33.
11. Beatty, *op. cit.,* p. 35.
12. Langtry, *op. cit.,* p. 33.
13. Ibid.
14. Ibid., p. 35.
15. Ibid.
16. Ibid.
17. Ibid.
18. Ibid.
19. Ibid.
20. Ibid.
21. Ibid.
22. Ibid.
23. Ibid., pp. 36–37.
24. Ibid., p. 38.
25. Beatty, *op. cit.,* p. 39.
26. Ibid., p. 40.
27. Ibid., p. 43.
28. Langtry, *op. cit.,* p. 147.
29. http://fannycornforth.blogspot.co.uk/2011/06/myth-and-mainstreaming.html.
30. Ibid.
31. Langtry, *op. cit.,* p. 54.
32. Ibid., p. 44.
33. Ibid.
34. Ibid.
35. Ibid.
36. Warwick, *op. cit.,* p. 43.
37. Ibid.
38. Langtry, *op. cit.,* p. 38.

39. Ibid.

40. Beatty, *op. cit.,* p. 81.

41. Langtry, *op. cit.,* p. 43.

42. Beatty, *op. cit.,* p. 47.

43. Langtry, *op. cit.,* p. 54.

44. Ibid., p. 62.

45. Ibid., p. 65.

46. Ibid., p. 64.

9. THE REAL PRINCE CHARMING

1. Lillie Langtry, *The Days I Knew* (North Hollywood, Calif.: Panoply Publications, 2005), p. 64.

2. Ibid.

3. Ibid., pp. 64–65.

4. Ernest Dudley, *The Gilded Lily* (London: Odhams Press, 1958), p. 40.

5. Theo Aronson, *The King in Love* (New York: Harper & Row, 1988), p. 41.

6. Laura Beatty, *Lillie Langtry: Manners, Masks and Morals* (London: Vintage, 2000), p. 97.

7. James Brough, *The Prince and the Lily* (London: Coronet, 1975), p. 145.

8. Aronson, *op. cit.,* p. 86.

9. Brough, *op. cit.,* p. 144.

10. Langtry, *op. cit.,* p. 66.

11. Aronson, *op. cit.,* 41.

12. Langtry, *op. cit.,* p. 40.

13. Ibid., p. 42.

14. Ibid., p. 41.

15. Ibid.

16. Ibid., p. 42.

17. Ibid., p. 40.

18. Ibid.

19. Ibid., p. 43.

20. Ibid.

21. Ibid.

22. Ibid.

23. Ibid.

24. Ibid.

25. Frances, Countess of Warwick, *Life's Ebb and Flow* (New York: William Morrow, 1929), p. 44.

26. Langtry, *op. cit.,* p. 102.

27. Beatty, *op. cit.,* p. 89.

28. Aronson, *op. cit.,* p. 129.

29. Langtry, *op. cit.,* p. 137.

30. Ibid., p. 139.

31. Ibid., p. 138.

32. Langtry, *op. cit.,* p. 139.

33. Ibid., pp. 139–40.

34. Ibid., p. 91.

35. Ibid., p. 92.

36. Ibid., p. 95.

37. Ibid., p. 94.

38. Ibid., p. 92.

39. Ibid., 93.

40. Ibid., p. 94.

41. Ibid., p. 95.

42. Ibid.

10. ROYAL MISTRESS

1. Lillie Langtry, *The Days I Knew* (North Hollywood, Calif.: Panoply Publications, 2005), p. 117.

2. Ibid., p. 119.

3. Ibid.

4. Ibid.

5. Ibid.

6. Ibid., p. 120.

7. Ibid., p. 119.

8. Ibid.

9. Ibid.

10. Ibid., p. 120.

11. Ibid., p. 48.

12. Ibid., p. 49.

13. Laura Beatty, *Lillie Langtry: Manners, Masks and Morals.* (London: Vintage, 2000), p. 81.

14. Ibid., p. 108.

15. Ibid., p. 117.

16. Ibid.

17. Langtry, *op. cit.,* p. 144.

18. Ibid., p. 145.

19. Ibid.

20. Ibid.

21. Ernest Dudley, *The Gilded Lily* (London: Odhams Press, 1958), p. 22.

22. Beatty, *op. cit.,* p. 144.

23. James Brough, *The Prince and the Lily* (London: Coronet, 1975), p. 190.

24. Ibid., pp.189–90.
25. Ibid., p. 190.
26. Beatty, *op. cit.*, p. 145.
27. Ibid.
28. Ibid., p. 147.
29. Ibid.
30. Ibid.
31. Ibid.
32. Langtry, *op. cit.*, p. 121.
33. Ibid.
34. Beatty, *op. cit.*, p. 150.
35. Ibid., p. 151.
36. Brough, *op. cit.*, p. 197.
37. Ibid., p. 152.
38. Brough, *op. cit.*, p. 198.
39. Ibid., p. 197.
40. Langtry, *op. cit.*, pp. 105–6.
41. Ibid., p. 106.
42. Ibid.
43. Brough, *op. cit.*, p. 199.
44. Ibid.
45. Beatty, *op. cit.*, p. 153.
46. http://www.balmoralcastle.com/acatalog/My-Dear-Paradise-5037903000009
.html.
47. Brough, Ernes *op. cit.*, p. 198.

11. THE WHEEL OF FORTUNE

1. Lillie Langtry, *The Days I Knew* (North Hollywood, Calif.: Panoply Publications, 2005), p. 54.
2. Laura Beatty, *Lillie Langtry: Manners, Masks and Morals* (London: Vintage, 2000), p. 156.
3. Ibid.
4. Ibid.
5. James Brough, *The Prince and the Lily* (London: Coronet, 1975), p. 200.
6. Ernest Dudley, *The Gilded Lily* (London: Odhams Press, 1958), p. 50.
7. Beatty, *op. cit.*, p. 158.
8. Dudley, *op. cit.*, p. 50.
9. Brough, *op. cit.*, pp. 201–2.
10. Ibid.
11. Brough, *op. cit.*, p. 202.
12. Ibid., pp. 202–3.
13. Ibid., p. 202.

14. Ibid., p. 203.
15. Ibid.
16. Ibid.
17. Dudley, *op. cit.*, pp. 51–52.
18. Brough, *op. cit.*, p. 203.
19. Langtry, *op. cit.*, p. 121.
20. Ibid.
21. Ibid., p. 66.
22. Ibid., p. 122.
23. Ibid., p. 123.
24. Ibid., pp. 124–26.

12. JENNIE AND RANDOLPH

1. Anita Leslie, *Jennie: The Mother of Winston Churchill* (Maidstone, UK: George Mann, 1969), p. 61.
2. Ibid.
3. Ibid.
4. Ibid., p. 59.
5. Ibid., p. 103.
6. Ibid., p. 69.
7. Ibid.
8. Ibid.
9. Ibid., p. 93.
10. Ibid., p. 97.
11. Anne Sebba, *Jennie Churchill: Winston's American Mother* (London: John Murray, 2008), p. 139.
12. Ibid., p. 137.
13. Jane Ridley, *Bertie: A Life of Edward VII* (London: Vintage, 2003), p. 245.
14. Sebba, *op. cit.*, p. 145.
15. Ibid., p. 138.
16. Ibid., p. 139.
17. Ridley, *op. cit.*, p. 245.
18. Leslie, *op. cit.*, p. 111.
19. Sebba, *op. cit.*, p. 152.
20. Ibid.
21. Leslie, *op. cit.*, p. 112.
22. Ibid.
23. Ibid.
24. Sebba, *op. cit.*, p. 154.
25. Ibid.
26. Leslie, *op. cit.*, p. 114.
27. Ibid.

28. Ibid.
29. Ibid.
30. Ibid., p. 115.
31. Sebba, *op. cit.,* p. 151.
32. Ibid., p. 162.
33. Ibid.
34. Ridley, *op. cit.,* p. 246.

13. MY DARLING DAISY

1. Frances, Countess of Warwick, *Life's Ebb and Flow* (New York: William Morrow, 1929), p. 3.
2. Ibid.
3. Ibid., p. 5.
4. Lang, Theo Lang, *My Darling Daisy* (London: Michael Joseph, 1966), p. 32.
5. Warwick, *op. cit.,* p. 5.
6. Ibid., p. 6.
7. Ibid.
8. Ibid., p. 90.
9. Ibid.
10. http://www.eastonlodge.co.uk/content/early-history.
11. Warwick, *op. cit.,* p. 7.
12. Ibid., p. 19.
13. Ibid.
14. Ibid.
15. Ibid.
16. Ibid., pp. 19–20.
17. Ibid., p. 8.
18. Ibid., p. 20.
19. Ibid., p. 19.
20. Ibid., pp. 22–23.
21. Ibid., p. 25.
22. Ibid.
23. Ibid.
24. Ibid.
25. Ibid.
26. Ibid., p. 26.
27. Sushila Anand, *Daisy: The Life and Loves of the Countess of Warwick* (London: Piatkus, 2008), pp. 12–13.
28. Lang, *op. cit.,* p. 33.
29. Warwick, *op. cit.,* p. 27.
30. Ibid.
31. Anand, *op. cit.,* p. 13.

32. Warwick, *op. cit.*, p. 31.

33. Ibid., pp. 31–32.

34. Ibid p. 32.

35. Ibid., p. 33.

36. Ibid.

37. Ibid.

38. Ibid., p. 34.

39. Ibid.

40. Ibid., p. 35.

41. Ibid.

42. Ibid.

43. Theo Aronson, *The King in Love* (New York: Harper & Row, 1988), p. 114.

44. Warwick, *op. cit.*, p. 69.

45. Ibid., p. 71.

14. THE HEART HAS ITS REASONS

1. Theo Aronson, *The King in Love* (New York: Harper and Row, 1988), p. 117.

2. Frances, Countess of Warwick, *Life's Ebb and Flow* (New York: William Morrow, 1929), p. 82.

3. Ibid., p. 44.

4. Ibid.

5. Ibid., p. 83.

6. Ibid., pp. 83–84.

7. Ibid., p. 41.

8. Frances, Countess of Warwick, *Afterthoughts* (London: Cassell, 1931), p. 66.

9. Aronson, *op. cit.*, p. 118.

10. Theo Lang, *My Darling Daisy* (London: Michael Joseph, 1966), p. 38.

11. Aronson, *op. cit.*, p. 118.

12. Ibid.

13. Ibid., p. 119.

14. Lang, *op. cit.*, p. 40.

15. Aronson, *op. cit.*, p. 120.

16. Ibid.

17. Ibid.

18. Lang, *op. cit.*, p. 45.

19. Jane Ridley, *Bertie: A Life of Edward VII* (London: Vintage, 2003), p. 265.

20. Ibid.

21. Ibid.

22. Aronson, *op. cit.*, p. 121.

23. Ridley, *op. cit.*, p. 265.

24. Aronson, *op. cit.*, p. 121.

25. Ibid.

26. Lang, *op. cit.*, pp. 34–35.
27. Aronson, *op. cit.*, p. 131.
28. Ibid., p. 124.
29. Ibid., p. 125.
30. Warwick, *Life's Ebb and Flow,* p. 67.
31. Aronson, *op. cit.*, p. 126.
32. Ibid., p. 128.
33. Warwick, *Afterthoughts,* p. 97.
34. Aronson, *op. cit.*, p. 126.
35. Sushila Anand, *Daisy: The Life and Loves of the Countess of Warwick* (London: Piatkus, 2008), p. 54.
36. Ibid., p. 158.
37. Aronson, *op. cit.*, p. 128.
38. Ibid., p. 129.
39. Ibid., p. 130.
40. Anita Leslie, *Edwardians in Love* (London: Hutchinson, 1972), p. 163.
41. Ibid.
42. Ibid.
43. Ibid.
44. Ibid.
45. Ibid.

15. SHE STOOPS TO CONQUER

1. Ernest Dudley, *The Gilded Lily* (London: Odhams Press, 1958), p. 55.
2. James Brough, *The Prince and the Lily* (London: Coronet, 1975), p. 223.
3. Ibid.
4. Dudley, *op. cit.*, p. 56.
5. Ibid., p. 60.
6. Ibid.
7. Ibid., p. 64.
8. Ibid.
9. Ibid.
10. Lillie Langtry, *The Days I Knew* (North Hollywood, Calif.: Panoply Publications, 2005), p. 164.
11. Ibid., p. 151.
12. Ibid., pp. 161–62.
13. Ibid., p. 12.
14. Dudley, *op. cit.*, p. 63.
15. Brough, *op. cit.*, p. 228.
16. Langtry, *op. cit.*, p. 152.
17. Ibid., p. 154.

18. Dudley, *op. cit.*, p. 64.

19. Ibid., pp. 63–65.

20. Ibid., p. 65.

21. Ibid., p. 66.

22. Ibid.

23. Langtry, *op. cit.*, p. 156.

24. Dudley, *op. cit.*, p. 67.

25. Ibid.

26. Ibid.

27. Ibid., pp. 67–68.

28. Brough, *op. cit.*, p. 235.

29. Ibid.

30. Dudley, *op. cit.*, p. 68.

31. Ibid.

32. Ibid., p. 69.

33. Ibid., p. 70.

34. Langtry, *op. cit.*, p. 161.

35. Dudley, *op. cit.*, 70.

36. Langtry, *op. cit.*, p. 166.

37. Ibid., pp. 156-70.

38. Ibid.

39. Ibid., p. 159.

40. Ibid.

41. Dudley, *op. cit.*, p. 75.

42. Langtry, *op. cit.*, p. 166.

43. Dudley, *op. cit.*, p. 70.

44. Ibid., p. 73.

45. Langtry, *op. cit.*, p. 166.

46. Dudley, *op. cit.*, p. 75.

47. Ibid.

48. Langtry, *op. cit.*, p. 167.

49. Dudley, *op. cit.*, p. 75.

50. Langtry, *op. cit.*, p. 168.

51. Brough, *op. cit.*, p. 230.

52. Ibid., p. 244.

53. Langtry, *op. cit.*, p. 169.

16. THE UNFORGIVABLE SIN

1. Theo Aronson, *The King in Love* (New York: Harper & Row, 1988), p. 131.

2. Michael Havers, Edward Grayson, and Peter Shankland, *The Royal Baccarat Scandal* (London: Souvenir Press, 1988), p. 22.

3. Ibid., pp. 24–25.

4. Frances, Countess of Warwick, *Life's Ebb and Flow* (New York: William Morrow, 1929), p. 37.

5. Jane Ridley, *Bertie: A Portrait of Edward VII* (London: Vintage, 2003), pp. 280–81.

6. Anita Leslie, *Edwardians in Love* (London: Hutchinson, 1972), p. 143.

7. Havers, Grayson, and Shankland, *op. cit.*, p. 26.

8. Ibid., p. 27.

9. Ibid.

10. Ibid.

11. Ibid.

12. Ibid., p. 28.

13. Ibid.

14. Ibid.

15. Ibid.

16. Ibid.

17. Ibid., p. 29.

18. Ibid., p. 30.

19. Ibid.

20. Ibid., p. 31.

21. Ibid.

22. Ibid.

23. Ibid.

24. Ibid., p. 32.

25. Ibid., p. 33.

26. Ibid., p. 34.

27. Ibid., p. 35.

28. Ibid., pp. 36–37.

29. Ibid., p. 36.

30. Leslie, *op. cit.*, p. 142.

17. THE TRANBY CROFT TRIAL

1. Anita Leslie, *Edwardians in Love* (London: Hutchinson, 1972), p. 142.

2. Ibid.

3. "The Baccarat Case," *The Times*, February 9, 1911.

4. Michael Havers, Edward Grayson, and Peter Shankland, *The Royal Baccarat Scandal* (London: Souvenir Press, 1988), p. 24.

5. Ibid.

6. Leslie, *op. cit.*, p. 143.

7. Havers, Grayson, and Shankland, *op. cit.*, p. 62.

8. Ibid.

9. Ibid., p. 63.

10. Ibid., p. 62.

11. Ibid., p. 68.
12. Ibid., p. 70.
13. Ibid.
14. Ibid.
15. Ibid.
16. Ibid., p. 73.
17. Jane Ridley, *Bertie: A Life of Edward VII* (London: Vintage, 2003), p. 288.
18. Havers, Grayson, and Shankland, *op. cit.,* p. 64.
19. Ibid., p. 89.
20. "The Baccarat Case," *Illustrated London News,* June 13, 1891, p. 770.
21. Havers, Grayson, and Shankland, *op. cit.,* p. 97.
22. Ibid., p. 104.
23. "The Prince as Witness," *The New York Times,* June 3, 1891.
24. Havers, Grayson and Shankland, *op. cit.,* pp. 106–7.
25. Ibid.
26. Ibid.
27. Ibid., p. 186.
28. Ibid.
29. "The Baccarat Case," *The Times,* June 5, 1891.
30. Havers, Grayson, and Shankland, *op. cit.,* p. 154.
31. Ibid., pp. 168–69.
32. Ibid., p. 169.
33. Ibid., pp. 188–89.
34. Ibid.
35. "The Baccarat Case," *The Times,* June 9, 1891.
36. Gertrude Attwood, *The Wilsons of Tranby Croft* (England: Hutton Press, 1988), p. 111.
37. Ibid.
38. "The Baccarat Case," *The Times,* June 9, 1891.
39. Ibid.
40. Havers, Grayson, and Shankland, *op. cit.,* p. 219.
41. Ibid.
42. Ibid.
43. Ibid., p. 229.
44. Ibid., p. 233.
45. Ibid.
46. Ibid., p. 234.
47. Ibid.
48. Ibid., p. 235.
49. Ibid., p. 236.
50. Ibid.
51. Ibid.
52. Ibid.

53. Ibid.

54. Theo Aronson, *The King in Love* (New York: Harper and Row, 1988), p. 133.

55. Ibid.

56. Ibid.

57. "Leading Article: The Baccarat Case," *The Times,* June 10, 1891.

58. Jason Tomes, "Cumming, Sir William Gordon Gordon-, fourth baronet (1848–1930)," *Oxford Dictionary of National Biography,* online edition, September 2014. http://www.oxforddnb.com/index/39/101039392/

59. Leslie, *op. cit.,* p. 144.

60. See Havers, Grayson and Shankland, *op. cit.,* p. 251.

61. Ibid.

62. Ibid., p. 263.

63. Ibid., p. 268.

64. Ibid.

65. Leslie, *op. cit.,* pp. 141–42.

66. Havers, Grayson, and Shankland, *op. cit.,* p. 245.

67. Frances, Lady of Warwick, *Life's Ebb and Flow* (New York: William Morrow, 1929), p. 37.

68. Havers, Grayson, and Shankland, *op. cit.,* p. 267.

18. THE SOCIALITE SOCIALIST

1. Theo Aronson, *The King in Love* (New York: Harper & Row, 1988), p. 140.

2. Ibid.

3. Ibid.

4. Jane Ridley, *Bertie: A Life of Edward VII* (London: Vintage, 2003), p. 267.

5. Aronson, *op. cit.,* p. 124.

6. Frances, Countess of Warwick, *Life's Ebb and Flow* (New York: William Morrow, 1929), p. 92.

7. Ibid.

8. Ibid., pp. 92–93.

9. Ibid., p. 99.

10. Aronson, *op. cit.,* p. 164.

11. Sushila Anand, *Daisy: The Life and Loves of the Countess of Warwick* (London: Piatkus, 2008), p. 61.

12. Warwick, *op. cit.,* pp. 99–100.

13. Anita Leslie, *Edwardians in Love* (London: Hutchinson, 1972), p. 167.

14. Anand, *op. cit.,* p. 62.

15. Aronson, *op. cit.,* p. 164.

16. Warwick, *op. cit.,* pp. 99–100.

17. Ibid.

18. Ibid.

19. Ibid.

20. Ibid.
21. Ibid.
22. Ibid.
23. Ibid., pp. 100–103.

19. CAPTAIN LAYCOCK OF THE BLUES

1. Sushila Anand, *Daisy: The Life and Loves of the Countess of Warwick* (London: Piatkus, 2008), p. 81.
2. Anita Leslie, *Edwardians in Love* (London: Hutchinson, 1972), p. 171.
3. Jane Ridley, *Bertie: A Life of Edward VII* (London: Vintage, 2003), p. 313.
4. Leslie, *op. cit.,* p. 171.
5. Ibid.
6. Ibid.
7. Theo Aronson, *The King in Love* (New York: Harper & Row, 1988), p. 199.
8. Ibid., p. 200.
9. Leslie, *op. cit.,* p. 173.
10. Anand, *op. cit.,* p. 102.
11. Ibid., p. 105.
12. Leslie, *op. cit.,* p. 174.
13. Ibid.
14. Ibid., p. 176.
15. Ibid., p. 178.
16. Anand, *op. cit.,* p. 112.
17. Ibid., p. 108.
18. Leslie, *op. cit.,* p. 170.
19. Ibid., p. 171.
20. Anand, *op. cit.,* p. 113.
21. Ibid., p. 114.
22. Ibid.
23. Ibid., p. 115.
24. Ibid., p. 155.
25. Leslie, *op. cit.,* p. 237.
26. Ibid.
27. Ibid., p. 229.
28. Ibid.
29. Raymond Lamont-Brown, *Alice Keppel & Agnes Keyser: Edward VII's Last Loves,* (Stroud, UK: Sutton Press, 2005), p. 127.
30. Ibid.
31. Leslie, *op. cit.,* p. 237.
32. Ibid., p. 238.
33. Ibid.
34. Giles St. Aubyn, *Edward VII: Prince and King* (London: Collins, 1979), p. 380.

35. Leslie, *op. cit.*, p. 239.
36. Ibid.

20. THE LAST MISTRESS: ALICE KEPPEL

1. Anita Leslie, *Edwardians in Love* (London: Hutchinson, 1972), p. 199.
2. Raymond Lamont-Brown, *Alice Keppel & Agnes Keyser: Edward VII's Last Loves* (Stroud, UK: Sutton Press, 2005), p. 36.
3. Theo, Aronson, *The King in Love* (New York: Harper & Row, 1988), p. 188.
4. Ibid.
5. Diana Souhami, *Mrs. Keppel and Her Daughter* (New York: St. Martin's Press, 1996), pp. 17–18.
6. Aronson, *op cit.*, p. 188.
7. Lamont-Brown, *op. cit.*, p. 134.
8. Leslie, *op. cit.*, p. 233.
9. Ibid.
10. Ibid.
11. Ibid.
12. Ibid.
13. Anita Leslie, *The Marlborough House Set* (New York: Doubleday, 1973), p. 200.
14. Ibid., p. 205.
15. Lamont-Brown, *op. cit.*, p. 107.
16. Aronson, *op. cit.*, p. 106.
17. Lamont-Brown, op. cit., p. 70.
18. Aronson, *op. cit.*, p. 187.
19. Laura Beatty, *Lillie Langtry: Manners, Masks and Morals* (London: Vintage, 2000), p. 172.
20. Leslie, *The Marlborough House Set* (New York: Doubleday, 1973), p. 143.
21. Lamont-Brown, *op. cit.*, p. 79.
22. Souhami, *op. cit.*, p. 82.
23. Ibid., p. 48.
24. Leslie, *Edwardians in Love*, p. 232.
25. Aronson, *op. cit.*, pp. 213–14.
26. Ibid., p. 214.
27. Souhami, *op. cit.*, p. 8.
28. Ibid.
29. Ibid.
30. Vita Sackville-West, *The Edwardians* (London: Virago, 2004), pp. 146–47.
31. Leslie, *Edwardians in Love*, p. 232.
32. Ibid., p. 230.
33. Ibid., p. 231.
34. Ibid., p. 231.

21. GOLDEN YEARS

1. Raymond Lamont-Brown, *Alice Keppel & Agnes Keyser: King Edward VII's Last Loves* (Stroud, UK: Sutton Press, 2005), p. 111.

2. Anita Leslie, *Edwardians in Love* (London: Hutchinson, 1972), p. 233.

3. Diana Souhami, *Mrs. Keppel and Her Daughter* (New York: St. Martin's Press, 1996), p. 64.

4. Anita Leslie, *Edwardians in Love,* p. 234.

5. Souhami, *op. cit.,* p. 63.

6. Ibid., p. 65.

7. Leslie, *op. cit.,* p. 234.

8. Sonia Keppel, *Edwardian Daughter* (London: Hamish Hamilton, 1958), p. 20.

9. Lamont-Brown, *op. cit.,* p. 72.

10. John Pearson, *Edward the Rake: An Unwholesome Biography of Edward VII* (New York: Harcourt Brace Jovanovich, 1975), p. 170.

11. Lamont-Brown, *op. cit.,* p. 98.

12. Souhami, *op. cit.,* p. 65.

13. Leslie, *op. cit.,* p. 235.

14. Ibid., p. 235.

15. Theo Aronson, *The King in Love* (New York: Harper & Row, 1988), p. 236.

16. Lamont-Brown, *op. cit.,* p. 93.

17. Ibid.

18. Ibid., p. 94.

19. Ibid.

20. Ibid., p. 130.

21. Ibid.

22. Ibid., p. 201.

23. Ibid., p. 131–32.

24. Souhami, *op. cit.,* p. 66.

25. Ibid.

26. Jane Ridley, *Bertie: A Life of Edward VII* (London: Vintage, 2003), p. 364.

27. Allen Andrews, *The Follies of King Edward VII* (London: Lexington, 1975), p. 176.

28. Lamont-Brown, pp. 82–83.

29. Ibid., p. 84.

30. Giles St. Aubyn, *Edward VII: Prince and King* (London: Collins, 1979), p. 380.

31. Lamont-Brown, *op. cit.,* p. 100.

32. Ibid.

33. Ridley, *op. cit.,* p. 347.

34. Aronson, *op. cit.,* p. 219.

35. Pearson, *op. cit.,* p. 159.

36. Lamont-Brown, *op. cit.,* p. 116.

37. St. Aubyn, *op. cit.,* p. 369.

38. Ridley, *op. cit.*, p. 366.

39. Lamont-Brown, *op. cit.*, p. 121.

40. Leslie, *op. cit.*, p. 295.

41. Ibid.

42. Aronson, *op. cit.*, p. 251.

43. Ibid., p. 219.

44. Ibid.

45. Ibid., p. 218.

46. Ibid., p. 219.

47. See Aronson, *op. cit.*, p. 219.

22. FAMOUS LAST WORDS

1. Theo Aronson, *The King in Love* (New York: Harper & Row, 1988), p. 250.

2. Ibid.

3. Ibid.

4. Ibid., p. 251.

5. Ibid.

6. Diana Souhami, *Mrs. Keppel and Her Daughter* (New York: St. Martin's Press, 1996), p. 91.

7. Ibid.

8. Jane Ridley, *Bertie: A Life of Edward VII* (London: Vintage, 2003), p. 458.

9. Raymond Lamont-Brown, *Alice Keppel & Agnes Keyser: Edward VII's Last Loves* (Stroud, UK: Sutton Press, 2005), p. 149.

10. Ibid., p. 148.

11. Aronson, *op. cit.*, p. 252.

12. Ibid.

13. Ibid.

14. Ibid.

15. Ibid.

16. Souhami, *op. cit.*, p. 91.

17. Ibid.

18. Ibid., pp. 91–92.

19. Aronson, *op. cit.*, p. 252.

20. Ibid.

21. Lamont-Brown, *op. cit.*, p. 150.

22. Ibid., p. 151.

23. Ibid.

24. Ibid.

25. Aronson, *op. cit.*, p. 254.

26. Ibid.

27. Ibid.

AFTERTHOUGHTS

1. Frances, Countess of Warwick, *Afterthoughts* (London: Cassell, 1931), p. 179.
2. Ibid.
3. Ibid., p. 180.
4. "Burlington Bertie," a song by Harry B. Norris dating from 1900, was made famous by Vesta Tilley in her heyday as a cross-dressing music hall star.
5. Laura Beatty, *Lillie Langtry: Manners, Masks and Morals* (London: Vintage, 2000), p. 282.
6. Ernest Dudley, *The Gilded Lily* (London: Odhams Press Limited, 1958), pp. 213–4.
7. Laura Beatty, *op. cit.*, p. 302.
8. Raymond Lamont-Brown, *Alice Keppel & Agnes Keyser: Edward VII's Last Loves* (Stroud, UK: Sutton Press, 2005), p. 6.

BIBLIOGRAPHY

Anand, Sushila. *Daisy: The Life and Loves of the Countess of Warwick*. London: Piatkus, 2008.

Andrews, Allen. *The Follies of King Edward VII*. London: Lexington, 1975.

Aronson, Theo. *The King in Love: Edward VII's Mistresses: Lillie Langtry, Daisy Warwick, Alice Keppel and Others*. New York: Harper & Row, 1988.

Attwood, Gertrude M. *The Wilsons of Tranby Croft*. London: Hutton Press Ltd., 1988.

Beatty, Laura. *Lillie Langtry: Manners, Masks and Morals*. London: Vintage, 2000.

Bentley-Cranch, Dana. *Edward VII: Image of an Era*. London: Her Majesty's Stationery Office, 1992.

Brough, James. *The Prince and the Lily*. London: Coronet, 1975.

Cowles, Virginia. *Gay Monarch: The Life and Pleasures of Edward VII*. London: Harper 1956.

Dudley, Ernest. *The Gilded Lily*. London: Odhams Press, 1958.

Gould, Arthur, and Robert Fizdale. *The Divine Sarah: A Life of Sarah Bernhardt*. New York: Knopf, 1991.

Havers, Michael, Edward Grayson, and Peter Shankland. *The Royal Baccarat Scandal*. London: Souvenir Press, 1988.

Hibbert, Christopher. *Edward VII: A Portrait*. London: Allen Lane, 1976.

Hickman, Katie. *Courtesans*. London: Harper Perennial, 2003.

Judd, Denis. *Edward VII: A Pictorial Biography*. London: Macdonald and Jane's, 1975.

Keppel, Sonia. *Edwardian Daughter*. London: Hamish Hamilton, 1958.

Lamont-Brown, Raymond. *Alice Keppel & Agnes Keyser: Edward VII's Last Loves*. Stroud: Sutton Press, 2005.

Lang, Theo. *My Darling Daisy*. London: Michael Joseph, 1966.

Langtry, Lillie. *The Days I Knew: An Autobiography*. North Hollywood, Calif.: Panoply Publications, 2005.

Leslie, Anita. *Edwardians in Love*. London: Hutchinson, 1972.

———. *Jennie: The Mother of Winston Churchill*. Maidstone, UK: George Mann, 1969.

———. *The Marlborough House Set*. New York: Doubleday, 1973.

Macqueen-Pope, Walter James. *Carriages at Eleven: The Story of the Edwardian Theatre*. London: Hutchison, 1947.

Pearsall, Ronald. *Edwardian Life and Leisure*. Newton Abbot, UK: David and Charles, 1973.

Pearson, John. *Edward the Rake: An Unwholesome Biography of Edward VII*. New York: Harcourt Brace Jovanovich, 1975.

Richardson, Joanna. *The Courtesans: The Demi-Monde in 19th Century France*. Edison, N.J.: Castle Books, 2004.

Ridley, Jane. *Bertie: A Life of Edward VII*. London: Vintage, 2003.

Sackville-West, Vita. *The Edwardians*. London: Virago, 2004.

Sebba, Anne. *Jennie Churchill: Winston's American Mother*. London: John Murray, 2008.

Souhami, Diana. *Mrs. Keppel and Her Daughter*. New York: St. Martin's Press, 1996.

St. Aubyn, Giles. *Edward VII: Prince and King*. London: Collins, 1979.

Trewin, J. C. *The Edwardian Theatre*. Oxford: Blackwell, 1976.

Warwick, Countess of, Frances. *Afterthoughts*. London: Cassell, 1931.

———. *Life's Ebb and Flow*. New York: William Morrow, 1929.

INDEX